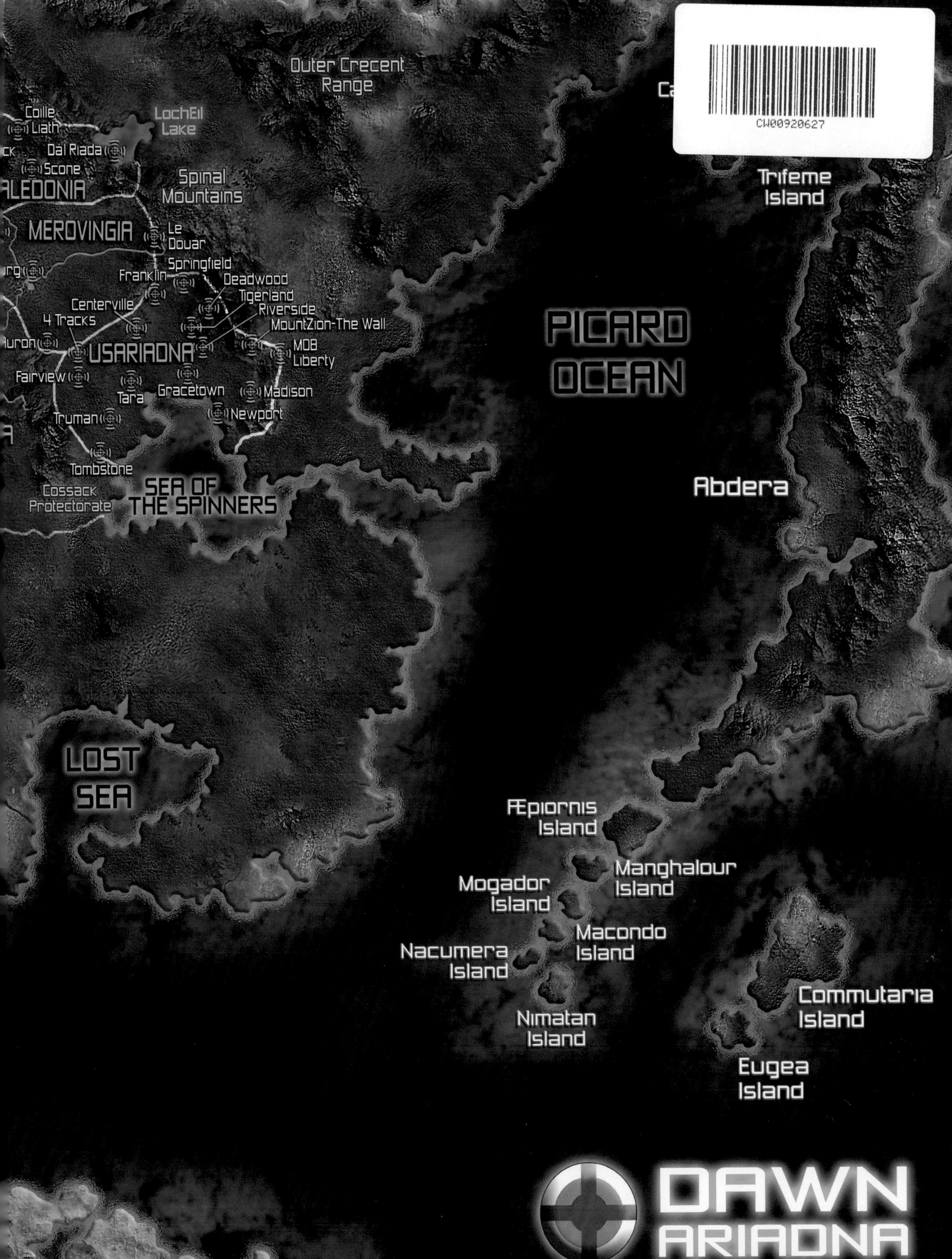

Outer Crecent Range
Coille Liath
LochEil Lake
Dal Riada
Scone
Spinal Mountains
MEROVINGIA
Le Douar
Springfield
Franklin
Deadwood
Tigerland
Centerville
Riverside
4 Tracks
MountZion-The Wall
MOB Liberty
USARIADNA
Fairview
Tara
Gracetown
Madison
Truman
Newport
Tombstone
Cossack Protectorate
SEA OF THE SPINNERS
PICARD OCEAN
Trifeme Island
Abdera
LOST SEA
Æpiornis Island
Manghalour Island
Mogador Island
Macondo Island
Nacumera Island
Nimatan Island
Commutaria Island
Eugea Island
DAWN ARIADNA

CREDITS

WRITING
Benn Graybeaton, Jonathan "Killstring" Herzberger, John Kennedy, Marc Langworthy, Mark Redacted, Rodrigo Vilanova

COVER ART
Ho Seng Hui

INTERIOR ARTWORK
Toma Feizo Gas, Ryan Harasym, Ho Seng Hui, Bagus Hutomo, Oh Wang Jing, Vincent Laïk, Vanni LoRiggio, Aituar Manas, David Nakayama, Cristian Picu, Antone "Chuck" Pires, Stanislav Poltavsky, Carlos Torres

ART DIRECTION
Marc Langworthy, Rodrigo Vilanova

LAYOUT
Thomas Shook

INFINITY RPG LOGO
Michal E. Cross

LEAD EDITOR
Colleen Riley

CARTOGRAPHY
Jose "Gigio" Esteras

SECTORIAL ARMIES LOGOS
Alberto Abal, Carlos Llauger "Bostria" and Hugo Rodriguez

PROOFREADING
Aric Wieder

INFINITY LINE DEVELOPER
Benn Greybeaton

ASSISTANT LINE DEVELOPER
Marc Langworthy

CORVUS BELLI APPROVALS
Gutier Lusquiños Rodríguez, Alberto Abal, Carlos Torres, and Carlos "Bostria" Llauger

ORIGINAL 2D20 SYSTEM DESIGN
Jay Little

GAME DESIGN
Benn Graybeaton, Nathan Dowdell, Mark Redacted, Justin Alexander, Marc Langworthy

PRODUCED BY
Chris Birch

OPERATIONS MANAGER
Garry Harper

COMMUNITY SUPPORT
Lloyd Gyan

PUBLISHING ASSISTANT
Salwa Azar

SPECIAL THANKS
Thank you to Corvus Belli—Alberto, Gutier, Carlos, and Fernando—for letting us play in your world!

PUBLISHED BY
Modiphius Entertainment Ltd.
2nd Floor, 39 Harwood Road,
Fulham, London, SW6 4QP
United Kingdom

Modiphius Entertainment Product Number: MUH050223
ISBN: 978-1-912200-34-4

TABLE OF CONTENTS

INTRODUCTION

CHAPTER 1

CHAPTER 2

CHAPTER 3

CHAPTER 4

CHAPTER 5

CHAPTER 6

CHAPTER 7

INTRODUCTION

WELCOME TO ARIADNA

"Dawn either makes you stronger, or it kills you: there's no middle ground. That's why you'll find more Teseum here than anywhere else in the Human Sphere: even our rocks are tougher than yours."

– Colonel Yevgueni Voronin, Cossack Diplomatic Corps

"Who braved the unknown stars, knowing full well the risks involved? Who travelled through an unstable wormhole, leaving everything behind? Who survived for two centuries, completely cut off from our support? Who tamed an untameable land, teeming with hostile aliens? And after all that, who resisted the colonial advances of the Human Sphere's military juggernauts?

The word you are looking for, commander, is Ariadnans. So tell me: after all that, what makes you think they have the slightest interest in listening to your orders? My advice? Cut them loose, take credit for their accomplishments if it suits you, but above all, stay out of their way."

– Saladin, O-12 Military Liaison. Second Paradiso Offensive.

Space was supposed to be the final frontier. Anyone still holding to that idea has obviously never been to Dawn. Harsh mountains, brutal winters, and native inhabitants that would be more at home in a horror story than a travel brochure? Everyday life for Ariadnans.

Tough, resilient, and impossibly determined are traits commonly attributed to members of this faction. While every faction has its share of patriots, Ariadnans feel a unique bond with their homeland; separated from their ancestors for more than two centuries, they're used to looking after themselves.

Self-reliant, independent, and every bit as tough as their planet's coveted Teseum, Ariadnans don't lack for determination, grit, or stubbornness which is a necessity when you're several technological revolutions behind the rest of the galaxy. It's not that only the strong survive, rather, it's in the defiant act of survival that they become strong in the first place.

WHAT'S IN THIS BOOK

More than just an expansion, this sourcebook aims to provide a "one-stop shop" for all things Ariadnan, including everything you need to create characters, run campaigns, or just immerse yourself completely in your character's faction.

CHAPTER 1 – FACTION: ARIADNA

An in-depth look at Ariadnan life. Take a journey through the fractious, yet unified, Ariadnan nations: their people and customs. Learn about the details of the different Ariadnan governments, their military traditions and organisation, as well as facets of daily life.

Travel to the highlands of Caledonia, where clans still settle disputes via claymore duels. Visit the tough-as-nails Cossacks of Rodina, where spycraft and diplomacy are both practiced the old-fashioned way, with little difference between them. Meet the independent truckers of the Merovingian trade caravans, and the last real cowboys of the USAriadnan frontier.

CHAPTER 2 – PLANET: DAWN

A planet so appealing that humanity flung itself through a wormhole to get there. A reality so appalling that galactics flee with their tails tucked between their legs. Dawn can be harsh, but no other crucible could have forged Ariadna into the irrepressible force that it is today.

Learn about the paradoxically familiar-yet-alien landscape: its flora, fauna, and untamed wilds. Take a closer look at Caledonian culture: from the superstitious citadel of Cailleach, to the regal splendour of Scone. Learn about metropolitan hubs of Merovingian art and culture like Mariannebourg, discover the heart and soul of Rodinanstanitsas, marvel at Tartary's Transtartaric Railway, and get acquainted with the six states that comprise USAriadna's freedom-loving population.

And if that's not enough, step into the Exclusion Zone and uncover the secrets of missing Yu Jing outposts, rumoured Teseum motherlodes, and the heated conflicts in the Outer Crescent.

CHAPTER 3 – MERCHANT TRADERS

Dive into the world of merchant traders, exploring their unique role in keeping Ariadna from fracturing, both in a historical and current context. Follow the Merovingian Commercial Agents through a competitive world of cutthroat intrigue. Enrich your adventures with a more detailed exploration of Assets, detailed cargo guidelines, and a framework for running encounters, scenarios, and even entire campaigns built around trade in Ariadna and beyond.

CHAPTER 4 – ARIADNAN GEAR

Low-tech, but high-quality, Ariadnans live and die by their equipment. New weapons like the Americolt Eagle hand cannon, Ojotnik rifle, and of course, Teseum claymores, offer a variety of ways to inflict serious damage, while defensive gear like Caledonian Duelling Bracers or Merovingian Métros Armour is designed to offer the reverse. New vehicles, survival gear, and ammunition abound: Ariadna isn't shy about putting its bounty of Teseum to creative use.

CHAPTER 5 – ARIADNAN CHARACTERS

Despite their technological disadvantages, Ariadnans hold their own against the heavyweights of the Human Sphere. With expanded rules for characters' homelands, new Adolescent and Career events, and twelve new careers – from the resourcefulness of the Irmandinhos Smugglers to the brutal tactics of the Spetsnaz – Ariadnan characters have a wealth of new options to explore.

CHAPTER 6 – ANTIPODES AND KIN

Of all the features of Dawn, perhaps none are so deadly and mysterious as the native Antipodes, and their kin, the metisy, or Dog-Blooded. Learn more about Antipodean tribes, the struggle of Wulvers and Dogfaces to find a place in society, even the urban legend of Omerzeniye: nightmarish monsters, allegedly created by the Antipodean cuckoo virus. Learn more about "Dog-Bowl", the supercharged athletic competition with its roots in Ariadnan ghettos, now transformed into a glamorous, lucrative enterprise.

You won't just learn about these creatures, though: with rules for Wulver, Dogface, and even Antipode player characters – and a custom Lifepath system, complete with twelve unique careers – these larger-than-life figures are ready to take their place in your *Infinity* campaign.

CHAPTER 7 – ADVERSARIES

Wild, untamed, deadly... and that's just the cities. Dawn's reputation as a dangerous place is decidedly well-earned. If the native wildlife wasn't threatening enough, Antipodes – and their genetic legacy – introduce an unpredictable danger to Dawn. This includes rare and terrifying hybrid creatures, complete with templates and guidelines for transforming any creature with the Antipode retrovirus.

Richly detailed NPCs round out the collection, with unique capabilities, and their own story hooks to introduce to your campaign. From Dozers and Desperados to the Wulver Pirate Arawn, Lord of Annwn, they'll each inject a unique flavour into your *Infinity* campaign.

CHAPTER 1

LIFE ON ARIADNA

Ariadna is a land of harsh weather, vicious predators, and an ever-present level of intrigue between four nations who until the past few decades believed they would only ever have to contend with themselves. The Ariadnans have since prospered across other worlds in the rest of the Human Sphere and continued to build cities and explore their home planet. The scars left by the Separatist Wars remain strong in their minds but for the moment peace reigns across Dawn as they struggle to survive against a planet they were forced to claim as their own when they lost contact with Earth centuries before.

Now Ariadna is at the forefront of galactic politics. It is simultaneously a relic and a game changer in the eyes of citizens throughout the Human Sphere. No one thought that a planet full of people that can only be described as hailing from the distant past would be able to not only survive without contact with Earth but also be able to stand up against the best fighting forces that the G-5 nations had to offer. Vids on Maya of Caledonian warriors resplendent in kilts and wielding claymores capable of slicing through ORC-clad PanOceania soldiers captivated the minds of millions, and the Dogfaces and Antipodes of Ariadna became feared and respected across the Human Sphere.

Ariadna now finds itself at a curious crossroads that was unforeseen despite being hoped for by the colonists since the landing of *Ariadna*. For years they were forced to fend for themselves and now they can trade for and pursue technologies and resources undreamed by their best scientists. The Ariadna Commercial Conflicts showed them an image of warfare beyond the stars, and now with the rising threat of the Combined Army and dealing with the constant threat of G-5 spies and operatives has led to all of Ariadna having to overhaul not just their equipment and military strategy but their way of thinking about their place in the galaxy.

Much to the surprise of their counterparts on Paradiso or Sol, life on Ariadna is very similar to life in the rest of the Sphere. Though life in the more rural portions of Ariadna is rough and the constant threats associated with living on the frontier might seem incomprehensible to those who have only known life on Tunguska or Neoterra, the people of Ariadna do their best to make do with what they can. Survival is one of the first thoughts on each citizen's mind, and one of the major issues the Ariadnan government must deal with.

THE PEOPLE OF ARIADNA

Life in the cities on Ariadna is similar to that of other planets. Throughout the day people go to their jobs, work until the day ends, then go home to be with their families. In their free time Ariadnans watch movies, listen to music, and attend plays just like their counterparts do. What is different is that their culture has evolved in radically different ways due to a significant bias towards survival over culture and a sense of nostalgia for the Earth their forebears left behind.

Almost every citizen has an affinity for the past, although this feeling is strongest in Caledonia and USAriadna. Schools teach the history of Ariadna and its founding, and although the vast majority of their cultural heritage comes from the memory banks taken from the *Ariadna* colony ship, there is still a strong love affair with classic movies and music. While it is not uncommon for people to hear USAriadnan Blues or Caledonian Metal, a passerby is still likely to hear classic hits by the Doobie Brothers and The Who on the radio alongside more modern music.

As drastically different as life on Dawn appears to those who see glimpses of it on Maya, life only becomes more varied as a visitor travels between the different nations. Rodina is more often considered the political face of the planet, and elegantly dressed Cossack politicians and well-drilled Kazak soldiers are often seen in press conferences and in news vids. Merovingia is the cultural and classy heartland of Ariadna, and the art scene of the country is experiencing a revolution as its own art styles make their way to collectors' houses across the Sphere.

All off-world imagery of the Ariadnans portrays them as caricatures and embodiments of the past as if they were nothing more than reenactors or paid actors putting on a performance. For a citizen of Haqqislam who stepped off a bus on the streets of Deadwood, this image would only be reinforced by the wide-brimmed hats and spurs that the people around him wear so casually. What the galactic scene does not realize is that by and large the majority of Ariadna dresses very casually in their off hours. Lacking the sophistication and finesse that two centuries of galactic fashion has shown to mankind has left Ariadna's own taste in fashion to go on at their own speed. On a hot summer day it is not uncommon to find Caledonians wearing kilts or shorts while hiking in the forested foothills around Scone. In Rodina during winter time, men and women are bundled up in long coats and scarves as they brace against the cold winds coming in off the bay. In USAriadna, fashion in springtime shifts dramatically depending on what state you are in, with several families going for Rockefeller Traditional style with men in slacks and button-up shirts and women in summer dresses, while those living in the cosmopolitan sprawl of Mount Zion may get away with tank tops and denim jeans. It is in Merovingia, however, that galactic fashions are starting to find a home among the most exclusive fashion scene. Both being unafraid to embrace new ideas and willing to pay exorbitantly in order to possess the latest in galactic fashions has made the streets of Mariannebourg home to several fashion boutiques from across the Human Sphere. The cultural elite are careful not to have their clothing clash with their surroundings but are always willing to embrace the new despite calls for others to remember their roots and the ruinous costs of even the simplest off-world apparel.

Despite all their differences with the other G-5 nations, it is cuisine that has helped form the best bridges for diplomacy. Ariadnan restaurants pressured their governments heavily in order for trade embargos to be lifted so that Ariadna could import traditional Sol foods such as Sol cattle, corn, and spices. Dishes that were impossible to replicate on Ariadna such as turkey now were able to be brought to Dawn, although at high prices. While food is not as critical for Ariadna commerce as advanced technologies and refined super materials, it has allowed diplomats on both sides to bring people together and share the distinctive foods of their cultures.

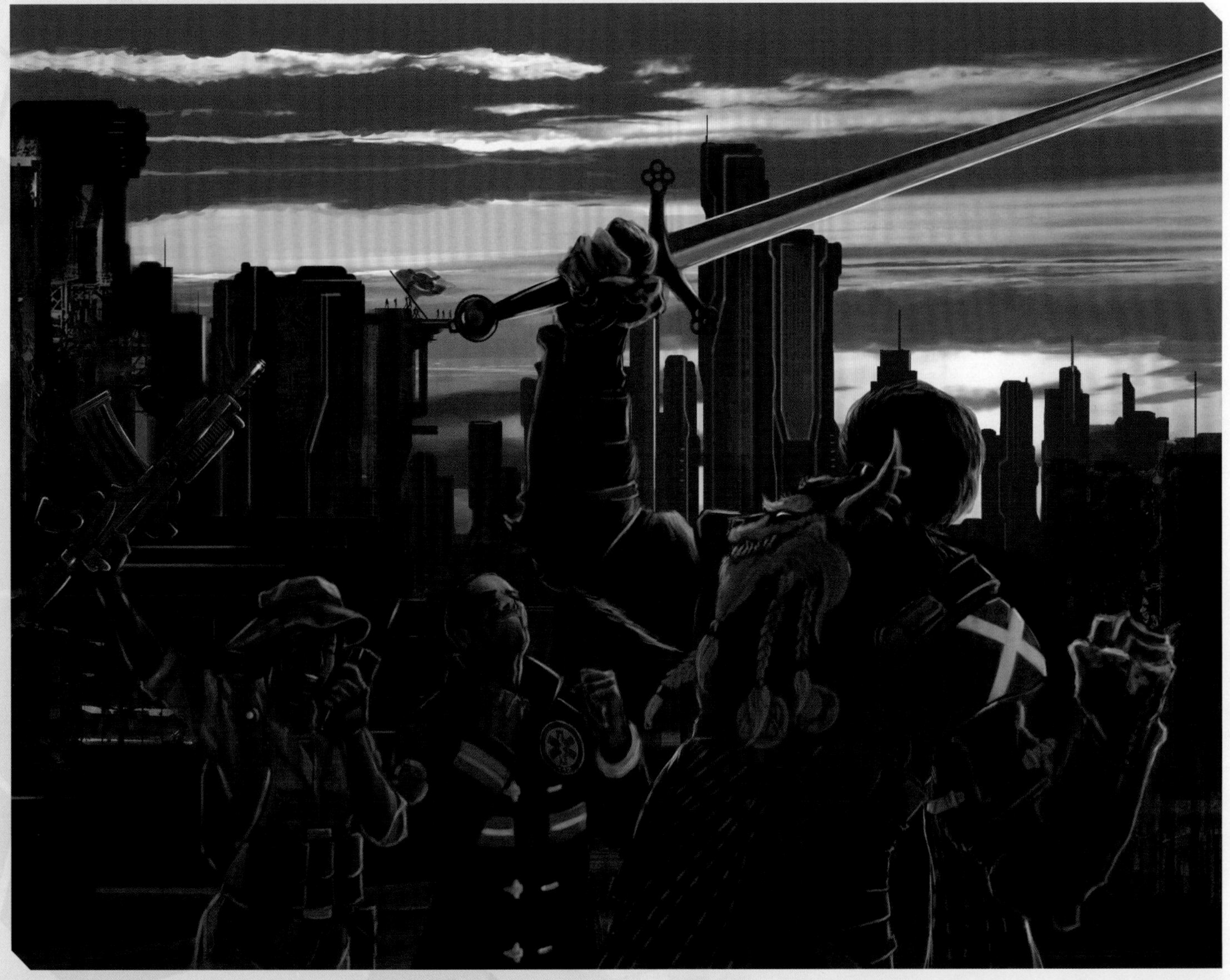

INVADERS FROM SPACE

The Ariadna Commercial Conflicts taught the Ariadnans much about modern warfare. Though military exercises had planned for the possibility of invaders from Earth coming to bring them back under their control, all of these scenarios either dealt with completely fantastical scenarios of ray guns and flying saucers or in comparative technology to what the Ariadnas currently had. When war came with G-5, it was brutal, ugly, and eye-opening but despite that, the Ariadnans learned they were capable of winning.

Early on in the conflicts, Ariadna was forced to fight a guerilla campaign on their own soil. Though the so called Galactic's never sought to dominate large portions of land or conspired to bring the whole of the planet under their control, the Ariadnans treated the Ariadna Commercial Conflicts as if they were trying to do so. Thanks to the Cossack *stanitsa* system they mobilised a large portion of their populace into fighting units and soon off-world bases across the planet found themselves constantly under threat of snipers and bombings. The few cities and settlements that were occupied by PanOceania and other forces soon saw themselves in a constant state of low-grade warfare where they found they could not trust the people they had occupied. Yu Jing incorporated brutal methods to suppress rebellion, but the Ariadnans held strong.

In addition to guerilla tactics, it was a combination of bold battle strategy and the bravery of Ariadnan soldiers that managed to inflict heavy losses on invading forces. Landing sites for off-world ships found themselves assaulted by special operatives who brazenly crossed occupied territory and took the fighting to the invaders. The technological advantage of power armour and monofilament blades were evened out by the ready availability of Teseum and its use in constructing weapons, bullets, and armour for the Ariadna armed forces. Though platoons of power armoured soldiers were capable of devastating entire regiments of Ariadnan soldiers, the advantage was mitigated when small squads of Caledonian Mormaers and Merovingian Moblots were able to stand toe to toe with the heavily armoured warriors.

Another unseen advantage that the Ariadnans managed to use to the surprise of the invaders was the presence of Antipodes, Dogfaces, and Wulvers on the battlefield. PanOceania had no idea of the existence these races and did not expect for the small groups of seemingly lightly armed men and women charging their lines to turn into massive monstrosities of fur and steel.

Though the Antipodes were not actively involved in the conflict, the tribes would almost always fight any off-world threat that landed on or crossed their territory. Early in the conflict, invading PanOceanians and Yu Jing forces were lured into using Antipode territory as landing sites. Reports of Antipode aggression combined with reports of the ferociousness of Dogfaces and Wulver commandos led to much confusion as the invading sides conflated the Antipodes with Dogfaces in early reports and believed the aliens to be in league with the colonists.

At the end of the Ariadna Commercial Conflicts, O-12, with vocal support from the unaligned countries, was keen to apply international law to Ariadna and end hostilities. Through hard negotiation and significant sanctions, the fighting nations were forced to sign a peace treaty with each other.

This established the sovereignty of Ariadna across the main continent in a region called the Ariadna Exclusion Zone. The exclusion zone is the area that constitutes the official borders of Ariadna. Foreign powers are not allowed within the zone except for scientific purposes and even then they must endure significant red tape from a committee of O-12 and Ariadnan representatives. In unexplored areas such as the archipelagos outside the zone, the other powers are permitted to operate settlements though the construction of new bases is subject to even fiercer red tape. To Ariadna, this compromise was taken as an insult to their national pride, but the Cossack High Command realised there were more invaders arriving every week and with the threat of atmospheric bombardment, they signed the treaty while planning for the day when they could reclaim all of Dawn for Ariadna.

SOLDIERS OF DAWN

The Ariadnan military is one of the most varied fighting forces to hail from a single planet. Though most modern militaries have done their best to codify and unite their soldiers into similar disciplines and classifications, Ariadna combines the men and women of four distinct militaries into one single, united force capable of withstanding any challengers. This is simultaneously Ariadna's greatest strength and weakness when it comes to organising their assets. It gives Ariadna considerable strength because each nation's army gives them the ability to field different fighting styles and keep their opponents guessing as to how their army will react in battle. It is a weakness because even the best trained commanders will not know how their soldiers will react with the combination of mixed units into a single force, and it is not uncommon for command structure to break down when the ranking officer of an Ariadnan detachment is killed and infighting occurs between the different commanders about who is in charge.

THE UNKNOWN RANGER

Classification: Lone Special Operations Asset

The Unknown Ranger is a myth that is told by soldiers as they share beers around the campfire late at night. In modern media, the Unknown Ranger is considered to be a recruitment tool meant to inspire boys and girls to join the Ariadna Armed Forces when they grow older, and to the enemies of Ariadna, the Unknown Ranger is considered a laughable idea that a single soldier possessing supernatural abilities could exist when real threats such as the Dogfaces and SAS commandos are actual threats to counter.

The truth is the Unknown Ranger is a tradition that originated with the philosophy of Old Man Ross. In one of his most famous recorded speeches he talked about how "one man, driven by purpose and possessing great skill, can be more effective than an army if we would simply let him do what needs to be done." The USAriadnan Ranger Force has taken this saying to heart and occasionally will designate a Ranger who has gone through great personal loss or shows tremendous skill to serve temporarily in the role of the Unknown Ranger. The Unknown Ranger does what needs to be done in order to win the day, whether this means taking over when the commanding officer is killed or bravely sneaking behind enemy lines to save captured soldiers.

LOUP-GAROU

Classification: Special Foreign Species Management and Tactics

When a fight starts in a bar, the police are called to keep the peace. When the fighters transform into 500-pound wrecking machines of toughened sinew and razor-sharp claws, the police call upon the Loup-Garous. Trained to be versatile, brave, and resourceful combatants, the Loup-Garous are able to switch between an arsenal of tranquilizer darts and other weaponry as needed to deal with a variety of threats.

Originally designed to serve as a controlling force capable of dealing with the rising internal threat of raging Dogfaces and the possibility of invading Antipodes, the Loup-Garous are more than an animal control team. Loup-Garou are highly trained agents of the Gendarmerie capable of keeping the peace and dealing with high-stress scenarios ranging from hostage situations to rampaging Dogfaces.

THE DEVIL DOGS

Classification: Mobile Aggressive Search and Destroy Operations

Though the Rangers may hold the hearts and minds of the USAriadnan public, the legend of the USAriadna Marine Corps is well known to their enemies. The 116th Marine Regiment was responsible for holding the line at the Battle of The Wall against the First Antipode Offensive and subsequently their descendants showed the highest tendency to be Dogfaces. Despite the growing resentment for Dogfaces and Antipodes across Ariadna, these men and women decided to serve their country and petitioned to join the Marine Corps as their forefathers did. Realising that a Dogface paired with an Antipode partner made for a devastatingly effective scout team whose senses would allow them to pick out specific enemy targets or search for concealed contraband faster than an ordinary human, the 2nd Assault Battalion of the USAMC was born.

Taking their name from the Marines who served in World War I on Earth, the Devil Dogs manage their responsibilities well. Their missions are dangerous and take all their skill and strength to survive. Though Dogfaces and Antipodes come from different cultures, they learned to put aside their differences and work as effective teams with the simplistic skill and natural tendencies of the Antipodes complimenting the training and discipline of the Marines.

9TH WULVER GRENADIERS

Classification: Elite Shock Troopers

The children of those who inherited the Dogface virus may have an easier time controlling their emotions but have a harder time hiding who they are in Ariadnan society due to the physical changes they exhibit at birth. Though some are able to hide who they are as they grow older through cosmetic means, the majority embrace their different nature and natural physical superiority to others. The largest colony of Wulvers is located in Caledonia where they are often shock troops capable of moving quickly around the battlefield to support Caledonian soldiers.

The Wulvers serving in the 9th Grenadiers may appear to be brazen and raucous on the battlefield but they take their role in the Caledonian Army seriously. They know that any mistake could cost the lives of their countrymen and though they may be mistreated on the streets of Scone, if they are able to save the life of a single countryman while inflicting heavy damages upon their opponent then they did a good job and more than earned their celebratory beers when they get back to the base.

HARDCASES

Classification: Irregular Warfare Specialist

To the members of the 2nd Irregular Frontiersmen Battalion the idea of being alone behind enemy lines is not a new one. They were formed during the Antipode conflicts to meet the need for dedicated scouts who could range beyond the Ariadna frontier and report the movements of Antipodes back to the military. Their name comes from the reputation these scouts earned for their resilience and survival skills; to survive beyond the frontier against the threat of Antipode tribes desiring only to track them down and kill them proves that they are truly Hardcases.

In modern times Hardcases serve both in and outside the Ariadnan military. Some have lived so long on their own in the wild that the thought of returning to the civilised world is almost unbearable and many prefer to stick to their lone campsites and trails that they call home. Others serve the general public by helping track down those lost in the wilderness or keeping an eye on Antipodes and their tribal boundaries. Many lost campers have had their lives saved when the Antipode stalking them was brought down silently by an arrow through its eye.

DOZERS

Classification: Combat Engineers

The Dozers are the engineering workhorse of the Ariadnan Army. Whether in peacetime or when at war, the Ariadna Corps of Engineers is constantly busy from constructing communication towers in the wilderness to repairing damaged military hardware in a hurry. Their name comes from a moment in Ariadnan history when a wrecked Cossack tank convoy blocked the central highway during the Separatist Wars. When asked how they would move the damaged tanks, their commander famously said, "Give me five minutes and a good dozer and we can move anything." Since then the name stuck and became the unofficial nickname for combat engineers serving in the Ariadnan Army.

The Dozers are trained for combat but are mostly taught to keep their heads down and focus on their task at hand. Capable of keeping their focus despite a hail of gunfire overhead, the Dozers know that while they may not be the best shots or the most ferocious in hand-to-hand combat, they have one of the most important tasks. The Dozers take great pride in their skills, and know they can count on their fellow soldiers to keep them safe as they go about their work on the battlefield.

5TH MINUTEMEN REGIMENT OHIO

Classification: Heavy Tactical Assault Force

Descended from part of the Ranger detachment that served to protect the original colonists, the Minutemen are more than just a unit descended from patriotic tradition. The Minutemen take their motivation from the brave souls who helped protect America from imperial control in its early days. In modern days, the 5th Minutemen serve a similar purpose and are deployed in situations where they must stand against enemy agents and inflict heavy damage.

Given the best armour and equipment that USAriadna has to offer, the 5th Minutemen Regiment Ohio are deployed across Dawn as a secondary response unit when military assets are required. They are not trained for covert ops but their Ranger training allows them to keep up with SAS and Spetsnaz agents in the field. When required to go loud, they go loud, and whether they are wielding sniper rifles or missile launchers they fire their weapons with skill, precision, and purpose.

SPETSNAZ

Classification: Elite Tactical Operations Specialists

The members of the *Voskya Spesialnogo Naznecheniya* are more than elite forces working for the Cossacks; they are the iron will of Rodina made flesh. The Spetsnaz are trained in brutal and sadistic methods designed to create the best soldiers possible and the methods are effective at what they create. Each Spetsnaz is trained to work both as a team and as an independent operative in the field but in either scenario they do not give way to flashy methods or blatant shows of bravado as other units will. The Spetsnaz strike like a scalpel, and know where and how to strike their opponents to achieve the desired results as fast as possible.

Spetsnaz training is considered controversial in that it has a higher turnover than Ranger or SAS training. While death is a possibility in other spec ops training, it is not uncommon for a Spetsnaz trainee's family to receive a note saying their child died during training. The Spetsnaz are also notorious for their reputation as ruthless enforces of the Rodina regime. Many believe that the government in Mat' uses Spetsnaz to strike out against dissidents. This may or may not be true but it is a rumour that the Cossack High Command enjoys spreading as it helps keep others in line through fear.

TROUBLE ON DAWN

Though Ariadna is a young nation, it does have its problems. From poverty, corruption, and internal dissidents, Ariadna is caught in a perilous place where it managed to maintain its own independence in the face of foreign invasion but it knows that between the threats of the Combined Army, aggressive acts from other nations in O-12, and internal strife, its newfound wealth and prosperity could be stripped away at any moment.

Not every Ariadnan is treated equally despite the Ariadnan constitution guaranteeing them this fact. Those fortunate enough to live in a major city often enjoy the fruits of their nation or do not have to worry about the threats of Antipode attacks or other dangers. Those living in a major city do not fear winters on Dawn and the threat of freezing to death or running out of food, but poor settlements do not have the same luxury. For some, the prospect of being caught off-guard by inclement weather or rockslides could mean people die, while other settlements are wary of Antipode attacks and keep a watchful eye at night for the predatory wolves at their doorstep.

There is also vast disenfranchisement for many Ariadnans. For some, it's as simple as not being born in the right class. The lower class in Rodina and USAriadna can expect few handouts to help ease their financial burden, and those born to a poor clan in Caledonia often never see the opportunities that are handed to those who hail from more noble lineages. Those born in the upper classes on Dawn are more likely to see pieces of off-world technology or be permitted to experience foreign foods and music while those living in lower class neighbourhoods may only get to deal with old and often dodgy Ariadnan technology.

Life is even worse for Dogfaces, Wulvers, and the Antipodes themselves. Dogfaces are treated like second class citizens and are required to register with the Ariadnan government. Though some do have inherent anger issues, the vast majority are treated like ticking time bombs and are often mistreated by law enforcement. Job opportunities for Dogfaces and Wulvers are almost always related with physical labour or service in the military, and although some relish using their abilities free of restriction there are some that find themselves trapped outside of the system and forced to resort to a life of crime in order to survive and feed their families. It is not uncommon for criminal syndicates to employ them as enforcers or body guards. Ironically, since the end of the Ariadna Commercial Conflicts it has become more common for off-world businessmen, gangsters, and PMC to hire Dogfaces and Wulvers to serve in their organisations, which gives them the best chance out of all Ariadnans to seek employment off-planet.

There are also the numerous growing dissident movements which have started to become more militant. The most recognised is DNAriadna, a hard-line group that is vehemently opposed to off-world settlements or in the exchange of culture with outsiders. They view immigrants from PanOceania and other nations as a threat to their way of life, and believe that Ariadnan traditions will disappear as they become beholden to the ways and technology of outsiders.

Other separatist movements include:

The Mummers, a Caledonian secessionist movement hoping to regain Caledonian independence from Rodina. They believe their homeland needs to stand on their own. They are often recognised by their use of a hand signal consisting of placing an index finger over the mouth to demonstrate that "mum's the word" and no one should talk about the group's motives in public.

L'Armée de la Rose, or the Army of the Rose. A political group that hopes to liberate the underclass of Merovingia from what they see as the corrupt and oppressive government, L'Armée de la Rose is responsible for the bombings, both successful and attempted, of several banks and mortgage companies across Merovingia. They are a tolerant organization that is known to welcome Dogfaces and Wulvers into their ranks.

Sons of Liberty, a USAriadnan-based movement that teaches their members that they are descended from patriots and rebels and that they do not need to be beholden to a government thousands of miles away in Rodina when they can govern themselves. The Sons of Liberty are problematic in trying to eliminate because of how well liked they are by the people, and because almost every USAriadnan harbours similar sentiments ever since the end of the Separatist Wars. Their demonstrations have grown more violent in recent years, and several acts of vandalism have been blamed on them as well as threats of bombings and assassinations towards Ariadnan government buildings and visiting off-world tourists.

The Red Star is controversial in Rodina because it fights back against the corruption of the government but unlike other separatist groups, they hope to extend their membership across Ariadna and have developed splinter groups in the other three nations. Citing a modern interpretation of old Soviet ideals, the Red Star aims to work at both the highest levels of Rodina's government while also organising workers to form unions to protect worker's rights.

CHAPTER 2

PLANET: DAWN

The similarities between Dawn and Earth were one of many factors that led to it being an ideal place for colonisation after the discovery of the wormhole, but the environment of Ariadna proved to be every bit of a challenge to the early colonists as dealing with the threats of starvation or the Antipodes. The planet is cooler than the world mankind was used to and the frequent rains and rocky terrain of the region where the *Ariadna* landed made survival difficult. Fortunately, the colonists were survivors and had brought with them the best gear and the best trained soldiers that Earth could provide, which was fortunate because it let them survive blizzards, hurricanes, and the scorching heat of the Ariadnan deserts and expand across Dawn.

CLIMATE AND GEOGRAPHY

One of the many reasons that made Dawn such an enticing planet for colonisation was how similar it was to Sol. Though its average temperatures are usually cooler than Sol, its atmosphere and ecosystem were remarkably similar to the types of terrain that humanity was used to. The environment of Dawn ranges from frigid mountains to burning hot deserts, but for the most part its vast hills and valleys provide home for the people of Dawn.

Dawn features a higher than average rainfall than Sol, with an intense rainy season that lasts from fall into spring. This weather is more severe in Rodina and Caledonia, where the settlements have adapted their buildings to the muddy grounds and threat of flooding. Caledonian villagers build their homes at the top of the valleys that line their country, while in Rodina the buildings along the coast are built to endure the monsoons that frequently roll in during the spring and summer.

Ariadnan winters are especially brutal and gruelling, and even in USAriadna snowfall is common. The need for warm clothing has given Ariadna a rugged look in the eyes of Maya broadcasts, and fur is a common accessory for Caledonian and Rodina fashion. Snowfall is particularly dangerous for those who live in USAriadna and Caledonia where heavy snowfalls can cut off roads and isolate border towns and outposts. In winter months, ATVs and snowmobiles are essential for travel between towns and most homes utilise fireplaces as well as gas heating in order to keep warm.

Summers on Dawn are warm and sunny, with temperatures in Merovingia and Rodina reaching as high as 35 degrees Celsius. Summer is typically seen as a time of travel and it is when trade convoys and delegations travel between the nations. Summer festivals are also common with each nation celebrating holidays from old Earth such as Independence Day in USAriadna or Bastille Day in Merovingia. On top of this are the holidays of Arrival Day, celebrating the landing of the Ariadna colony ship, and Unification Day, which was established by Rodina to celebrate the union of all nations on Dawn into one.

MIRROR SEA

One of the primary seas controlled by *Ariadna*, the Mirror Sea was named by original surveyors of the planet after its calm seas reflecting the sun brightly during the day. The Mirror Sea is where the majority of Rodina's fishing fleet operates and has been responsible for feeding Ariadnans since the founding of the colony.

SEA OF THE SPINNERS

Located on the eastern side of the primary continent, the Sea of the Spinners is named after the intensive storm activity on its surface. "Waterspout" tornadoes are known to form in the sea with some regularity, which has made the sea dangerous for USAriadna's shipping and commercial fishing but the abundant resources located in the waters and along the coasts have made the area a priority for Ariadna's economy.

SPINAL MOUNTAINS

Home to some of the oldest and most ancient Antipode ruins on the planet, the Spinal Mountains have been a battleground for mankind and Antipodes since the *Ariadna* landed. The region is also full of abundant natural resources and Teseum but is considered too dangerous for mining due to the threat of Antipode attacks. The Spinal Mountains serve as an important buffer for USAriadna and a proving ground for the regular troops that patrol them.

FLORA AND FAUNA

The animal life of Dawn is as varied as Sol though animals tend to lean more towards mammals with thick hides and coats of fur. The colder climate has pushed the majority of reptiles towards the deserts lining USAriadna, and the northern hemisphere of the planet features many larger mammals than their counterparts on Sol. Bears are common on Dawn and hold cultural significance to the many nations on the planet. The Tartary bear, with its thick grey fur, is often used as a mascot for military units out of Rodina and Caledonia, while the Golden Bear with its light brown pelt and long legs is a deadly predator. The Antipodes hunt the Golden Bear as part of their rite of passage, while human hunters trade the pelts and claws along the many border forts of Ariadna. The Golden Bear's claws have slight traces of Teseum in them, giving them an almost supernatural sharpness that makes them a threat even to Mormaers in heavy armour.

The seas of Dawn are dangerous and even experienced sailors lose their lives over the tiniest mistakes. Even calm seas never last long as heavy winds and tumultuous waves can capsize the sturdiest vessels or bring down flyers who lose themselves in sudden storm fronts that can appear along the coasts. The phrase "calm as the seas of Dawn" is used to describe something that appears deceptively calm but is actual a torrent of vicious riptides or dangerous predators waiting to come to the surface.

The ocean's biosphere is also a danger to explorers. The oceans team with wildlife in the deep waters, and the Dawn Tiger Shark is a voracious predator known to be highly territorial. Even the whales on Dawn are massive and uncaring creatures, and the Ariadnan Thunderwhale is a massive giant known to accidentally capsize unwary fishing vessels.

It is difficult to describe the environment on Dawn without mentioning the importance that it plays for Antipodes. Antipodes are still in an early stage of development and as such live off the land. The wealth and prosperity of a tribe is often determined by their access to ample hunting grounds and since the arrival of the colonists, the natural migration patterns of deer and elk have been disrupted, forcing the Antipodes to adapt their hunting patterns. Despite mankind's offers to help "civilise" the tribes by providing them with the technological means to produce their own food, Antipodes find that confining their prey to narrow cages spoils the meat. Antipodes have been forced to cede much of their traditional lands to the Ariadnans and this insult is a common reason for the tribes to go to war with humanity.

LEADING BANKS PER NATION:

Royal Caledonian Banking Union (Caledonia)

La Monnaie Financing and Loan (Merovingia)

Mat' Commercial Credit Union (Rodina)

Dodge Banking and Capital (USAriadna)

OF WOLVES AND MAN

Like on Sol, one of the more dominant species on Dawn was descended from wolves instead of apes, although there are still apes on Dawn. Though species on Dawn are still being documented, a popular species kept in Ariadnan zoos are Foxbears, which are small fox-like creatures with opposable thumbs and complex family structures. They are believed to be an evolutionary off-shoot of the Antipodes but do not possess their advanced cognitive skills.

ECONOMY

Ariadna's economy is split between how it functions internally and how it functions on the galactic stage. For centuries, Ariadna could only trade with itself, as even the Antipodes only wanted very limited trade with the colonists and were happy with receiving worked metal and agricultural products. Now that Ariadna is a small but growing power in the Human Sphere, it spends its time preparing its economy for an influx of foreign goods while at the same time doing its best to modernise and bring its people to the same technological level as PanOceania or the Nomads.

Although the government is based out of Rodina, Merovingia is the true trade centre of Ariadna. It sits in a prime location between the other three nations and it maintains the largest fleet of trains, transport trucks, and commercial aircraft out of its neighbours. Merovingia also doubles as the commerce capital of Ariadna, and several of its major banks have their primary headquarters based out of Mariannebourg. Mariannebourg is also home to the Ariadna Stock Exchange which keeps an eye on the growing investment network that has been expanding since the collapse of the wormhole.

The introduction of interstellar trade and O-12 has led to a mad rush for Ariadna to modernise their banking practices and deal with the influx of foreign currency and goods into their markets. Before the arrival of PanOceania and the other nations, Ariadnan businesses lived and died on providing the most cutting-edge products developed solely by Ariadnan businessmen and financiers. Now their market struggles with the influx of advanced and cheap equipment produced off-world and sold for prices comparable to Ariadnan goods. Sensing that this economic force could destabilise their entire industry, the Ariadnan government passed an emergency measure known as the Ariadnan Interstellar Commerce Act (AICA), which limits the amount of off-world goods that are allowed on the planet and places stiff fines and sanctions on any Ariadnan business that deals primarily in off-world goods. Many businesses are simultaneously grateful and hesitant about the AICA, since it does encourage Ariadnan businesses and keeps the Ariadnan ruble strong but deprives them of seeking out technological secrets that could give them an advantage over their rivals.

CALEDONIA

Caledonia is a modern anachronism made of a proud people who have managed to preserve their independence despite being absorbed into one

Ariadnan nation by the Cossacks many years ago. They are often made fun of in Maya comedies or even in jokes told by their fellow Ariadnans. The idea of brutish Scotsmen in long kilts and talking in a strange language is a source of amusement for many who think of Caledonia as a backwater nation. The truth is that Caledonia is not just proud, but they are rightfully proud, and though their customs are different from others their strength keeps them united and safe against all enemies.

Descended from the 45th Highlander Rifles, they were originally tasked with being part of the security forces for the first expedition. After all contact was lost with Earth, the 45th Highlanders and their families moved towards the north and began to establish a string of border forts and defences around sources of fresh water and game trails in order to provide protection from the Antipodes. Over time, contact between each outpost became sporadic and some became completely cut off from their neighbours. Owing to their survivalist tendencies, many of these outposts managed to thrive and became the ancestral homes for the noble families that comprise the Caledonian government today.

Contrary to popular belief, the Caledonian dialect is a mixture of English, Gaelic, and Danish, and most Caledonians are able to speak Caledonian as well as English. Each household maintains their ancestors as heroes, and it is not uncommon for pictures of their original ancestors to be found in homes above the fireplace or bar. Caledonians are proud of their heritage and view themselves as true survivors who held the line against Antipodes.

Part of this pride shows itself in their martial lineages. Though the idea of sword-wielding warriors who are not bound in high-tech suits of armour may seem suicidal to people watching videos on Maya, the truth is Caledonians practice with martial weaponry from a young age. Simultaneously considered a rite of passage as well as a sport for Caledonian youth, it is not uncommon for Caledonians to spend their Sundays on the village green practicing with bows and heavy metal practice swords so that they can learn to protect themselves. This helps those Caledonians who decide to join the house guard of local dukes or who seek careers in the Ariadnan military, where their training with bows and steel claymores is supplanted with training in Combi Rifles and Teseum-laced claymores.

Caledonians are deeply spiritual people, and view the world around them as a gift that is earned through survival and duty to their families and to their country. A Caledonian who does not contribute in some way to their village or city is considered a traitor to their countrymen. This comes from the days when survival was not guaranteed and every soldier in the 45th Highlanders were required to spend sixteen-hour days protecting their families and building structures in the wilderness. Even the nobility are not immune to this worldview, and a decadent and out-of-shape noble is considered reflective of their people. Nobles are encouraged to spend time in the fields helping farmers or on the Green practicing with the soldiers that live or die at their command.

Superstitions are also considered a major part of Caledonian life. Most Caledonians believe that Dawn is a planet of mythic wonder, and many families have stories of heroes prevailing against the monsters that lurk beyond the threshold of each village. Many of these superstitions are bastardisations of traditional myths and legends from old Earth, although most have been given a modern Ariadnan twist. Stories of Antipode chieftains with enchanted swords or massive dragons lurking in the mountains are undoubtedly taken from Antipodes wielding Teseum or wildlife lurking in the ranges but for most Caledonians, they maintain a strict code of conduct when it comes to the supernatural and refuse to break some traditions for fear of bringing bad luck down upon their families.

CALEDONIAN CUISINE AND CULTURE

Caledonians are firm traditionalists despite having come up with their own unique culture on Dawn. They favour sticking with the ways of their forefathers and although change is occasionally welcomed it is seen with disregard by older members of their society who view life in Caledonia as rapidly changing ever since the renewed contact with the rest of the Human Sphere.

Caledonians traditionally prefer two meals during the day, with a light snack in the morning holding them over until they can have a heavy meal for lunch and dinner. Caledonians prefer stews and heavy slabs of meat and vegetables, although those who live near lakes prefer meals of baked or fried fish. Caledonians also prefer stouts and dark ales, and the Dawn barley grown in Caledonia provides them with a thick, peaty taste.

When it comes to the arts, Caledonians prefer pieces that detail their view of bawdy heroism. Statues are often depicted with weapons and most paintings show Caledonians triumphing over adversity. Many homes and public places will have paintings illustrating glorious moments in a clan's history, often regaling their viewers with a mythical account of a clan's ancestors doing battle with Antipodes or during the Ariadna Commercial

SUPERSTITIONS

Traditional Caledonian customs for warding off black magic include wearing iron and Teseum torcs around their neck when they leave the house, turning three times and spitting on the ground when the name of a hated rival is uttered in their presence, and lightning massive piles of Dawnwart weed during full moons in order to keep the Antipodes away.

THE GREEN

Referred to as the Green, the village green in the centre of many Caledonian settlements is where impromptu games of football, American football, and Dog Bowl take place when it is not used for training.

Conflicts. Most families maintain an ancestral weapon from the early days of Ariadna, though contrary to the belief of avid Maya viewers these are not ancient suits of armour and longswords but instead aging assault rifles and combat knives often wielded by the original soldiers who landed on Dawn.

A LAND OF EMERALD AND WHITE

Two qualities stand out in the landscape of Caledonia. The first is how spread out the country is, with most cities and villages being a substantial distance from each other. Though this is not always the case, it is possible that farmers in a village near Inverloch may never see someone hailing from Cailleach. Though trade is encouraged between all villages, most Caledonians prefer to stay in their hometowns around their families and do their best to avoid the complicated and convoluted life in major cities.

The second is the pristine nature of Caledonia's forests and mountains. Though Caledonia is an up-and-coming nation, they prefer to build simply and do not cut down more trees than they need to. Sources of water are kept pristine and pure in case they are needed to feed the settlement, and conservationists do their best to make sure that the local herds of Ariadnan deer and elk are protected from excessive hunting. They do their best to keep their homeland a pristine beauty as much as reverence to God and Ariadna as it is for their Antipodan neighbours. Knowing that senseless slaughters of animals or despoiling the environment may anger neighbouring tribes, Caledonians try to take only what they need. The Caledonian mindset does permit them to take what they want, as the survival of humanity will always trump the preferences of their alien neighbours.

CAILLEACH

One of the greatest forts in Caledonia, it was established early during the First Antipode Offensive and is the centrepiece of Caledonian defences along the west. Originally a short, flat bunker lined with turrets and narrow walls for defenders to aim rifles out of, the fort has become a veritable fortress that is seen from miles away. Cailleach is topped with a massive lighthouse that provides a beacon for travellers lost in the countryside with a light to show them home.

Though the city is known for its heavy military presence, it is also considered one of the most visible representations of Caledonian culture and this is best exemplified by the cuisine found in the city. The Cailleach cattle yards and other farms supply meat to most of Caledonia and it is here that travellers can find traditional Scottish meals as well as culinary styles hailing from the rest of Ariadna. During a windy day the pungent smells of the cattle yards can find their way into the city while at night the smell of smoked and spiced meats hangs heavily in Cailleach's centre district.

Cailleach is known for its strategic importance, and few can doubt the sheer firepower of its mounted guns. But it is perhaps more well known

to other nations as one of the more superstitious of Caledonian places. All who live here abide by a strict code of conduct meant to keep away the evil spirits that lurk around the city. Named after an ancient hag from Gaelic folklore, the people of the city take their superstitions seriously. So seriously, in fact, that they have designed their city along several lines of metaphysical thought as well as practicality in warfare.

The southern gate of the city is only used for visiting Antipodes, Dogfaces, and Wulvers as they are already seen as having a touch of the devil upon them (a cruel stereotype enforcing racist mindsets that have stubbornly clung on in Caledonia). This is due to the belief that the southern gate is where all negative energy is channelled but also has historical precedent. During the Grief of the Clans, Jock McDougall led his men through the southern gate into the city and it was in Cailleach where he struck down Robert McDougall, the head of the clan. Since then the people of Cailleach avoid the southern gate if possible and go out of their way to enter the city through its other entrances. More devout followers of superstition believe that the negative energy flows straight from Cailleach and all the way towards Mat', leading credence to the Caledonians distrust of Rodina in general.

Cailleach also has become the centre for exotic faiths in Ariadna. Several followers of the Old Faith, or witchcraft as it is known on Earth, have set up numerous shops and spiritual sites in the city. For the most part, the people of Cailleach do not mind these places and it is not uncommon for gifts of protective herbs or artwork inscribed with warding spells to be bought as housewarming gifts or as a present for someone's birthday. Visitors from USAriadna and Merovingia love the kitschy nature of these shops, and tourism is one of the major sources of income for the city.

CALONACK

Considered by many to be the party capital of the planet, the city is renowned for its whiskey distilleries and for Calonack University. Whiskey and scotch produced by the town's many distilleries is prized across Ariadna and recently the two largest distilleries, Magh Bae and Loveless Spirits, have secured government contracts to trade their goods with PanOceania. This has led to a large influx of money for the small city and across the city's horizon townsfolk see the sight of construction cranes and half-built buildings.

Calonack University is the largest university of its type in Caledonia. Though many settlements and cities boast trade schools and centres of learning, Calonack University is the largest to exist outside of a capital city. The university's focus is in engineering, and the wait-list to get into the university is often very long and they are highly particular in who they accept. The school also receives funding from the military and the famous Dozers are often trained at CU before being sent into the field. The CU Centre for Robotics is considered the best on the planet, and the laboratories there are said to be producing the next generation of Muls for the Ariadnan military.

COILLE LAITH

Coille Laith is a brutal, cold fortress that stands as a major barrier between the Antipodes as well as an important holding ground for Caledonian goods on their way from mines in the north of Ariadna to the south. It has a reputation for being a draconian and harsh place and it is not undeserved, with the military having to serve as police officers and where the highest state of battle preparedness and security is maintained at all times. This has led to a brutally effective system but has done little to help with civil rights for those who feel like they are targeted by this oppressive system, and many of those who are happen to be Dogfaces or outsiders from other nations.

The city is still heavily involved in operations against the Antipodes, and sorties are routinely launched from the city. When not involved in monitoring and countering actions taken by the Antipodes in the Exclusion Zone, Coille Laith is vital in Caledonia's attempts to control smuggling throughout the region. Soldiers serving at Coille Laith do not know if the next threat they face will be by an Antipode's claws or a smuggler's gun, but this tense atmosphere has created some of the toughest soldiers in Caledonia who take great pride in serving "where the action is".

DAL RIADA

"Before you can own the land you must first own yourself." It is an inscription that is carved into the massive stone at the centre of the town's village green and one every citizen knows by heart. Founded by scouts and rangers who desired to make their home on the lake's scenic shores, there is a joke that if Ariadna ever establishes another nation then it will have Dal Riada as its new capitol. A city of hunters and survivalists, Dal Riada is not as weak or as peaceful as it may appear, as every member of the city is expected to learn how to fire a weapon by the age of ten and is required to attend weekly drills in the town militia.

INVERLOCH

Inverloch is as controversial as it is iconic in the minds of modern day Caledonians. Built on the edge of Caledonian territory, it was also built across carefully assigned treaty lines as laid out by local Antipode tribes. Inverloch itself is a statement to

LOCHEIL LAKE

The lake has more stories told about it then the founding fathers of Ariadna, and some range from the strange and magical to the cold and real. The lake's bounty of fish has drawn fishermen to its banks and is the lifeblood of Dal Riada, but the lake is also home to a much darker tradition. It is said that a secret cult of survivalists meet at night along its shores and settle disputes with hunting knives and fists. The loser of said fight has their body wrapped in heavy fishing lines and dropped to the bottom of the lake where it is said their body will nourish the fish.

the Antipodes: "We are here, and we will prosper" is inscribed on the city's flagpole in English as well as the trinary language of the Antipodes. The fort is also a test site for Antipode detection equipment and surveillance systems, and for miles around the city there are carefully hidden sensors and cameras that allow for the city to be aware of any sudden invasions.

Despite Inverloch being controversial, it is also regarded as an important installation for the Caledonian military. It greatly aids the Ariadnan military in monitoring the Exclusion Zone and provides an important link in the local supply chain. Bureau Aegis maintains a small field office in Inverloch, where a skeleton crew of four agents work tirelessly and thanklessly to handle the Concillium's affairs within the region.

TUATHCRUITHNE

Nestled under the eaves of the Boceliande Forest, this rugged and enduring rural colony is a refuge for anyone seeking a simpler life free of the clan rivalries that dominate Scone's political arena. Most residents of Scone forgive the fiercely independent Tuathcruithneans their oddities, as the master brewers of the Boceliande forest brew the most renowned beer in all Caledonia. Though the forest has been declared an Antipode-free zone, the settlement itself has become something of a haven for Dog-Blooded in need of sanctuary – including the Firbolg of Cailleach, a hybrid almost as legendary as the settlement's beer.

SCONE

The wealthiest and most powerful of all Caledonian cities, Scone is the seat of government for Caledonia. At night the city is a literal beacon across the countryside as a mixture of torchlight and modern lighting gives the city a regal glow. It is here that all manners regarding Caledonia are decided by the Caledonian Parliament, and it is here that the struggle between tradition and the future is fought on the front lines as modern Caledonians plead with their brethren to think of the benefits of technology and the traditionalists implore their radical brethren to remember the benefits of the ways of their forefathers.

Scone's architecture is a mixture of classic Earth medieval fortifications, 20th century Edinburgh buildings, and, in stark contrast, modern communication towers and satellite relays. Each clan maintains a home in the city and the larger and wealthier clans are able to create massive fortifications resembling ancient castles belonging to the old Highland lords of Earth. By contrast, the western side of the city is home to towering skyscrapers and modern apartments. A tourist travelling from the west side into downtown Scone will often feel like they have travelled in time, while a farmer who has only known his clan's keep as the largest building he has ever seen will regard the western half of the city as alien and off-putting.

A stark divide that has occurred within Scone is the patronage of many neighbourhoods by Caledonian dukes seeking to expand their reach and power within the city. Although the city is under the control of the mayor of Scone and the city council, each neighbourhood proudly displays tartans at their intersections showing their support for several noble families. The larger and more prominently displayed a tartan is represents how much control they have in the area, while those families who do not possess the resources to patronise any neighbourhoods in the city are often forgotten by its citizens.

It is here that the quickly shifting alliances between the many clans of the nation are often felt by the people of Scone. Family loyalists are quick to be vocal and proud of their clan's achievements, while those from rival families are quick to argue back. Every few years violence between the citizenry occurs when supporters of two clans make their grievances violent, though the clans often rely upon the police and their public relations specialists to smooth over these incidences and keep the peace.

The night life in Scone is vibrant and alive, as theatres across the city show off the latest in Merovingian artwork, USAriadnan films, and Rodinan plays. Half the city's restaurants are Caledonian, leaving the rest to incorporate foods such as USAriadnan barbeque and Merovingian French cuisine. The city's one major flaw is that due to rising costs and rent within the city, more and more Caledonian businesses are starting to be pushed out in favour of exotic and foreign establishments that cannot be found in towns across Caledonia and are able to afford the high taxes.

THE STONE

Officially known as the Caledonian Parliamentary Building, the building's nickname of the Stone is earned from its appearance of having been chiselled from a mountain. Made of solid granite with seams of Teseum reinforcing its super structure, the Stone is a dizzying display of turrets, battlements, and power lines. Sitting at the centre of Scone and taking its name from a relic of Scottish kings, the Stone has never fallen to enemy invaders and as many believe, never will. The numerous hidden cannons and machine gun emplacements along with the miles of tunnels dug beneath the fortress guarantee that if it were ever besieged, it would be almost impossible to assail.

The entrance to the building is made up of two large doors constructed from oak and reinforced with bands of Teseum. The only times the doors are ever shut outside of security reasons is when the parliament is in session. Armed guards keep watch outside the entrance while conducting intensive security screenings for everyone passing inside the gates. Upon entering, visitors are first greeted by the Hall of Trophies, a massive hall that is full of trophies taken from all conflicts Caledonia has been involved in. The ceiling is covered in the tartans and battle standards of every Caledonian clan, and the walls are lined with the torcs and weapons of Caledonian heroes. It is every Caledonian soldier's hope that their deeds are worthy enough to be remembered here.

Past the Hall of Trophies visitors are greeted with the modern side of the Stone, where new hallways and offices line the inside of the building and signs indicating the offices of each noble house are clearly laid out. The halls are almost always bustling with activity as lobbyists, politicians, visiting diplomats, and other visitors move through the halls conducting the business of the nation. The largest office is reserved for the Caledonian Justiciar, who is elected from amongst the nobles to serve the needs of the nation. The Justiciar is also responsible for dealing with delegates from other nations and is expected to be available to travel to Mat' at a moment's notice whenever the Rodina President asks him to.

SKARA BRAE

A city known for its violent history, Skara Brae is a fortified outpost that was established by Caledonia to be the first line of defence against invading Rodina forces and now serves as a vital stronghold in protecting those traveling through the area. Patrols operating out of Rodina and Caledonia routinely meet at the city, and at night the sounds of Scottish drinking songs and Russian military anthems can be heard echoing across the city.

The city is divided into two sections, both of which represent a different stage in Skara Brae's history. The first section that visitors encounter is Old Brae, where the foundations of ruined buildings and plots full of debris and destroyed hardware still lie in the open. These places are leftovers from the time when Skara Brae was destroyed by triumphant Kazak forces during the Separatist Wars. The other sections of the city, known optimistically as New Brae, show how far Caledonia has advanced in the years since the Separatist Wars as newer technologies are incorporated into their design.

The city is occasionally home to short term outbreaks of violence between the Caledonian and Rodina garrisons stationed there to guard travel between their respective nations. For the most part, the violence is often limited to soldiers being arrested while on patrol and then being driven back to their garrison while their commanders and politicians argue with each other. On rare occasions, these conflicts turn violent, and small exchanges of gunfire occur in the hills and cliffs along Hadrian's Range. Neither side has escalated the conflict with each other, and leaders on both sides do their best to keep these conflicts away from the prying eyes of Ariadna news agencies.

MEROVINGIA

The future is a weird concept on Ariadna which spends much of its time wallowing in the traditions of its past. Orthodox Christian families gather in Rodina for Mass on Sunday while USAriadnans proudly display their genuine reproduction sidearms and cigars as a point of pride. But for Merovingians, they have always and only looked ahead to the future rather than behind. They value their past but see it as stepping stones leading to greater glory for Ariadna and refuse to be bogged down by sentimentality or tradition if it hinders progress.

Merovingia is a place of commerce and trade, where they prefer their politics be settled through business and do their best to avoid damaging commerce and trade if they can. But Merovingia is proud, and their military is second to none, as they refused to roll over quietly when Rodina expanded their armies into their territory and chose to fight for the freedom of their homeland for as long as possible. Even today, the Force de Réponse Rapide Mérovingienne (FRRM) is a modern, mobile force pulling double duty protecting Merovingia's borders and travelling abroad to fight in the Ariadnan Expeditionary Corps. The soldiers of the FRRM are trained in multiple disciplines including tactical response and emergency services.

Often viewed as vain and arrogant by their neighbours, the truth is Merovingia feels rightfully proud because of their achievements. Their cities feature great works of art and their economy is thriving. Merovingian businesses do the most trade with off-world companies and even Rodina is forced to rely upon Merovingian business advisors to help predict where their economy is going. The great wealth their republic generates has been paid back to the people in the form of entitlement programs and massive public works. Even the more practical-minded USAriadnans are forced to admit that Merovingian cities are beautiful, if not as utilitarian as they might prefer.

Merovingia must also play a dangerous game of politics with their neighbours as they are surrounded on all sides. Though this gives them an advantage when dealing with the threat of Antipode raids or during the heavy fighting of the Ariadna Commercial Conflicts, this also means that Merovingia does not have the luxury of ignoring any of their fellow nations and is often caught in the web of complex politics that ties them all together. Merovingia must carefully consider the wants and demands of USAriadna when making a treaty with Rodina while at the same time hoping Caledonia does not object in any form, and the same is true for the nations neighbouring Merovingia. Even off-world businesses from PanOceania and Yu Jing find that when dealing with the internal politics of Ariadna they almost always find themselves having to negotiate with Merovingia in some way.

THE GOLDEN LANDS

Merovingia may be situated between three other nations and the Antipodes, but their choice of land is an immeasurable bounty in the form of raw materials and agricultural products. Though their territory is lighter in its amount of Teseum than other nations they make up for this imbalance by maintaining sophisticated foundries capable of refining the ore and incorporating it into items used through Ariadna. The sophisticated Moblot suits of armour employed by Merovingian infantry feature delicate yet sturdy layers of Teseum in their construction, and though their output of Teseum falls behind Caledonia, they are able to trade for the valuable ore with ample quantities of Ariadnan wheat and water purification technologies.

The weather in Merovingia is also equally suited for farming, and one of the more common professions outside of the cities is that of a farmer. To the haughty Merovingians living in cities farming may seem like a lowbrow profession meant for those who lack the education to get ahead in life, but the truth is that the difficult Ariadnan winters and threats from raiders make farming a dangerous and challenging business. Merovingian food products are also responsible for feeding the majority of Ariadna, and as Merovingia struggles to get their own products into the hands of foreign markets, it is clear that their ample farm lands and plentiful rivers will be a hot commodity even for interstellar markets.

AURON

Surrounded by fields of golden wheat and featuring the latest in Ariadnan architectural styles, Auron is well known across the planet for its fantastical reputation of being the City of Spies. Popularised by spy movies and novels, the city has embraced the notion of it being a mysterious place with restaurants and gift shops selling the latest in "spy gear". The truth of the matter is that the city is the focus of numerous special forces operations and spies and government agents are almost constantly involved in operations involving everything from drug trafficking to illegal import of off-world goods. The city's real importance comes from Montgolfier Airport, which provides transportation and air support for the FRRM. The airport is a major hub for all civilian air travel across Ariadna.

LE DOUAR

Built upon the Spinal Mountain range and guarding the main transit line across the mountains, Le Douar is a fortress built with intimidating fortifications and a tightly patrolled perimeter. A relic from the Antipode offensives, the city is meant to intimidate local Antipodes and stands as the first line of defence against local tribes. It is here that technologies and weaponry designed to combat Antipodes and Dogfaces are tested, and new recruits to the Loup-Garous are often assigned here for their first tour in order to learn how to best deal with the Antipodes.

MARIANNEBOURG

All capital cities on Ariadna are modern metropolises with advanced feats of civil engineering and the most sophisticated in Ariadnan technology but of all four cities, Mariannebourg possesses the most beauty and most modern designs of any city on Dawn. One of the most modern Ariadnan cities, Mariannebourg is reinventing its city centre with tall glass buildings designed to reflect light and appear like a shining city from far off, while their parks and restaurants reflect not only hundreds of different cultures and styles but also a uniquely Ariadnan way of doing things. All of this is built around the most powerful economic force on the planet, where trade houses and the Ariadnan Stock Exchange continues to make sure money flows through the lifeblood of the Ariadnan economy.

The origins of the city are a sad story often retold in opera or in poem. When the research teams settled around Lake Chetain not long after the initial diaspora from the colony ship, their families built several research labs with the hope of discovering a way to regain contact with Earth. Their efforts were a failure, but not just because of their lack of technology, but because the First Antipodan Offensive shattered the serenity of Lake Chetain with the first full scale conflict seen on Ariadnan soil.

Though the researchers had brought their own security forces and were reinforced with soldiers hailing from nearby US Rangers and Cossack Infantry, the settlement took heavy casualties, and the death of the head researcher's daughter brought the stark realisation that the colonists were never going home. Dedicating themselves to building a new capital for their descendants, the city of Mariannebourg rose up along the waters of Lake Chetain. The settlers of the city decided to focus their efforts building for the long term and constructing everything needed for a new nation to emerge on Dawn. Though originally the other nations refused to acknowledge the importance of building a stock exchange or global hospitals, these efforts have paid off considerably in an age where all of Ariadna is united.

A CITY OF STAIRS

The city is split into three sections, each having their own notoriety and prestige for living there. Though Mariannebourg is an expensive city to live in, thousands enter the city each year hoping to find their place and their fortune among its gilded lanes. The largest section of the city is referred to as the Le Rivage, and this is because of many buildings being built downriver from the original Lake Ravel. Le Rivage is where the majority of people live in the city. Living accommodations differ drastically, with most living in cramped tenements or in cheap housing constructed in a basic colonial style but following a progressive and modern urban design

Those who live in the upper middle class make their homes in La Barbacane. This section of the city boasts some of the older parts of the city, and the aging bunkers and buildings here are a relic of the city's founding and stand at odds with the chic and modern architecture of the rest of the city. The streets of La Barbacane also serve as a gateway to the city's industrial section, where massive factories create everything from touch screen computers to helicopter engines. Mariannebourg does its best to keep the industrial section of the city from despoiling its clean and modern view, but the city does not shy away from any business that is of importance to the nation just for the sake of preserving its architectural splendour.

The centre of the city, known as Le Cercle Splendide, is where politicians and the rich make their homes alongside several of the city's most beautiful and splendid museums and opera houses. Named for the planned nature of the city's circular streets, Le Cercle is crowded with tourists and citizens going about their day and enjoying the many opulent restaurants and tourist sites. The streets of Le Cercle are considered some of the safest of the city, but the Merovingian security forces strictly enforce their laws in the interior of the city.

FREEDOM FOR ETERNITY

The two largest buildings in the heart of Mariannebourg are the Merovingian Parliament Building and the Presidential Palace, and both sit at opposite sides of each other across the Mariannebourg Government Mall. These towering buildings represent the things they stand for, with the Parliament Building possessing a simple yet stoic façade surrounded by the numerous flags and symbols representing all the districts in Merovingia. The office of the Prime Minister is located within, and each day the sidewalks around the Parliament Building are crowded with government employees seeing to the business of the nation.

By contrast is the opulence of the Presidential Palace. Its grounds are full of flowing fountains and bushes carved in fantastic shapes of mythical animals and knights from a bygone era. The seat of power for the nation and where visiting dignitaries and ambassadors are seen by the Merovingian President, the grounds feature some of the most advanced security systems and are guarded day and night by Moblots in gilded Teseum armour. The Palace appears gaudy, but it is meant to portray wealth and power, and it signifies the history of Merovingia in its carefully carved bricks.

Located beneath the park that makes up the Mariannebourg Government Mall is the headquarters of the FRRM. Deep beneath the surface in reinforced bunkers capable of surviving an orbital bombardment, the FRRM's complex is capable of coordinating the military resources of Merovingia and is tied directly in with their counterparts in Mat'. Access to the complex is highly controlled and few know about it outside of Merovingia.

POICTESME

The Iron Heart of Merovingia, Poictesme is the manufacturing capital of the country. Vast fields of factories and outdoor construction yards surround the city and the air, rivers, and roads are always crowded with transports bringing in Teseum from Caledonia and taking finished goods from Merovingia across the planet. The city is heavily garrisoned, and the famous Special Intervention Regiment, "The Zouaves" has been stationed here to insure security. The city boasts an intensive security system on par with the capitol as any acts of sabotage or terrorism could cripple Merovingia's economy. The city's Dog-Bowl team is considered one of the best in the country, and their brutal name of Les Guillotines reflect a harsh but deserved reputation on the field.

LAFAYETTE

Lafayette was built out of a need for mutual cooperation between Merovingia and USAriadna when the need for a dedicated Ariadnan space program necessitated the building of laboratories and research parks that could better help Ariadnans build a program that could build upon a field of technology that Ariadna had abandoned over a century ago in favour of focusing on survival. The local Teseum mine provided funding for the city while the numerous labs and companies established in the city meant a steady stream of scientists and researchers traveling to the city to offer their expertise in the hope that they could bring Ariadna's space capabilities on par with their neighbours. The city boasted the finest libraries and laboratories across Ariadna and their research advanced the cause of Ariadnan space travel considerably.

In the end, it was not to be. Lafayette's Teseum mine ran dry and funding shifted away from growing Ariadna's own space program in favour of retrofitting purchased spacecraft from the Nomads and Haqqislam. Though Mat' still considers developing Ariadna's own space program to be an important mission, funding has shifted away dramatically causing half of Lafayette to become abandoned. Now the city fights for funding between its Merovingian and USAriadnan investors, and businessmen from both countries are now beginning to view the city as a poor investment.

DAUPHIN

Known as the Princely City, Dauphin sits upon Lake Cherbourg and is known across Ariadna as a city of living art. Originally designed as an experiment by the Merovingian Council of Artists, Dauphin is a call back to an earlier time with castle turrets and vast gardens spanning the length of the city. The city's many aquariums and amusement parks make it a luxurious retreat for those who can afford it. During the Ariadna Commercial Conflicts the city was damaged by a Yu Jing strike team but the city has embraced the damage from the war and now great works of art dot the city showing off the bravery of Merovingia's noble defenders and the savagery of their Yu Jing invaders.

RODINA

If a nation could be considered the true motherland of Ariadna, it is Rodina. It is the place where the colony ship landed and was the first nation to spread its roots and come into being. Though the colonists splintered and their respective cultures left to found their own nations, Rodina is the oldest and most powerful nation with the supremacy of its government over the other nations made clear by the Ariadnan Constitution and the force of its economy. Although each nation is unique and has their own strengths, Rodina maintains dominance and it is through their voice that all Ariadnans are represented to their neighbours and to the rest of the galaxy.

The Cossacks consider themselves the most practical and forward-thinking of their neighbours. Though they recognise the value of Caledonian, Merovingian, and even USAriadnan philosophy, they view their way of life as the best because of one simple fact: it works. They view the world as being between several simple choices that every person must face in their lifetime. If your neighbour's house is burning, you do not wait for the fire department but pick up a bucket and help out. If a neighbour's house burns down, you let their children sleep on your couch while you help them dig through the rubble. If someone threatens your neighbour's life, you help protect them, because the same threat could come for you next.

Since uniting the Ariadna Federation after the Separatist Wars, Rodina has grown to become the formidable economic and political powerhouse of the planet, falling only behind Merovingia in terms of wealth and capital. They maintain one of the planet's few space ports, and it is in Mat' that the Roving Star Satellite System that maintains everything from Dawn GPS to communications

with ships in orbit is housed. Though the Cossacks place great emphasis on excelling in all fields of thought, they consider academics to be the principal strength of their nation. Rodina is home to the most universities on *Dawn* and has surprisingly well-funded research centres dedicated to the expansion of Ariadnan knowledge.

Although the government in Mat' has the strongest military and access to the best researchers and medicine on the planet, the Rodina Parliament is well aware that they are holding on to the Ariadna Federation only by maintaining as tight a grip as possible. Though in the years since the end of the Separatist Wars the other nations have come to accept Cossack rule, the government knows that between dealing with their nations, O-12, and the ever-encroaching threat that is the Combined Army, there is always the chance that their control could slip through their fingers. This has led to an encouragement by Rodina for other nations to take up practices such as the *stanitsa* program in order to help bring the other nations into their line of thinking.

DYNAMO

The electrical powerhouse of Rodina, Dynamo is situated along a series of waterfalls known as the Torrents. Its importance to Ariadna is obvious as it provides the majority of electrical power for not only the nation but thanks to Teseum-infused power lines it is able to send power to substations as far away as Merovingia and USAriadna. Although the sight of fierce fighting during the Ariadna Commercial Conflicts with the PanOceania war effort focused on depriving Ariadna of the bulk of its electrical power, Dynamo stayed free of foreign occupation thanks to the skill and ferocity of its the defending Kazak soldiers.

The city's ample electrical power fuels its many factories. Processed ores arriving from Caledonia and Merovingia are turned into tanks, aircraft, and suits of heavy armour by the thousands of Cossack workers who live in the city. The city is also the home of Dynamokon' Motorcycles, which is responsible for building the light motorcycle that has become the iconic symbol of the Rodina Dynamos, the motorised Kazak Light Cavalry. Though civilian models are available, there is a burgeoning black market for official government parts to be retrofitted into their owners' vehicles.

Though Rodina portrays Dynamo as an example of pure Cossack ideals, the Rodina Mafia has a considerable hold on the city. Bratva gangsters do their best to keep under the radar of the government but in Dynamo it is said that if someone has the rubles they can get anything they want. The city is also home to a large population of Dogfaces whose strength is valued in heavy industrial work. The city boasts one of the largest Dog-Bowl arenas in Rodina, although there are rumours that during the off season it doubles as an underground pit fighting arena run by the Bratva.

GÖK-BURGO

As Mat' is the capitol of Ariadna, Gök-Burgo is the capital of naval trade. Dozens of ships ply their way through its harbours daily and the waters off the coast are lined with oil platforms and off-shore storage facilities. Gök-Burgo is also the largest shipyard on the planet, and its facilities struggle with not only keeping up with the demand for their ships but in keeping up with the latest designs. Recently Gök-Burgo created a deep-water construction site for the construction of submarines, a fact that worries the off-world settlements in the islands surrounding Dawn's main continent. Submarines of this type could give Ariadna the ability to deploy hidden first strike weapons within close proximity of their mining sites.

MAT'

Though a Merovingian may scoff at the lack of grand architecture and a Caledonian may wonder why there are so few buildings dedicated to the might of individual families, Mat's beauty comes from its practicality and simple design. Though there are a dozen towering buildings that are considered skyscrapers in Mat', the nation's carefully measured and devised planning insures that public transportation operates efficiently and that the city does not feel too crowded or too spacious. While these measures might seem boring to others, it suits the Cossacks well as it allows them to focus their efforts and finances elsewhere rather than feeling the need to make grand statements with the capitol.

At the centre of Mat' is the remains of the *Ariadna*. Though the ship has long been dismantled for every usable resource possible, the massive girders that made up its frame were left in place as a memorial to the expedition's original goal. The girders rise up to surround the Ariadna Building, which is the chief government centre for the nation, like metallic talons. The Ariadna Building is the only structure that could be considered extravagant in Mat' as it was built with the finest architectural materials from across Ariadna. Its bricks are inscribed with the names of famous Ariadnans across the planet's history and inside the lobby are paintings dedicated to the Antipode Offensives and Ariadna Commercial Conflicts.

Though officially there are no separate and distinct neighbourhoods in Mat', the city has developed its own various cultures over the years. The north-eastern section of the city is known as the Rynok

STANITSA VILLAGES

The greatest strength of Rodina is its ability to summon large numbers of skilled personnel to handle almost any kind of emergency imaginable. When the Russian contingent realised they were on their own and understood the enormity of the problems they faced in taming the vast wild regions of Ariadna, the Cossack High Command set about recreating several programs that had served the old Russian empires well throughout their history. These programs, which would centre around villages called *stanitsas*, helped enable the Cossacks to forge not just a powerful army but also an equally formidable economy and distribution system that helped aid the Cossacks in becoming the dominant military force on Ariadna and unite the other nations during the Separatist Wars.

The model for the *stanitsa* villages starts with having smaller, more closely connected settlements that are arranged in a controlled fashion during their settlements. Unlike the vast fields of Caledonia or USAriadna, most villages and cities in Rodina were laid out in a carefully arranged grid pattern with clear lines of transportation and communication between them. Each new settlement was built with strong walls and their infrastructure was completed before moving on to another settlement.

The second was in the organisation of who got to live in these settlements. Though Rodina fought to keep clear of the tyrannical laws and programs that plagued Russia during the 20th century, the government in Mat' set up clear guidelines that were followed strictly. Before the foundations for a new settlement were laid, the government had already chosen the provisional mayor and his staff. They had already designated which units would be detached from the Cossack regiment in Mat' and whose families would be allowed to move with them. The reason for this was not to install dictators but to give each settlement a strong start, with elections being allowed to happen two years after the initial founding. The *stanitsas* also introduced a new form of official for each village known as the Hetman. This "head man" would have absolute control over all military assets in the community and in times of emergency would be given complete control over the civilian government as well. Though in the beginning *stanitsas* were slowly phased out in favour of allowing nations to expand as they saw fit, in recent years Rodina has begun to enforce the *stanitsa* system in all nations as the frontier of Ariadna expands across Dawn.

What gives the *stanitsas* their strength is that not only are they carefully laid out but each village trains a portion of their populace in skills and trades that can help them mobilise quickly in the face of an emergency as well as allow a civilian militia to organise into a ready combat regiment within a short amount of time. This system helps provide Ariadna with vast reserves of trained military personnel to call on as well as insuring that all settlements have a means to protect themselves in the face of foreign invasion or Antipode attacks. The close-knit organisation of each *stanitsa* also enables them to mobilise their forces quickly to help local settlements that come under attack or suffer large scale disasters, as the trained personnel appropriate for the mission are able to be called up, equipped, and mobilised in as short a time as possible.

(Market) district, where it possesses hundreds of businesses and stores selling everything from off-world fashion to Merovingian delicacies. In order to get permission to open a business in the city a company applies for permits that must be renewed each year. If the company fails to meet government regulations on safety and profit (or fails to pay bribes to the right officials) then their permits are revoked and the business is quickly replaced by a new business. This has the added benefit of helping the Ariadnan economy stay fresh while encouraging businesses to be competitive and prosper.

The northwestern section of the city is the home to the numerous garrisons and military bases for the Rodina army. Each member nation in the Ariadna Federation is allowed to maintain their own delegations there although the base falls under the purview of the Stavka, the Ariadna High Command. All military planning is based out of the Yadro (Ядро, the Core), which is a massive military bunker with the most sophisticated communication systems allowing Ariadnan generals to communicate with units across the planet. The Yadro is also responsible for coordinating Dawn's air and space defence, and although it is unable to receive the up-to-the-minute reports that their rivals in the rest of O-12 are able to receive with their sophisticated equipment, it has grown by leaps and bounds in recent years.

Although the northwestern section is home to multiple military bases, the streets lack the raucous bravado that is found around Caledonian and USAriadnan installations due to the strict control that Cossacks place on the conduct of military personnel in their free time. Although soldiers are allowed, and even encouraged to relax and unwind in their free time, the last thing that the Cossacks want is for the population to get the mental image that their armed forces are not professional. This has led to a burgeoning underground club scene in the city, where speakeasies and night clubs offering confidentiality and privacy for soldiers are common.

The southern section of the city is home to most of Mat's population. The southern side of the city could be described as drab and plain, with a stark and simple brutalist aesthetic paying homage to the pragmatism of the Rodinian people. Buildings in Mat' are subject to strict government guidelines that limit the size, colour, and placement of the building for safety reasons, but it is also done to keep the people content with what they have. By limiting the amount of extravagant homes in the city they help keep the people thinking all are equal.

PRIDE OF THE PEOPLE

Although its headquarters is located near the Ariadna Building, the home of the Rodina Stellar Authority is actually based around the Roving Star Spaceport. This spaceport was maintained after the landing of Ariadna out of the idealistic belief that contact with Earth would be recovered not long after contact was lost, but stood abandoned for decades as the priorities of the burgeoning Ariadnan economy demanded that money be focused in other areas. With the realisation that Ariadna is far behind the rest of the G-5 nations when it comes to space travel, a new priority has been placed on modernising and upgrading not only the Roving Star Spaceport but the fields of spacecraft design and maintaining satellites. Captured and purchased spacecraft belonging to other nations are brought to Roving Star and stored in special hangars located on the eastern side of the facility, where a regiment of Kazak soldiers stands guard vigilantly. As for the rest of the spaceport, hangars and apartments belonging to the crews and delegates from PanOceania, Haqqislam, and other nations are located alongside a tightly patrolled perimeter known unofficially as the Walk of Stars. Protests are common along the Walk of Stars as people wary of increasing foreign interference in Ariadnan affairs and who remember the wounds suffered during the Ariadnan Commercial Conflicts keep the hatred between Ariadna and outsiders alive.

A secret that few citizens of the city are aware of (or perhaps are aware of but do not acknowledge) are the large number of underground munitions storage depots in the city. The tunnels were originally dug to store supplies taken from the *Ariadna* but after the Cossacks decided to build up their military they realised that their production capacity started to outstrip their need for weapons in peacetime. Not willing to cut back on the amount of munitions and arms produced on Ariadna because the Kazak High Command was sure they would be needed some day meant they needed safe, secure, and dry areas to store these munitions. Many of these depots are kept under heavy lock and key but otherwise do not draw a lot of attention to themselves. Children playing in a park may not realise that the sealed door next to the tunnel by the creek leads to a stash of anti-tank weaponry, or that the charming bistro overlooking the canals is situated over a storage facility full of ten million rounds of high calibre ammunition.

NOVOCHERKASSK

Though Mat' represents the full might of the Rodina government, Novocherkassk represents the fist that gives it strength. Once a small hamlet that served as one of the first *stanitsas* built in Rodina, Novocherkassk is significant in that it is home to one of the finest military academies on Ariadna but is also home to the shipyards of the Zapadnyy Flot, the mighty western fleet of the Rodina navy. The purpose of the city is as simple as it is important: to turn generations of Rodina men and women into the soldiers needed to preserve Ariadna and keep it free from oppressors.

Currently, the Novocherkassk Military and Officer School is a sprawling campus where flights of helicopters and Ariadnan aircraft fly overhead routinely and its many parade grounds are full of cadets drilling under the watchful eyes of their drill sergeants. Getting into the school is no easy task as it is highly competitive, but for any who hope to advance far in the Ariadna military it is considered an almost essential stepping stone. The academy differs from other schools on Dawn in that it does not cater solely to Cossack students, although they make up the majority of the student body. The school takes very few applicants from the other nations and those it does take are trained to be liaison officers working to help each nation operate under Rodina's control.

Though the Rodina mindset is to consider practicality and necessity in their approach, the academy pushes their officers to consider all forms of military strategy in their decisions. The academy's primary goal is to teach officers to follow the orders they have been given and to get their soldiers to do the same, but the Ariadna Commercial Conflicts proved that radical change is needed to keep Ariadna on pace with the more modern stratagems incorporated by PanOceania, ALEPH, and Yu Jing. Foreign mercenaries and military advisors hailing from the Nomads and other parts of the Human Sphere are paid a considerable sum to immigrate to the city and take up teaching positions, although these teachers are monitored carefully for any signs of being spies working on behalf of any G-5 nation.

The Zapadnyy Flot is home to smaller shipyards than their counterparts in Dynamo but they serve an even more important function. The fleet is kept on active duty and they are responsible for patrolling the entirety of Dawn's oceans, and as such the city's port is moving day and night with military ships returning from long range missions to be refit and sent back out to sea. The Zapadnyy Flot tries to stay at the forefront of Ariadnan ship design but their fleet keeps ships in service for decades as long as they have a use for them. It is not uncommon to find smaller destroyers and minesweepers left over from the Separatist Wars kept in service to escort Ariadna commercial shipping or to patrol the coasts for smugglers.

VOLGOGRAD

The City of Rivers is considered a pale offshoot to its sister city of Dynamo but the people of the city consider themselves proud and hardworking members of Rodina society. The city is remarkably different from other cities in Rodina in its sheer opulence and seedy nature. Billboards advertising gentlemen's clubs and dozens of bars line its streets, and the streets are more often lit by the neon glow of street signs then by actual lighting. Some believe the Bratva made an arrangement with the Rodina government so that they could have absolute control over one city so long as taxes were always paid and the Cossacks could have a city where they can facilitate any kind of business that needed to be done. Though some believe this is an urban legend, the city does have a very high crime rate but also a very low arrest rate. Some believe this is due to the brutal retribution methods of the Bratva families and their interest in solving any wrongs done to them as brutally and efficiently as possible.

PROKLYATIV VOLK

Although the independence-minded USAriadnans may joke that their cities have been occupied by Rodina ever since the end of the Separatist Wars, only in the City of the Wolf is there an active and armed occupation. Although people living in the city are free to come and go as they wish, the Cossacks prefer that Dogfaces live in there along with Wulvers and the few Antipodes whose lands have been taken and now have nowhere to live in Rodina. It is a city that advertises itself as a healthy place for those "afflicted" with the genetic curse of being a Dogface where they can seek treatment for their condition, but in reality, it is a brutal training ground used to keep the numbers of Dogfaces small and under strict control.

Though tolerance for Dogfaces is on the rise across Ariadna, the armed guards of Proklyativ Volk see their duty as more that of zookeepers than as security guards. The Handlers, as the specially trained Kazak peacekeepers are known, only give one warning to a rampaging Dogface before they open fire with their array of toxic sedatives and tranquilizers. Unlike the Loup-Garous of Merovingia, the Handlers are not trained in multiple methods for bringing a Dogface under control. The Handlers will attempt to subdue a Dogface once, and then they will respond with lethality.

Despite the harsh methods that are employed by the Handlers, the city's Teseum mines are a lure for those unfortunate Dogfaces who cannot find employment anywhere else on Dawn. The city's mines are teeming with Dogfaces and Wulvers using specialised equipment and their inherently superior strength to extract heavy loads of Teseum and other ores. Those who work in the city are paid well, but the Dogfaces rarely get a chance to enjoy their money as it is often spent on bribes for guards in order to keep the peace. Several Dogface separatist groups have been rumoured to be planning a massive attack on the city to liberate it for their comrades, but the garrison is well defended and the guards are willing to utilize absolute force to maintain control.

TARTARY

The breadbasket of Rodina, it was in Tartary that the *stanitsa* system gave Rodina the resources to overwhelm Caledonia during the Separatist Wars. Once a vast plain with scattered mineral deposits and tribes of Antipodes resenting human expansion into their territory, Tartary is now filled with dozens of interconnected villages that provide Rodina with ample reserves of food, resources, and personnel. Troops from Tartary helped defeat Caledonia and drive out the Rasher Falls Antipode tribe which had previously held back all attempts to colonise the area.

CASTROPOL

The fishing heart of Tartary and home to the powerful Vostochnyy Flot, the city of Castropol is essential to the prosperity of Ariadna thanks to its massive fishing fleets that provide food throughout the year. The city's squat homes and simple aesthetic is due to the fact that for the citizens of Castropol, everything revolves around the sea. Sailors and their families spend the majority of their time tending to the needs of the sailing vessels and their crews, and the fish markets of Castropol are one of the main sources for exquisite Ariadnan fish such as Storm Sea Swordfish. The Vostochnyy Flot, or Eastern Fleet, is responsible for patrolling the eastern nations on Dawn and also doubles as the main force assigned to blockade duty around areas in the Exclusion Zone where offshore drilling rigs have been set up. Though they are warned to avoid starting renewed conflicts with the other G-5 nations, the Vostochnyy Flot take their duty seriously and are quick to punish anyone caught exploiting Dawn's resources inside Ariadna's sovereign waters.

The city is also home to the main headquarters for the Irmandinho Brotherhood. These sea scouts and sailors are considered a vital part of the Ariadnan armed forces despite their reputation keeping them from being completely trusted. Their reconnaissance and subterfuge skills are highly respected by the Ariadnan chain of command and counterbalance their recklessness, rough reputation, and the unconfirmed certainty that they engage in smuggling and other black-market activities. They have been gifted a small headquarters to maintain in Castropol, which is where they receive intelligence updates and provide reports on activities observed while at sea. It is also home to the Curican Bar, where Irmandinhos can relax surrounded by fellow Galicians and conduct business away from prying eyes. The walls are lined with photographs and mementos of those Irmandinhos who are politely described as having disappeared in deep waters. The Curican is said to be one of the best places on Dawn for obtaining off-world technologies. This reputation is fairly accurate though the pickings can be slim at times and what the black market traders exchange for these gadgets is subject to some speculation. More than one complaint has been filed with O-12 about "saboteurs of unknown origin" breaking into warehouses, vandalising technology, and stealing supplies.

DALNIY

Known throughout Rodina as one of the farthest Cossack settlements and considered a dangerous, almost foolhardy, place to devote resources, Dalniy is the home of the Novyy Yuzhnyy Flot. This "New Southern Fleet" is a combination of the military and research vessels designed to not only expand Rodina's control over the seas but also expand the knowledge that can be gained from it. It is also one of the few fleets to be staffed by scientists and researchers from the rest of the galaxy, although they are often forced to use ships and research equipment provided by their Ariadnan counterparts. Of particular interest to the researchers at Dalniy are the southern algae blooms that occur in the region. They only happen a few times a year but when they do, the seas take on a beautiful green glow at night as solid masses of algae ascend from the bottom of the ocean. These algae blooms are not only beautiful but are able to be converted into an environmentally friendly fuel that some believe could replace the use of fusion reactors in planetary vehicles. This sense of scientific adventure is aligned with corporate desires both on Ariadna and off-world who seek a way to exploit the algae for their own benefits.

OVSYANKA

Considered an abandoned dream by the few who call the city home, Ovsyanka is an aging city built upon crumbling docks. The streets are cracking as green land starts to retake it despite the presence of a major Transtartaric rail spur in the area. Unfortunately, the city's economy was crippled as resources for the Transtartaric were shifted to other sections of the planet, driving many Ariadnans towards ports near the Tsitadel or Castropol. Interest in the city has been on the rise in recent years thanks to a push to redevelop itself as a centre for galactic trade. Ovsyanka now gets by as a trade route for the Yu Jing colonies in the Snark Lands and seems to be inhabited by more off-worlders every day.

Rumours that an unknown force has taken over the abandoned naval base south of the city have spread across Dawn, with onlookers claiming to see ships landing there late at night. Twice Ariadnan patrols investigated the base but found no signs of activity. However, pictures of strange aircraft still circulate across the planet as people claim that some force has made the base their home.

TSITADEL

While military bases built in the four Ariadnan nations have the responsibilities and duties of keeping their homelands free and secure from all enemies, none have as enormous a responsibility as the air base of the Tsitadel. While air bases in the northern part of the planet have the luxury of numerous air fields and watch towers with which to patrol their skies, the Tsitadel must rely upon an endless array of sorties and satellite images to help them monitor the skies of nearly half the planet. Aircraft flying out of the Tsitadel often spend long hours in the sky, usually with the deep blue of the Dawn seas or endless fields as the only scenery.

The Tsitadel's mandate is twofold: they are responsible for monitoring Antipode aggression from the south and keeping a watchful eye on foreign settlements operating in the Exclusion Zones. Both of these missions are critical for Ariadnan survival and neither can be ignored in favour of the other. Though some would consider keeping an eye on foreign powers occupying their planet to take priority, time has shown that if the Antipode threat is ignored then it can lead to calamity as hordes of Antipode warriors surge across southern settlements and defences.

Ariadna's air force requires a vast variety of aircraft to manage their many needs. They need to maintain several squadrons of helicopters and drop ships capable of moving their soldiers swiftly across the planet at a moment's notice. Though they know their best fighter aircraft are outgunned

TRANSTARTARIC RAILROAD

The Transtartaric Railroad is the greatest engineering marvel created on Ariadna. Though it lacks the flashy appeal of the spaceport or the colonial charm of Deadwood or Scone, the Transtartaric Railroad not only unites all of Ariadna by allowing for easy travel between the nations but it is also the fastest and easiest way to send resources across Ariadna. Its armoured hull bristles with guns and the most sophisticated scanning equipment known to Ariadna; its presence is one of an unstoppable juggernaut roaring across the landscape with Kazak Railway Troops watching from sniper nests and fortified positions as civilian passengers relax in relative safety. Thanks to the railroad, ore from Caledonia can reach the manufacturing yards in Dynamo in just a matter of days.

Originally the brainchild of engineer Nicolai Korlokov, a Russian researcher whose work in the early days of colonisation on Dawn was essential for the survival of the colony, the Transtartaric Railroad's plans sat idle for years as the colonists struggled to hold off Antipode raiders and stay alive during brutally cold Ariadnan winters. When the Cossack President Nicholai Alexandrov Totemkin desired a symbol to show Ariadnans that was not just the bayonet of Kazak rifles, he revived the Transtartaric Railroad plans as a means to not only keep the country united but to grow it economically. These plans were deemed a monumental undertaking by the other nations who felt that traditional highways or the use of aircraft would be more practical then beginning such a huge endeavour, but Totemkin realised that the symbol of the Transtartaric Railroad was more important than just what it could do for the economy. It was a real, tangible thing that they could construct to show their citizens that they were free to travel across Ariadna as they wished, and that not all transit had to have the appearance of dishevelled and mud-covered transports traveling alone through dangerous Antipode lands.

The construction of the railroad became possible when Totemkin dedicated one year of military output from Rodina's factories to building it. Considered unthinkable and almost certainly an impeachable offense to the practically-minded Cossacks, Totemkin's arguments swayed his fellow politicians to the necessity of the project. Within a year, the major groundwork for the railroad had been laid and lands were set aside for building the thousands of miles of tracks necessary for it. Though the other nations were wary of its construction, they soon saw the merits of the Transtartaric Railroad when it came online and they experienced having a fast but secure way of transporting goods across the continent. Soon auxiliary lines and trains were built that fed back into the central hub in Mat', and now it is possible for a Caledonian to ride a circuit of trains through Merovingia to Rodina and to USAriadna before returning home without ever having to leave the train system.

The railroad is not without its problems. Resources needed for the continual expansion of the railroad have been diverted towards developing Ariadna's space program. Though the Tartary Army Corps patrols the rail system, the massive length of the tracks, Antipode raiders, bandits, and even sabotage from off-world forces makes safety a constant challenge. While it is still one of the fastest ways to move cargo and people across the planet, some are beginning to wonder if the booming space industry will forever eclipse the Transtartaric, though considering the unpredictable nature and costs of space flight it is an argument best held off for the future.

One of the ways the railroad continues to stay profitable is through the government offering discounts and simplified bureaucracy to corporations and miners who ship their goods via the Transtartaric Railroad. The subsidies offered by Ariadna are one of the major bartering points with O-12 and off-world corporations, as they look at the Transtartaric as a potential means to ship their goods to the Exclusion Zone where they can be trade with the local population.

by their PanOceanian or Yu Jing counterparts, they still maintain several squadrons of attack aircraft and bombers for use in war. They also need easy to maintain, reliable aircraft for patrolling and exploring the rest of Dawn. Several popular aircraft designs out of USAriadna allow for the pilots to be able to land their planes and conduct simple repairs in less than ten minutes.

Built as a series of ingenious overlapping rings, over half of the Tsitadel's air fields are underground. Realising the importance of shielding their jets from atmospheric bombardment, the air fields possess the ability to launch planes straight down runaways carved into rock. Despite the fact that engineers have assured pilots that takeoffs from these lanes are perfectly safe, only the most skilled aviators are assigned to take off from these lanes out of an abundance of caution.

The Tsitadel is also home to the Ariadna ВИПЕРА (VIPERA) pilot school. Before the Ariadna Commercial Conflicts, the most action that Ariadnan pilots saw after the Separatist Wars was dropping bombs on Antipode settlements or striking sorties against smugglers' bases. Each year mock drills and contests were held between all four Ariadna countries to see who had the best pilots, but even these exercises did not prepare Ariadna for the devastatingly powerful ships and aircraft employed by PanOceania and Yu Jing during their invasion.

Now the VIPERA school teaches their pilots the best methods to deal with their more modern counterparts. Owing a lot of their technical expertise to Nomad military advisors and foreign mercenaries, the Ariadna air force was able to rebuild itself into a modern force capable of dealing real damage to even the most advanced PanOceanian craft. Realising that surprise is key to defeating the advanced weapon systems of foreign aircraft, Ariadnan pilots have adopted the hip-shooting methodology utilised by the old US military.

USARIADNA

No matter what words are used to describe the culture of the USAriadnans, they are never portrayed as anything other than bold and larger than life. Some see them as brutish, loud, and stubborn while others would say they are brave, determined, and resourceful. There is one thing everyone can agree on about USAriadnans: they are survivors. They have stood against invasions by massive wolf-like predators, their neighbours to the west, and the forces of their former home system intent upon bringing Ariadna to heel. Though USAriadna was defeated by the Kazaks, they view themselves as having more freedom than ever and they intend for the galaxy to hear their ideals.

USAriadna is a place of extremes. From their deserts to the south and cold forests to the north, it takes more than top-of-the-line Merovingian coats or Rodina GPS equipment to keep safe in their territory. Their territories along the infamous Wall are some of the most dangerous on the planet and every man, woman, and child is taught how to survive because someday their lives may depend on it. This comes from centuries of planning, training, and tradition that defines Ariadnans.

Most of this survivor instinct comes from the worship of heroes. It is not just that USAriadnans venerate their forebears or seek to emulate them but that they try to be better than them. The average citizen of Deadwood knows that George Washington was not a saint and the soldiers who serve on the line at MountZion know that there were many things Old Man Ross got right and many he did not. This does not shake their unwavering fealty or loyalty to the past. They believe that for someone to succeed in the world, they must continually seek to improve upon themselves. The USAriadnans will freely share this concept with their neighbours and to any who cross their path. It is not unheard of for a USAriadnan to meet someone for the first time and spend a few minutes sizing them up.

To a USAriadnan first impressions are key, and it will set the tone in how they continue to deal with someone. They will watch how a person walks, the words they choose, and how they carry themselves when dealing with opposition and hardship. They will then point out the many flaws they see and offer to help teach them to be better. This has led to a phenomenon known derisively across Ariadna as "USArrogance" but to the USAriadnans, they are not doing this to be cruel or to earn the enmity of others. They do this so that people know how to improve.

REAL USARIADNAN HEROES

In Caledonia, it is not uncommon for a family to be able to recite the members of their family tree back to their ancestor who landed on Dawn. In Rodina, they teach about the great deeds their family did in service to Rodina. In Merovingia, a family's name is associated with class and how highly regarded they are by others. But in USAriadna, a family's name is important but nowhere near as important as the heroes that helped define the country.

All children are taught the importance of the American Constitution from old Earth. They are taught about Washington and Jefferson and how they managed to free their country and bring about the greatest democracy on the planet. They are taught that even on Dawn, that the ideals of American freedom are worth living for and definitely worth dying for. This is reiterated in their daily lives with the endless displays of jingoistic patriotism in USAriadnan towns and cities, where the starry banner of USAriadna is displayed outside of most businesses and some houses fly both the USAriadnan flag as well as the more traditional flag from the old United States of America.

In USAriadna, people are given the heavy burden of trying to prove themselves worthy of being remembered. A family who is descended from a proud line of Minutemen is not regarded highly outside of their military service if they have not achieved bold deeds in combat. Likewise, a family of farmers who defended their homestead from a pack of Antipodes using only their wits and old rifles are remembered in song and in stories as a reminder of what a common person can achieve. Even their leaders must work hard to inspire their soldiers. While everyone knows the names of their local government representatives, they are more likely to hear about the exploits of Van Zant and his soldiers fighting against Antipodes or engaging in heroic operations against Combined Army soldiers in the Ariadna Expeditionary Corps.

Tradition is a powerful force in USAriadna and much of their current fashion is based around their idolisation of their forefathers. Although the stereotypical image of a USAriadnan is of a tall man wearing a bomber jacket, a Stetson hat, and armed with a Colt pistol, the true image is not far off. USAriadnan fashion goes through periods that are based on classical periods from the old USA, and it is not uncommon to see men in suspenders, long coats, and wide-brimmed hats walking the streets of Deadwood while youth with slicked-back hair race motorcycles on the outskirts of MountZion wearing leather jackets. Once a year the country celebrates Independence Day based around a loose approximation of when July 4th is on Earth.

MOUNTZION—THE WALL

The capitol of USAriadna and arguably the most heavily fortified city on the planet after Mat', the city is famous because it has two ubiquitous names. Outside of USAriadna, it is known as MountZion, as it was named when explorers surveyed the planet from orbit centuries before. To the people living in USAriadna and to the trappers and hunters operating outside of Ariadnan territory, it is known simply as The Wall, and it serves as a barrier against the world beyond Ariadnan territory capably and effectively.

During the Antipode Offensives, The Wall was a bastion against the majority of the invading Antipode tribes. Originally a chain of hills connected to MountZion-The Wall was a series of border forts and artillery installations that were supported by a system of roads and tunnels dug behind them to allow soldiers to travel between them with ease. As time went on, the forts' walls became larger and interconnected until the region was one massively long fort. Over ten miles in length, The Wall is crewed day and night by USAriadnan soldiers and at night it is not uncommon for the artillery guns to "go loud" and launch bombardments at Antipodes or other raiders caught operating too close to the fort. There are thousands of signs and fences in every direction spanning outward from The Wall warning those who are within range of their guns, which is a courtesy that USAriadnans feel is more than enough to justify their heavy artillery fire.

The Wall is not only famous among Ariadnans but also particularly infamous among the Antipodes. Antipode legends of "The Wall with Teeth" spread across the planet, and almost every Antipode thinks of MountZion as the capitol of humanity on Dawn before they think of Mat'. Despite, or perhaps because of, the utilisation of Antipodes in the USAriadnan military's famous Devil Dogs unit, most Antipodes have nothing but contempt for The Wall and many tribes tell stories of clashes between their warriors and the humans who hide behind walls and massive cannons rather than meet them on the field of battle.

Today, MountZion is made up of six major installations, which each have their own specialty and purpose. Each installation serves as a neighbourhood and is often split into two separate sections, with the first being the Civilian Section and the second being the Military Section. The difference between these two sections is not just a matter of keeping military personnel separate; those who live in the Civilian Section are expected to do their best to support the soldiers in the war effort and are allowed more freedoms and luxuries while those living in the Military Section go through their daily life treating each other as if they were in the military even if they were not. In the Civilian Section the common greeting is "Hello, Citizen" while those living in the Military Section often address each other by "Greetings, Soldier".

The six neighbourhoods of MountZion are:

Fort Patton: Known as the Steelworks, Fort Patton is responsible for the construction of vehicles and heavy armour for the USAriadnan military. The streets outside of the neighbourhood are often clogged with off-duty military personnel racing their civilian counterparts to improve their skills and increase their reputation.

Fort Eisenhower: The major communications hub of MountZion, it is also one of the more luxurious parts of the city. This neighbourhood is home to high-ranking officers and politicians as well as most of Ariadna's upper class. The streets are paved in brickwork and colonial artwork and sculpture is common along its streets.

Fort Lazarus: Known more colloquially as "Fort Custer", this neighbourhood of the city is the only section of MountZion to have been razed not once but twice by enemy attacks. Though the city has always managed to hold out against invaders, this northernmost neighbourhood was once devastated by fires set by Antipode scouts who managed to slip behind the city's walls during the First Antipode Offensive and later it was heavily damaged by missile fire from a PanOceanian attack. Despite efforts by the city to rebuild the area, it still suffers economically and is home to the city's poor and destitute. This neighbourhood is also where the majority of The Wall's Dogface and Wulver population reside, and it is not uncommon to see tattooed Ariadnan Dogfaces roaming the streets.

Fort Yeager: The primary airfield and landing pad of the city, Fort Yeager is home to the USAriadnan Air Force as well as the Wright Co Package Company. It is from here that the majority of packages and shipments sent through USAriadna are catalogued and organised, and Wright Co offers its famous "Pony Express" package where shipments can be sent to remote homesteads and settlements by motorbike or light truck. The airfield maintains its public channel as well as a private one used predominantly for visiting dignitaries from across Ariadna as well as delegates from O-12.

Fort Grant: The idea of mixing casinos and theatres with an armed military garrison may seem out of place but for those living in Fort Grant it is a way of life. The entertainment heart of the city, the streets of Fort Grant are lined with billboards and advertisements for everything from genuine USAriadnan bourbon to the latest in athletic shoes. The city also boasts one of the oldest and most extensive film libraries on the planet, and its monthly film festivals allow visitors to see classic American cinema such as *Yankee Doodle Dandy* or *Independence Day* along with more modern films such as *The Last Squad* and *An USAriadnan Dogface in Mariannebourg.*

Fort MacArthur: Day and night the lights at the factories of Fort MacArthur never go out as the neighbourhood's primary industry of munitions and arms is constantly moving. Responsible for the majority of bullets, missiles, and other weaponry needed by the Ariadnan armed forces, Fort MacArthur is the most fortified section of the city as well as one of the most dangerous. Though security is high, past incidences of sabotage have led to the presence of Cossack Diplomatic Corps stationing their agents as well as Kazak soldiers inside the neighbourhood to "assist" in security, a fact that has many in the city angry about so-called "foreign occupation".

A NATION OF STATES

Though the other nations have divided their land into small territories centred around major cities, it is in USAriadna that the divide between states is not just more rigidly enforced but a matter of pride. The six states that form USAriadna almost seem to come out of the passage of history, and it is here that visitors can find gunslingers, 20th century industrialists, and modern citizens rolled into a single nation. Though some places seem like they come from another time it would be a mistake to think that their citizens are in any way backwards or unintelligent. Though an insulting foreigner in Deadwood might find themselves greeting the heavy end of a barstool. They'll wake in the hospital handcuffed to a bed as the Sheriff's deputies wait with eager ears to hear why they shouldn't issue charges of incitement.

There is a stark divide culturally between the states themselves, with the northern and southern states considering themselves descended from the values and traditions of their counterparts back in the old United States. This divide has led to the same differences that America found itself in around the time of its civil war: the southern states, with a few exceptions, have the majority of the farmland and textiles while the northern states possess the most factories and technological centres. Fortunately, both sides work together amicably and although both tout the superiority of their ways of life, they are united in their devotion to the USAriadna nation.

JACKSON

The poorest of the southern states, Jackson has constantly had to live leanly and lacks the comparatively modern comforts found in other nations across Ariadna. They have less arable farmland than their neighbours and have recently begun to suffer a steady increase in poverty due to a continual decline in the output of the region's mines. The proud Jacksonites refuse to lean on their neighbours for support, however, causing the alarming shortages of basic needs to lead to ever-increasing unrest.

Gracetown: "Amazing" Gracetown is known for its quaint surroundings, its simple homespun values, and its idea of being a place where someone can raise their family in peace. The city does boast a peaceful nature but beneath its surface lies a core of martial might. The state capital of Jackson, Gracetown controls the flow of Teseum and other valuable materials as it flows through the state. Gracetown is a city where soldiers go to retire and take up a contemplative life. Beneath the town's gentle demeanour is the tendency for its people to speak their minds about the government in Mat'. Though the locals will feign politeness each citizen will gladly tell visitors how they feel about their political views.

MADISON

Madison is considered the last stop to anywhere, and has the unfortunate mental image in the minds of most Ariadnans as little more than a seedy town where everyone is plotting to murder you and steal your wallet. The truth is that Madison was built around a Teseum mine that went dry early in its development and now all that sustains the city is coal mining and cattle herding. With almost a fifth of the citizens of Madison on government welfare and record levels of drug addiction cross the city, it is the perfect place for criminal elements to meet when they are trying to lay low and carry out their business far away from prying eyes.

NEWPORT

In almost every single way, Newport is a military town. Some consider it simply a military base that has grown so large it decided to elect its own mayor, but the truth is that Newport is home to both the Nimitz Naval Academy and Farragut Shipyard. Soldiers, sailors, airmen, and marines come from across Ariadna to study there. It is also home to the 5th Marines regiment, and it is not uncommon to encounter armed forces personnel enjoying much needed R&R throughout the city. The city is known for its violent confrontations between personnel, and it hosts the championships for both the USAriadnan Military Football and the USAriadnan Military Dog-Bowl teams.

JEFFERSON

A land of heat and heated tempers, Jefferson is situated north of the Velasco Desert. The Velasco, named after the leading officer of the first scouting party to survive its dangers, is said to be the most fearsome desert on Dawn. During the day its scorching heat and dry, cracked mud ground hides nests of Dust Trail Rattlers and the dreaded Desert Dragon, a 3-metre-long reptile whose venomous bite guarantees death if not treated.

The state is home to two iconic USAriadnan sites: the American Wild West-era city of Tombstone and the Fathers' Memorial. The memorial is seated at the Plisqibi Dam, which provides hydroelectric power to the entire state. It is carved into the nearby granite that lines the valley floor and features massive statues of the founding fathers. Each statue is accompanied by plaques extolling the deeds and popular sayings of each man. The Fathers' Memorial is one of the few places on Ariadna that the Antipodes respect and refuse to go near. While it's generally held that the constant hum from the turbines is what keeps them at bay, it's been suggested more than once that Antipodes see it as a sacred place for mankind and afford the statues a distant respect.

TOMBSTONE

The dusty city of Tombstone is an anachronism and a modern marvel. Though most of the city is built as if it came out of the American frontier from the 1800s, the city boasts electric lights and it maintains a standing army capable of holding off Antipode raids. Though the men and women who walk its streets appear like they've come out of legend, they are every bit as real and ferocious as those legends say they are.

The city was built to provide a way station for miners seeking Teseum mines in the surrounding brutal landscape. Founded by US soldiers and their families, they quickly realised the danger and complexity of the region and started to adapt themselves to a frontier lifestyle similar to that of the Old West of the United States. As the mystique and legend of the city grew, those who made their home there started emulating more than just the clothing and style of the Wild West but also the lawlessness and ethics of the period. Soon duels at high noon became an acceptable way of settling conflicts and gambling in saloons while sipping sarsaparilla or whiskey became the norm.

The city of Tombstone is split in half by Main Street, where the majority of businesses are located. Each day hundreds of people step along the wood planks of the sidewalks to look at goods and wares kept behind glass windows. The street itself is unpaved and dust thinly coats almost everything in town but adds to the frontier aesthetic. Even the arrival of mining cars or other transports does little to break the look of the city looking like it fell out of time, and visitors in modern Merovingian fashions stick out like sore thumbs.

The rest of the city is split into the four neighbourhoods of Wayne, Eastwood, Rogers, and Elliott. Wayne and Eastwood are home to the city's upper class as well as the majority of the city's bars and attractions. Rogers neighbourhood is home to dozens of Teseum processing facilities, and ore brought in from the desert is refined and shipped off to MountZion to be turned into processed goods.

Elliott neighbourhood is home to the city's military garrison as well as the helipad and fuel depot. Though all military personnel are required to wear the USAriadnan standard uniform while on duty, the garrison allows its soldiers to wear special desert kits that feature extra water rations and outdoor gear for survival in the harsh terrain. A special dispensation granted to the garrison allows them the option of wearing their Americolt Peacebreaker pistols as an additional sidearm.

TRUMAN

The city of Truman has a fiery reputation, and not just because its namesake was the only US President to authorise the use of atomic weapons. The city is home to firebrands of all types, from environmental activists to doomsday preachers. It is rumoured that the city has been infiltrated by spies from other planets hoping to start a revolution in USAriadna by appealing to the angriest and most vocal of its citizens, but so far, all investigation into the matter has drawn a blank. There are reports of unidentified spacecraft sighted in the hills, but whether these are actual ships from off-world or the rantings of lunatics is up for debate. Truman also doubles as a centre of religious revival in USAriadna, and every street corner has a church dedicated to an old Earth faith (Catholicism, Methodist, etc.) or one of the many versions of Christianity that have grown on Ariadna since its separation from Earth such as the Rossist movement and the New Ariadnan Church of Christ.

As Jefferson's state capital, Truman is marginally more settled than other towns and cities in the state. It has a very traditionalist culture and takes the role of the preacher very seriously. While a significant minority of senators and civic leaders are preachers, political power very much rests in the hands of the farmers. This hierarchy adds to the unrelenting resentment against Rodina and Merovingia, as the farmers take serious issue with basic necessities and much-needed profit being sent elsewhere. The land surrounding Truman is a vibrant sea of cereal fields made up of massive farms worked by hands who are billeted in large dorms while the farmers themselves live in the city. This intensive farming has led to several attacks from nearby Antipode packs, who find the change to their environment unsettling. The current debate in the USAriadnan senate is to what measures should be taken to secure the farms against Antipode incursion. While all sides accept that a military option will likely be required the question is how big the offensive should be.

LINCOLN

The manufacturing heart of USAriadna's north, Lincoln has revolutionised its factories over the past decade and incorporated many adaptations and technology provided from off-world. The governor of Lincoln has declared that with these new enhancements, they will see USAriadna outpace Rodina and Merovingia and become the greatest source of manufactured goods on Ariadna. Combined with the state's philosophy of "Be yourself, and speak for yourself" the state has started to develop an arrogant reputation, although it is not entirely undeserved with how far their manufacturing capacities have come.

Centerville: Located at the centre of the state, Centerville is an industrial city where dozens of factories producing everything from industrial construction equipment to military components keep the city's skyline full of thick plumes of smoke and exhaust day and night. The drab nature of the town may be to blame for the city's preoccupation with violence, and across the city are numerous Dog-Bowl fields and Aristeia! duelling arenas. The city is best known for illegal fight clubs. Though the clubs are banned under the law, the police and the clubs have an understanding that has allowed them to remain an underground sensation drawing in competitors from across Ariadna.

FRANKLIN

Known as the hometown of Old Man Ross and the USAriadna Line Rangers, Franklin is known for making the toughest and meanest soldiers in the whole of USAriadna. The black and yellow riveted white star of the Rangers is seen on countless bars and monuments throughout the city and its western section is home to the 1st Line Ranger Regiment and Ross Army Base. It is here that the Rangers train in the toughest simulated conditions before being shipped out across USAriadna to be tested in real environments with real dangers around them. Over half of each class repeats training, with 2% washing out. An emphasis on personal resilience and the overcoming of obstacles, including failing training, leads to solid infantry soldiers who understand that while mistakes can be costly, it is only when you cease to persevere that you fail. Rangers are legendary for always continuing on and snatching victory from the jaws of defeat.

SPRINGFIELD

Razed to the ground in the First Antipode Offensive, many thought Springfield would be forgotten until the USAriadnan Congress announced the city would be rebuilt into a modern marvel. Many aspects of the city seem to fulfil this promise and half the neighbourhoods reflect modern Ariadnan architecture and technology. Unfortunately, after most of the city had been built, funding for it dried up and it has been forced to deal with massive debts. This changed when Bracco Limited, a small government contractor with diversified interests in construction, transportation, and security, stepped

FIGHT PUBS

The underground fight clubs in Centerville each have colourful names such as The Broken Fingers and the Teeth & Toes. Champions do not remain on top long except in the case of Mad Mouth McGee, a Wulver champion of the Dead Rabbit Inn whose signature weapon is a glove pierced with Teseum fragments.

in and purchased the local Dog-Bowl team. The influx of capital and the newly upgraded stadium led to many aspiring football and Dog-Bowl players coming to Springfield. Many of those who either wash out of playing sports or whose own debts prove too much for them find plenty of work as security guards and muscle for Bracco.

KENNEDY

The heartland of commerce and agriculture in USAriadna, the state of Kennedy was at the fore-front of the Separatist Wars. When Rodina troops crossed into USAriadna, the soldiers of Kennedy held out long enough for the rest of the country to organise its troops in defence. Though they lost the Separatist Wars, Kennedy has held on to its belief in freedom, and adopted the Golden Bear as its symbol. Since the Separatist Wars, the rest of USAriadna believes the state to be living off the protection provided by their soldiers. Residents of Kennedy point to the hard work they put in maintaining the trade that is the life blood of the country's economy as an important task they provide to Ariadna.

4 TRACKS

Trade is the lifeblood of any nation, and in USAriadna the heart of its trade is 4 Tracks. Named after the road system that runs through it, 4 Tracks is not just a place that goods get shipped through but is the strategic hub where everything runs through the nation. Although Merovingia considers itself the economic heart of Ariadna, if trade is disrupted in 4 Tracks the economy of Ariadna suffers. One of the largest minorities in 4 Tracks is the Merovingian traders who use the city as a major stopping point for their caravans. The caravans have the added benefit of letting the USAriadnan government ship things through unofficial channels when they need to, allowing for spies and soldiers on special missions to find transportation out of USAriadna without being noticed.

FAIRVIEW

While Fairview is famous for manufacturing a refreshing cola beverage which was famous during the 20th and 21st centuries, it is also home to numerous technological companies and an airport that rivals that of MountZion. This airport results

in a significant temporary population that includes not just business and political leaders but also their respective entourages, and a variety of travellers simply passing through.

ROOSEVELT

Home to people of strong character and traditional values, Roosevelt is more than a recreation of the American South. Roosevelt is considered by some to be the last haven of honour and grace in Ariadna. Unlike the boorish towns of Deadwood or Tombstone, cities in Roosevelt represent honour and grace from a time when women were expected to act like ladies and men were noble like the knights of old.

Tara: If Roosevelt is the home of culture and civility in USAriadna, then Tara is its zenith. A city spread out across sloping plains and where manor houses built like palatial estates are common and the emerald gem of its verdant forests and massive plantations are an icon shared across the planet, and land owners ride like the knights of old across the land. Despite its noble reputation, Tara is also highly discriminatory against Dogfaces and Wulvers, and it is unlikely that one of these groups will find a warm welcome in its borders.

WASHINGTON

One of the strongest states economically in the union, Washington is home to numerous financial firms and military defence contractors. The state's economy means that their cities often have the best tech and defences. Of all the states in the nation, Washington is perhaps the most diverse and welcoming. Though there are many who would prefer that the state stay purely USAriadnan, the largest population of immigrants can be found in Washington. It also has one of the largest populations of Dogfaces in the state, with one of the few all-Dogface cities in the nation.

DEADWOOD

Located in the middle of a vast forest and besieged by regular Antipode raids, Deadwood has managed to thrive thanks to the tough demeanour and survival skills of its citizenry. Everyone in Deadwood maintains their own weapons, which has given rise to the resurgence of duels to settle disputes and the police force keeps a careful eye out to make sure that brawls do not become deadly. Despite the raids from the nearby Antipode tribes, the town is home to one of the top Dog-Bowl teams in the region, the Deadwood Dukes.

LUNAR HILLS

Originally founded on the need to keep the newly born Dogface population in one place for study, Lunar Hills has grown from a Dogface ghetto to one of the largest research centres into the Dogface condition. Lunar Hills boasts one of the few hospitals that focuses solely on treating the needs of Dogfaces and Wulvers and its research has made several essential breakthroughs into transformation control and methods to keep rage in check.

RIVERSIDE

If The Wall were to disappear overnight then Riverside would likely become the next capitol of the nation. Built in a grid-like pattern and surrounded by a series of sophisticated bunkers and anti-aircraft emplacements, the city is capable of withstanding long sieges and can support a large army inside its walls for years.

Though its population is not the largest, it is the financial and political capital of the state. Politicians routinely pass through Riverside to speak to interest groups and to drum up cash for their re-election campaigns while meeting with their colleagues to discuss legislation. Early in the city's history the mayor hit upon the idea of lacing several of the most important buildings with Teseum. Though only one building was built with those specifications, the Hamilton Financial Group is not only as the tallest building in USAriadna but also the most secure.

Though Hamilton Tower is the largest building, the second most recognizable has to be Government Plaza. Here the movers and shakers of USAriadna are able to meet with representatives from the rest of Ariadna as well as foreign dignitaries in its many parks and cafes. At the end of Government Plaza is the old USAriadnan Chamber of Commerce building, which has been converted into a lavish hotel and convention centre where dignitaries and diplomats meet with lobbyists from other Ariadnan nations as well as diplomats representing O-12 nations.

EXCLUSION ZONE

The Exclusion Zone is one of the most heatedly contested places on Ariadna. The term refers to all territories on the main continent that have not yet been colonised by Ariadnans and includes more than half of the planet, though much of it is untouched wilderness that is nearly uninhabitable by humans due to harsh weather or threats from neighbouring Antipodan tribes. The Zone is also open to exploration and scientific research by the other nations from the Human Sphere. Set aside by treaties at the end of the Ariadna Commercial Conflicts, the Exclusion Zone exists as a reminder of the threat of off-world colonisation in the minds of every citizen on Ariadna and it is seen as a treasure waiting to be taken by those wishing to flaunt the

law with clandestine mining activities. While these illegal mines are rare enough that only a couple have been legitimately sighted, it has led to a situation where the Ariadnan authorities assume that even the most innocuous activities are a cover for mining.

LIFE IN THE EXCLUSION ZONE

Maya broadcasts depict mining on Dawn as a luxurious affair complete with the latest in high-tech mining equipment and vast perimeters of land patrolled by the best soldiers their nation can provide. A popular advertisement broadcast by ALEPH depicts mining in the zones in a heroic light, with miners bravely trucking out loads of Teseum for the war effort against the Combined Army and shows how a miner spending only a few months on Ariadna will return home with their pockets full of riches and a prosperous future ahead of them.

Like most commercials, the positive side effects of mining on Dawn have been greatly exaggerated. Mining on Dawn is a disorganised mess at the moment. Though each nation's outposts do offer the latest in off-world mining equipment, each nation has had to equip all of their mining outposts with the capacity to pack up quickly and move out. After a disaster claimed the Yu Jing mining settlement of Prosperous Dream when a series of rock slides wiped out half of the settlement, each nation made sure to approach mining with a careful and measured approach.

Each encampment possesses a tightly defended perimeter usually made up of fences or sensor outposts. There are three reasons for high security around each mining outpost: the first being to keep out the wild animals and Antipodes that may come near the camp. Though Antipodes are known to be intelligent by the rest of the Human Sphere, most nations prefer not to deal with them and do not show the same kind of tolerance and respect towards the tribes that Ariadnans try to. Many times have Antipode tribes tried to remove armed miners from their lands which has led to small conflicts between garrisons of off-world soldiers in power armour and TAGs.

The second reason is to keep an eye on Ariadnans that find their way towards these outposts. Though Rodina has urged all of their citizens to give the Exclusion Zone a wide berth, the outposts are one of the best glimpses into life in the Human Sphere that many Ariadnans will ever be able to see. It is not uncommon for miners to slip away from these outposts to meet with trade caravans from Merovingia or to meet with Irmandinho smugglers who trade rare Ariadnan delicacies for anything that might remotely interest people and bring in a profit. These items range from off-world food and beer to pieces of valuable technology, although it is not uncommon for miners to trick these traders by offering them broken pieces of advanced equipment or to charge outrageous prices for common items found at a waystation's tourist stop on the way to Dawn.

The third reason is the most important because while mining on Dawn would be tricky enough without the threats from Antipodes or Ariadna security forces, the risk of sabotage from competitors makes every nation incredibly wary of any visitors approaching their camp. Each firm wants to keep their mining equipment and the layout of their mines a secret from their competitors while at the same time hoping they can find a way to sabotage their rivals and drive them out of business. Security firms working for these mining outposts can make a fortune but they must maintain constant vigilance or else they will see their employers driven out of business or worse, suffer heavy casualties from raiders and attacks by rivals.

MINING FOR PROFIT

Mining on Dawn is one of the most common professions and whether a miner hails from Caledonia, Rodina, or is one of the few miners working in the Outer Crescent for an off-world company, it is one of the most lucrative jobs. It is also among one of the most gruelling.

Teseum, in its raw form, resembles a silvery ore that is often found along cobalt and iron seams. No one knows why the metal is so prevalent on some worlds and non-existent on others, but what is known is that it is a metal that is prized across the galaxy. When forged with the right ores and polymers Teseum is sturdy but light and can be used to create beautiful pieces of artwork, circuits capable of channelling immense amounts of power, and suits of power armour and other weapons.

Though the market value of Teseum is always in flux, mining several pounds of it in a day should be enough to make any miner a tidy profit. The problem is that the majority of mines across the planet are already owned and any Teseum recovered from these mines is seen as the property of the owner, with the miners receiving a fixed wage regardless of how much they recover. In Caledonia, the mines are owned by the nobility, while corporations in Merovingia and USAriadna own the majority of Teseum mines there. In Rodina all mines are owned by the government, which helps provide the government with an immensely lucrative source of income.

There are vast differences in how miners in Ariadna and miners working in the Outer Crescent go about obtaining the ore. In Ariadna, miners work under the auspices of their governments to run their mines as environmentally friendly as possible while still maximising profits. Though it is very dangerous work, with cave-ins being common and the dust from the mines causing hundreds of injuries each year, the mines are run with government inspectors making sure that they do the least amount of environmental damage as possible. This is to help keep the environment pristine, but also to avoid upsetting the Antipodes, who view the defilement of Dawn as an act of war and view the exhaust and pollution coming from mines as a reason to renew their conflict with the Ariadnans.

By contrast, things are much different in the Outer Crescent. Companies keep strict control of their mines but report directly to the nations that control them. Despite the advanced technologies employed by each nation, the preferred method is strip mining. Gigantic machines, sometimes made from Teseum themselves, tear great holes in the ground and massive sifting machines toil day and night to get as much Teseum as possible. Though this method is incredibly profitable, it is also highly toxic, and it is not uncommon for local streams and lakes to become heavily polluted and for thick clouds of smog to linger around each mine. Despite protests from the government in Mat', O-12 refuses to pass any meaningful legislation to change mining operations in the Exclusion Zone. Lone bands of environmental terrorists do their best to sabotage these mines, often earning the ire of O-12 and putting their treaty with Ariadna in jeopardy.

THE GREAT FRONTIER

It is romanticised in USAriadnan ballads and in tall tales told around Caledonian campfires. For citizens of Sol, who have seen every portion of their planet mapped, recorded, and colonised by towns and villages of humanity it is unnerving to imagine a major world whose people only maintain control over half of their planet. Each day explorers set out from the edges of Ariadnan civilisation and seek to map out the planet and find new places for settlements and mines in spite of the imminent dangers. Even the sophisticated mining settlements of PanOceania and Haqqislam are but small outposts of civilisation in a massive, untamed wilderness that spans across several continents.

Abdera: One of the largest islands in the Exclusion Zone and also one of the more permanent ones, the settlement of Abdera is the closest thing that off-world miners and military personnel have on the planet to a place where they can relax and mingle with miners from other settlements. Abdera's squat,

A DAY IN RODINA

There is no city on Ariadna that is more strictly in a routine than Mat', but the people are happy as they go do their jobs. The majority of the people in the city either work for the government or for businesses that facilitate it, and each day the skies are lined with shuttles arriving from off-world coming with ambassadors and executives hoping to make special arrangements with the government in Rodina. The newest tech and excitingly exotic foods from off-world make their way into the cuisine served in the city and people come from across Ariadna to buy the latest piece of technology approved for circulation to the masses.

A DAY IN CALEDONIA

It's either cold or rainy or some mixture of both in Caledonia. There is a rush of workers heading out to the mines in the morning and long lines of people waiting outside Ducal residences hoping for a word with the noble that represents them. Vendors selling warm clothing with the colours of several clans' tartans line the streets along with those selling artefacts (or reproductions of artefacts) from old Earth. At night, Caledonians spend the first part with their families and enjoy hearty dinners before heading out to local pubs to watch the latest Dog-Bowl game.

THE UNITED, DIVIDED

Both Yu Jing and PanOceania are jealous of the smooth relations enjoyed by the Nomads and Haqqislam when it comes to mining rights in Helios and seek to find a way to disrupt this arrangement using back channels such as diplomats, saboteurs, and the hiring of Yuan Yuan pirate crews to harass miners and stop all operations.

square buildings are made from old interstellar shipping containers and simple structures built from prefabricated designs. What the city lacks in aesthetic it more than makes up in culture, as the citizens of Abdera come mostly from Paradiso and Acontecimento and the streets are lively at night with PanOceanian miners engaging in drinking games and restaurants serving PanOceanian takes on local Ariadnan cuisine.

Abdera's reputation for being a neutral meeting ground between diplomats from Ariadna and O-12 is well deserved, as many government officials hoping to use back channels to communicate the wishes of their government meet with their Ariadnan counterparts far from prying eyes. It also has a dangerous reputation as it is not uncommon for these same government officials to become the victim of crimes or even be murdered by spies.

Novîy Cimmeria: In the bars of Rodina it is not uncommon for older miners to offer to sell the coordinates of supposed Teseum motherlodes or places with vast seams of gold and diamond just waiting for young, ambitious explorers to come and claim them. If even a tenth of these stories were true, the majority of Rodina's youth would be millionaires, but sadly the majority of the region is full of small outposts and abandoned settlements from the hundreds of explorers who have lost their fortunes and sometimes their lives in the area. Novîy Cimmeria is a cold, desolate place where the frigid temperatures make it difficult to establish settlements and where supply lines often fall apart in the wake of heavy snowfalls and below freezing temperatures.

Yu Jing continues to send out survey teams to find seams of Teseum on the planet, and materials are often imported from Yaochi, their settlement with direct contact with the Yu Jing bases on the Snark Lands. There is also Kurage Station, a large Japanese settlement that was established by Yu Jing in an attempt to send citizens considered too dangerous to be kept around their compatriots on Shentang. The settlement is a known gathering place for members of the Kempeitai who use its remoteness to hide operatives on the run from Imperial Agents.

VOLKSTRANA

Volkstrana carries out an important mission on behalf of the Ariadnans: it is responsible for monitoring the Antipode threat and in understanding ways to deal with the Antipodes whether it is through force or manipulation. The settlement is home researchers and scientists working to understand the Antipode trinary mind and new technology is constantly being developed to allow Antipode controllers to better communicate with their charges. The city's defences are formidable, and most entryways into the city are through heavily guarded trenches in order to prevent the Antipodes from breaking through.

THE SNARK LANDS

The Snark Lands are under Yu Jing control and it is here that they do the majority of their biological research on Ariadna. Home to one of Ariadna's more curious animals, the Snark Lands have been left alone by much of Ariadna due to the need to focus resources elsewhere. The majority of the land mass is dotted with Yu Jing outposts and most of these are dedicated to researching the strange atmospheric and biological phenomena that are common to the continent. The main city on the continent, Yâshān City, is named after the mountain from Chinese mythology and offers shelter from the numerous flood plains that fill with water during the rainy seasons. The Ariadnan Snark, a short bipedal ape capable of blurring light around its skin naturally, is of particular value to off-world researchers as well as Ariadnan scientists hoping to reproduce their own versions of the advanced forms of camouflage employed by ALEPH or PanOceania.

HELIOS SYSTEM

The Helios System is one of the few star systems to have the majority of the ships and commercial satellites in its system owned by foreign powers and still be independent from the control of others. Though Ariadna maintains its own vessels and satellites, the system is full of ships from every corner of the Sphere hoping to conduct trade with Ariadna. Large ore loaders from PanOceania, interstellar gunboats from the Nomads, and ornate yachts containing trade delegations from Concillium are among the many vessels found in orbit above Dawn. The star system's many unexplored planets and asteroids also offer multiple opportunities to the corporations that are fortunate enough to win permits to survey them, but only if they can survive the double-edged sword that is the Ariadna Stellar Trade Commission O-12 bureaucracy. It is this reason, and the lack of Ariadna possessing any real power to control their own system, which has led to Helios becoming swarmed by pirates and corporations seeking free rein to do as they please.

TITHONUS

Considered by the original colonists as nothing more than a molten slab floating around Helios, Tithonus has become increasingly important over the years due to the presence of the research firm Andlestar. Andlestar's CEO hopes to use Tithonus as a test bed for new materials and technologies designed to take advantage of the planet's molten state to generate power. To date the majority of

Andlestar's attempts to harness energy on the planet have ended in failure but somehow the corporation is able to provide enormous kickbacks to the Ariadna government for allowing them to continue work on the planet.

USHAS

Ushas is a test bed for the Ariadna space program, and it is there that they test numerous technologies such as new launch systems and atmospheric survival gear. The planet's surface is covered in meteor strikes and while valuable ores have been discovered on its surface, it lacks the ease and value of simply mining the nearby asteroid belts or on Dawn itself.

SARANYU

A cold planet dominated by fields of crushed rock and mountains of iron, Saranyu was one of the first planets claimed by foreign powers during the Ariadna Commercial Conflicts. Used as a base to marshal forces from Yu Jing and PanOceania, it now serves as the major trade centre for those two nations. Both nations maintain strong defences around their bases, and Ariadnan craft are refused entry. No one is sure what military assets are kept on Saranyu.

ARMSTRONG ASTEROID BELT

Known as the Heroes' Grave by some explorers from Ariadna, the Armstrong Belt is rich in resources such as iron, cobalt, and frozen hydrogen. The belt has been the focal point of Ariadna's space industry. The asteroid belt suffers from micro-meteor storms, unstable asteroids, and even the occasional pirate, but despite these dangers freighters make the journey between the belt's space stations and *Dawn* every day.

ALBINA

Albina is a massive gas giant with an extremely charged atmosphere that is in a state of constant storms. All probes attempting to enter the planet's atmosphere are almost immediately overwhelmed by the intense static charge of the planet's atmosphere and those that do survive long enough to break orbit are destroyed by the horrendously strong winds. The intensive radiation given off by Albina does provide cover for ships attempting to evade detection by hiding in orbit.

EOSTRES

Eostres is a very profitable planet and a sign that peace between Ariadna and other nations can work for the best interests of others. Leasing the rights to mine methane, helium, and hydrogen from the atmosphere of the massive gas giant has resulted in the Nomads and Haqqislam establishing massive trading outposts on the threshold of the planet's atmosphere. The workers of these stations are allowed to visit Ariadna for three days at the end of each month, which has boosted trade on the planet and helped build relations between the three nations.

TERESHKOVA ASTEROID BELT

Referred to by some Ariadnans as "New California", the Tereshkova Belt is a gold mine of valuable ores including Teseum. When ample samples of the ore were recovered by PanOceania during their first surveys of the system, Ariadna declared that the belt was off limits and would only be mined by crews from Ariadna. Considering the vast size of the asteroid belt, this claim was mostly ignored by the other nations who were quick to set up their own mining operations along the belt. Ariadna has no ships capable of patrolling the belt and the belt was not covered by O-12's treaties regarding Ariadna. Mining rights in the belt remain a sore issue in all negotiations between Ariadna and the rest of the Sphere. Ariadna is keenly aware that they are reliant on a single overworked O-12 vessel for any information about the belt. Information about the ship's presence is publicly discussed amongst miners from all factions and the vessel has utterly failed to provide any real deterrent.

A DAY IN MEROVINGIA

The highways surrounding Mariannebourg are busy in the morning as hundreds of trucks and civilian vehicles travel to and from the city. The sidewalks are full of Merovingians on their way to work in the glamorous skyline. Merovingians enjoy their lunches in cafes and restaurants surrounded by gorgeous fountains and intricately carved statues that span the city. After work, they can take their pick of activities from the vibrant nightlife. Dozens of theatres and cinemas offer Ariadnans a chance to view classic films such as *Casablanca* along with new pieces created by the burgeoning Merovingian film industry.

A DAY IN USARIADNA

You're serving breakfast and the morning is full of a rush of people seeking something quick and sugary to go along with their morning coffee, and the streets are bustling with cars and trucks taking people to their jobs. A pair of Dogfaces stop in for a quick drink to take the edge off night duty at one of the security towers that make up the first line of defence against Antipode raiders, and a troupe of Rangers sit at their usual table eating their breakfast of black coffee, burnt bacon, and eggs. The radio plays an old 20th century western tune while a couple of Minutemen sit outside discussing everything from the construction of new border forts, the latest bawdy joke one of them heard while in Deadwood, and talks of renewed conflicts with PanOceania miners caught sending survey drones outside of the Exclusion Zone.

CHAPTER 3
MERCHANT TRADERS

THE ULTIMATE RESOURCE

FLEDGLING TRADITIONS

In the early days of Dawn's colonisation, life was more than tough for the Ariadnans. It was brutal, isolating, and almost decimating for the brave pioneers. Commerce in the face of such extreme adversity became virtually meaningless; technology was a rapidly dwindling resource and the concerns of most settlements centred on providing sustenance for their swiftly declining populations. Trade and barter, therefore, became a central function of basic survival. Either that, or banditry and pillaging, though this always brought swift and brutal reprisal from Rodina and any neighbouring communities. Although the bleak times of the Ariadnan Depression were tragic and almost fatal for the fledgling colonies, the seeds for many trading traditions were planted that would eventually grow into a fundamental aspect of life for the descendants of its survivors.

Despite being unable to put aside their differences, grudges, and inherent dislikes related to nationalistic divides, the distinct Ariadnan subcultures knew that their nations would soon become extinct if they were unable to barter internally for basic supplies. Not only did trade become a necessary and vital means for survival, it also became a means to maintain social and spiritual links between the fragmented settlements. An almost ceremonial emphasis was placed on dealings where trade crossed patriotic boundaries – though this would all too often devolve into conflict long before any discussion began. Nevertheless, some forms of these ceremonies are still re-enacted today, particularly among the formidable clan holdings of the stoic Caledonians, where they remain almost as wary of each other as they do outsiders.

TRADING WITH FINESSE

Mariannebourg also successfully endured the Depression. Of course, if any nation were to survive the cruellest of times with some sense of grace and culture intact, it was certain to be the Merovingians. Although sporadic, trade links were maintained with Mat' throughout, which allowed a productive alliance to flourish as the Age of Exploration began. The city had not only endured, but had almost managed to thrive somewhat thanks to serving as an attractive lure for any Ariadnan who caught wind of its success stories and who could feasibly make the trip.

EVOLVING ECONOMY

As always, Rodina seemed to stay one step ahead in preparing for Ariadna's uncertain future by ensuring that some form of commerce remained present within the marketplaces and sparsely stocked shops of Mat'. In addition to their greater power and influence as a colonial majority, the fact that the Ariadnan ruble has remained in continual circulation in some form throughout the entirety of Ariadna's short history is also a major factor in its dominance as the international and interplanetary coin of trade. Cossacks quote this as a point of national pride, citing that they remained civilised even in the harshest of times while every other nation regressed. A minority of historians – who are often quickly silenced or discredited – attribute it to luck and corruption, rather than foresight; the wealthy of Mat' clung to the virtually useless system of currency as a means of blackmail and control in the face of severe adversity. Clever forecasting didn't ensure the dominance of the Ariadnan ruble, rather a desperate bid to cling to power – or so they say.

Regardless, the Cossacks did convince their compatriots on the Ariadnan Council to institute the *stanitsa* system. This system of mutual support further helped to solidify trade dealings between closely situated settlements, which quickly helped the economy to recover as the colonists pulled themselves free of the Ariadnan Depression. Despite all but disappearing during those unremittingly tragic days, commerce rapidly became a means to exchange goods and services once again thanks to the deep local connections and traditions that had been forged.

The Ariadnans had staved off extinction and clung on to civilisation. Their tenacity and resolve were rewarded with the discovery of Teseum. Unearthing the properties this neomaterial possesses brought about a renaissance of industry and technology in communities. Found in abundance in Dawn's soil, the unique qualities of the ore enabled the nations with the necessary means of extraction and refinement to begin reclaiming and upgrading their crumbling infrastructures and decaying technologies. The rapid period of growth known as the Consolidation Phase firmly entrenched trading traditions within the fractured Ariadnan cultures, particularly among the Merovingians, who had taken to viewing trade as a form of bloodless combat between two opponents. "Bartering with a Merovingian can cost more than dealing with the devil" is frequently spoken advice freely given to non-residents of Dawn.

SEPARATION, FEDERATION, AND STAGNATION

The Age of Exploration took flight on the wings of adventure and rebirth. Most Ariadnans saw this as a period of renewed hope and vigour, as settlements began to prosper for the first time since the colonists' arrival on Dawn. The broken links – both physical and spiritual – between each nation were repaired, and new joint ventures such as the Naval Exploration Corps were undertaken. The Merovingians, however, saw an opportunity beyond the immediate growth taking place and took steps to ensure they were perfectly placed to coordinate (some would say dominate) Ariadna's fledgling commercial markets. Merovingian Commercial Agents were traversing new highways and haunting the hulls of the latest ships before the final stones had even been laid or the keels had been fully commissioned. Merovingian trading caravans and outposts not only helped establish many of the international trade routes that are now firmly entrenched on Dawn, but also enabled the Republic to pull itself rapidly ahead of its counterparts in the international markets. So far ahead, in fact, that no other nation has ever topped their influence in any arena except Teseum, where the Caledonians largely lead the way.

The emerging economies of the territories also established their own currencies during this time, which allowed the Merovingians to stake their claim on another burgeoning, but undeniably important arena of trade: the stock markets. A fledgling stock exchange was established in Mariannebourg, though its function was put on hold as the Separatist Wars erupted. As the Wars wound down and the Federal Nation of Ariadna emerged, each contributing nation settled into the trading roles that had either been dealt to them, or they had forged for themselves: Caledonia the Teseum markets, Rodina the international currency and policies, USAriadna the timber, meat, and grain markets, all neatly tied together by the Merovingian trade caravans and enclaves.

Although the Contraband Wars threatened to once again unravel the fabric of Ariadna's trade, the arrival of the *POS Nirriti* actually served to solidify each region's area of expertise. If someone needed Teseum rounds to take down some bothersome mercs harassing their backyard, the Caledonians were again relied upon. If an authority was needed to front negotiations, the Cossacks were given the lead, and so on.

Thanks to the establishment of the Ariadnan Interstellar Commerce Act, little has changed concerning the balance of power since the end of the Ariadnan Commercial Conflicts. Having been burned twice now by their ancestors – in their opinion at least – the Ariadnans instituted the Act as a means to stabilise their own planetary economy against an interstellar marketplace that could potentially and catastrophically undermine their own. The largest problem the Ariadnan Council currently faces is how best to enforce the Act. Luckily, the Caledonians have shown little interest in sharing a dram with the off-worlders in order to discuss their Teseum stockpiles, although the Merovingians are becoming ever more forceful and insistent in their requests to connect the Ariadnan Stock Exchange to Maya – so much so that they are actively seeking to conduct meetings with their own Commercial Agents as the lead negotiators, rather than relying on members of the Cossack Diplomatic Corps.

As the dust begins to settle from the Commercial Conflicts, the future is once again looking uncertain for the fiercely individualistic regions of Ariadna, with some seeing value in rapidly absorbing the technologies on offer from the other G-5 factions, but most fearing a loss of the rich history and ancestry that has forged the Ariadnan people into who they are today. Trade must continue regardless, however, and that is something that the Merovingians are holding on to with a tight grip as they look ever forward towards a new Dawn.

PLYING THE HIGHWAYS

THE TRADERS' NETWORK

Some say the Merovingians are waging a bloodless, systematic war that will eventually net them the preeminent position on the Ariadnan Council. They certainly seem to have invaded every nook and cranny of Dawn's transport and trade infrastructure to the point that very few major transactions take place without the Merovingian Presidency eventually being made aware. Every main highway, train depot, port, and airport – and most minor ones in fact – contain a set of offices or a dedicated building to host their Commercial Agents. Most often, these agents also double as customs officers or border inspectors, which is a service that the Merovingians offered to their Ariadnan counterparts during the rapid expansion of the Exploration Age that has largely remained uncontested. This ensures that they are well-placed to police the movement of goods of course, but leaves their military rather fragmented; as was the case during the Separatist Wars, though this is something they have since taken steps to prevent from becoming a detriment should a similar scenario occur.

The transport of assets across the highways, byways, and railroads of Dawn takes place fairly freely and unrelentingly. Not only does this ensure that the economy continues apace, but also keeps the far-flung extremities of the planet resupplied;

THE MALT CLAVIE

An auld tradition that allowed the Caledonians to avoid conflict numerous times, particularly during the Consolidation Phase, the malt clavie came about as a means for a clan to signal its intent to enter peaceful negotiations. To begin, the clan desiring to open discussions sends an envoy team towards their intended associates. The envoys carry a small burning cask held aloft inside a metal basket to signal their intent. Their opposite numbers share a stout malt if amenable, or water if not. Meetings can therefore be short affairs over a cup of crisp water, or boisterous exchanges over a cask of whisky or keg of beer. With a history laden with internecine clan bloodshed, the Caledonians might well have made themselves extinct but for this innocuous tradition.

EAR ETIQUETTE

The Merovingian practice of earlobe tugging to signify the closing of a deal came about during the Depression, when folks from all nationalities drifted towards Mariannebourg to escape their own plight. The Merovingians had yet to cultivate the multilingual skills for which they are renowned, but rather than holler uncouthly at refugees during a trade they established a rudimentary system of hand signals to conduct business, including the tugging of the earlobe which continues to this day.

civilisation needs a solid foundation to prosper, after all, and the Merovingians are determined to ensure that culture has an opportunity to evolve where Ariadnans are concerned. The other nationalities can call them all the names that they like, the Merovingians consider it a small price to pay for the dedication and service they provide in insuring future generations against any future economic collapse of the Federation.

PAPER TRAILS & REGULATION

Every major shipment of goods being moved across Dawn needs to be catalogued prior to its departure, including its intended route and ultimate destination. Failing to do so can invoke heavy fines and penalties. The Commercial Agents know exactly what is moving across the networks and when. The system was designed to minimise the need for inspections, though unscrupulous merchants soon took to including additional, unregistered goods with their shipments. A trickle of off-world technologies such as scanners, measurement devices, and security equipment has reduced the number of instances of smuggled goods on the main networks, although physical inspections are still a routine priority. It's easy to move merchandise, just so long as the rules are followed.

DELICATE BALANCE

Some of the haughtiness ascribed to the Merovingians can be attributed to their constant need to traverse the minefield of the varying degrees of Ariadnan sensibilities and regional traits. Not every town, village, or outpost welcomes, or indeed feels they require, a relative outsider telling them what can and can't be imported or exported. The authority and presence of the Commercial Agents can therefore wax and wane by region and location.

In major settlements and hubs, the Merovingians often maintain extensive offices and warehouses, with their customs and supervisory duties regularly supported by either local law enforcement or military delegation, or by a small unit of the FRRM – which is the lesser occurrence, as non-Merovingian nations bristle at foreign troops on their soil regardless of their remit. Telling a Caledonian or USAriadnan that a Merovingian unit will be taking over from their own will soon escalate beyond shouts and threats to violence.

In the smaller towns, villages, and outposts, there may only be a token presence in the form of a single Commercial Agent or delegate, though the Merovingians make efforts to support such isolated individuals with frequent visits from their own trading caravans and affiliated businesses. The fact that they have a presence at all in some of the more far-flung, less tolerant settlements is a testament to their skill at brokering deals and their determination to ensure that trade flourishes under their delicate, practiced touch.

INTERNAL AFFAIRS

The Merovingians don't control every aspect of the trade routes, but they oversee enough to ensure that they are at least aware of all major mercantile movements, not least to be able to influence the outcome of the trade if need be. Most internal trade within a region is still also conducted without Merovingian influence; if one clan chief wants to seek a deal with another, they will go directly to their opposite number without any fuss or deliberation. Internal movements, therefore, can be undertaken without any influence or input from the Merovingian contingents at all. Placing those goods onto the Ariadnan trade infrastructure, however, is a different story, as described above. In an attempt to make inroads on the entirety of the Federations' commercial infrastructure – both internal and international – the Merovingians point to their lack of participation in each region's internal economic affairs as a direct contribution to the opportunity for smuggling to flourish. They have been not so politely told to keep their noses out.

This also doesn't mean that the Merovingians directly participate in every trade or transportation of goods. Neither would they want to. If the Caledonians are exchanging a supply of Teseum with the USAriadnans for an equivalent – and likely protracted in this case – value of grain, that's all for the good of Ariadna as a whole and clearly requires none of their input (unless their expertise and objectivity is specifically requested, or the trade will create a major detriment elsewhere). Likewise, the transportation of the goods across the Ariadnan network – whether by road, rail, sea, or air – will be conducted by each region's own personnel. What the Merovingians *will* be interested in are the effects the trade will have on the stock market and the commercial markets.

LIFE ON THE TRADE HIGHWAYS

Like almost any walk of life, a career as a Commercial Agent is exactly what each individual chooses to make of it. It can be a daily challenge in search of new adventure and opportunities along the frontiers and internal regions of the Federation, a rather sedentary posting as a customs agent at a minor trade post, or a fast-paced and cultured appointment in the Ariadnan Stock Exchange. There is always opportunity for those seeking advancement, particularly if they distinguish themselves as a trade broker. Similarly, there are also a plethora of desk assignments and clerk duties that need

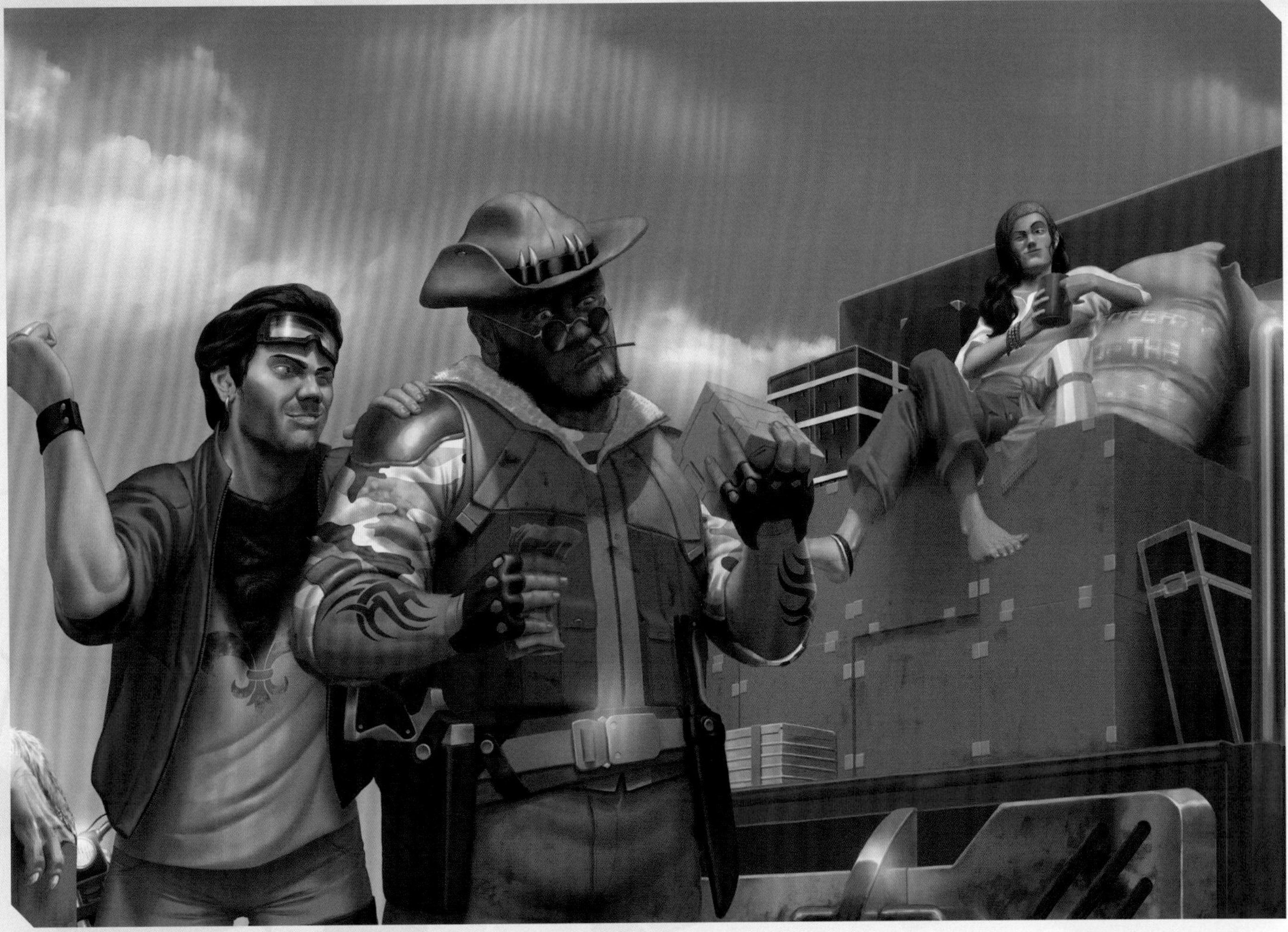

fulfilling for those that disgrace themselves or underperform.

The Merovingian trade caravans of today are civilised affairs that are designed to maximise transport economy and profit. With the in-depth knowledge that they have of the goods passing across their network, they can precisely time the depositing and collection of goods so that shipments arriving from various sources all bound for the same destination arrive in precise harmony, only to then leave as one cargo while their former transportation leaves with new goods bound for an entirely different terminus.

Maintaining this kind of network relies upon a large number of transport workers, administrative staff, logistical support operatives, and security personnel, many of whom are employed from within the local populations. It's a tough life, particularly for the manual workers that transport the goods or the support operatives who work hard to ensure that the goods can be delivered (by maintaining vehicles, roads, rails, and ports; manning fuelling stations; and other essential routine tasks), let alone the security personnel whose duty it is to fight off Antipode attacks or bandit raids. The benefits to the economies of each member state of the Federation speak for themselves however, particularly in areas such as employment and taxation.

INTERCONNECTING INDEPENDENCY

Ultimately, the Merovingians run the trade routes because it's what they do. Yes, they contribute arts, culture, and – arguably – class to the Federation, but if the best value for a deal is to be sought, then so should a Commercial Agent's opinion. The Caledonians drink, brawl, and bring tables made of Teseum to the party, the Kazaks rule with a tight grip and bring order, the USAriadnans provide large-scale industrial production and staple foodstuffs, while the Merovingians provide refinement and an assurance that everyone gets a fair deal.

BATTLE BAGS

Southern USAriadnans working on the transport network or roving the ranges never leave home without their battle bags. These tough satchels are a throwback to the extreme days of the Depression, when foragers and traders could walk for days or weeks in search of their next meal. The battle bags would contain the few meagre items the wanderer possessed, including extra ammunition, a change of clothes, and any vital spare parts. "Lose your battle bag, lose your life" is a word of warning that still resonates with many USAriadnans.

BEYOND THE HORIZON

The arrival of the other G-5 factions on the surface of Dawn brought immediate aggression, further disillusionment, and more conflict. They also brought opportunity. New and exciting markets were suddenly available to the Ariadnans, although they were all too soon placed behind a flood wall that slowed their imports to something less than a trickle. The forward-thinking Merovingians, however, understand that the barriers put in place won't hold back the tide forever, so they seek to prepare for the day when trade routes of the Human Sphere are once again fully accessible.

Some Commercial Agents have been given interplanetary scope, with remits to establish trade enclaves in any system that they can negotiate favourable terms. They have quickly learned from the disreputable tactics employed by both Yu Jing and Pan Oceania by brokering deals based upon the *potential* for favourable trade once the Ariadnan Interstellar Commerce Act has been repealed. Whether it ever will be, or whether the favourable trade terms materialise if it is, remains open to much conjecture.

INTERPLANETARY COMPARISONS

The remainder of this chapter deals with scenarios and campaigns that intend to provide a focus on trade and mercantile activities, with an intentional bias on the Ariadnan narrative of course. That doesn't mean that such tales should only take part under the auspice of the Federation. The scenario and campaign guidance provide additional notes on tailoring them towards other factions and groups, but also consider applying these guidelines in settings where they might not be usually considered, if for nothing more than a change of pace. If the PCs need to visit a Helot colony on Varuna, for instance, it could be immersive fun to send them to an underwater marketplace in search of something rare and exotic. Trade is a universal activity after all, not just the domain of the Merovingians!

INTERSTELLAR TRANSIT

Although they aren't exactly able to create commercial traction with off-world imports, Commercial Agents are busy exploring the length and breadth of the Human Sphere with a view to establishing interstellar export routes. In a similar vein to the international trade routes of Dawn, this of course requires a requisite amount of transportation vessels and personnel. Although imports are severely restricted where Ariadna is concerned, there are less limitations placed upon contracts for the purposes of conducting Ariadnan business. Bringing anything from off-world onto Ariadna can be an administrative nightmare, less so for anything Ariadnan made being sent in the opposite direction. Employing off-world couriers and mercenaries to satisfy a transportation void that will take decades for the Ariadnans to fill currently makes economic sense. In the meantime, Commercial Agents can harvest the very agencies that they employ for contacts, agents, and market access.

THE TECHNOLOGICAL GAMBIT

Although not exactly friendly with the Nomad Nation or Haqqislam, the Ariadnans have found common bedfellows in the unending goal to balance the power scales of the Human Sphere. For their parts, the Nomads and Haqqislamites try to respect the Ariadnan Interstellar Commerce Act by instead offering technological services in place of physical goods. Pan Oceania and Yu Jing hold no such reservations, with both seeking to gain an upper hand in the Ariadnan markets and political arenas by offering advanced technologies, equipment, and manufacturing processes. For now, the emissaries of the Cossack Diplomatic Corps remain resolute in their refusals, but more and more deals with other nations of the Federation are being sought with the intention to circumvent the Act.

With the Merovingians pushing hard to establish dominance as the Federation's interstellar commercial expertise, and the number of clandestine deals taking place outside of the Act on the rise, it may not be long before the aforementioned flood gates give way.

THE VALUE OF ASSETS

SIMPLICITY OVER INTRICACY

Assets, and their value towards Earnings, are introduced on p. 39 of the *Infinity Corebook*, then further expanded on within *Part IV: Gear, p. 327*. Some brief examples of these abstract resources are offered, which is fully in keeping with the light and flexible feel that the system is designed to provide. This is particularly appropriate for the Human Sphere, where cash and credit are fluid funds that can evaporate or manifest instantaneously. Most people have little need to catalogue every item of value, as they have geists or lesser AIs to take care of such mundane tasks. The Assets and Earnings system has been designed to also free the PCs of such laborious bookkeeping tasks. Occasionally, however, it may be necessary or prudent to note a description against a particular Asset – especially if the Asset or Assets in question represent something other than cash value, i.e. contacts, information, data, etc.

THE VALUE OF ONE

A single Asset can represent a great many things, each of a differing value in a monetary sense. An Asset may also have a high representative value in a certain scenario, but next to no value in others. This is particularly the case between factions and systems; a Cube 2.0, for instance, carries a high value in both social and fiscal terms for PanOceanians, but is of little interest to most Ariadnans. Maintaining Assets as an abstract item, therefore, can greatly vary and enhance their situational use. It's a fairly straightforward process to ascribe more detail to Assets for those that wish it, but GMs and PCs should be forewarned that doing so can limit their utility. That said, the personalisation and flavour brought to the table through this may well outweigh the cost for some.

Even the Cube 2.0 example given previously can be taken further, particularly on planets such as Dawn, where fiercely individualistic nationalities place a high value on their own customs and traditions over anything their neighbours may have to offer. Some descriptive examples of Ariadnan Assets with a value of 1 (plus an occasional 1N variable) might include:

- Caledonian ten-year single malt whisky, Rodinian triple-distilled vodka, straight bourbon from USAriadna, or lesser-quality red from Merovingia
- A USAriadnan battle bag or Commercial Agent's paper transaction book (blank – dependant on contents, notated copies fetch considerable amounts on the black market)
- A poor-quality Stetson or kilt, or an ushanka made from the fur of a common animal

ONE NEGOTIATION

The Merovingians are so successful in trade negotiations because they always enter discussions with one concept in mind: the value of one. In their opinion, everything has a singular value. To exploit an opportunity, a trader must establish that value prior to beginning discussions then negotiate towards it, which provides for a solitary focus during negotiations. Refining one kilogram of Teseum, for instance, may carry a comparative cost of one-thousand francs, which provides the Commercial Agent with a baseline to negotiate towards no matter the amount of Teseum being discussed. Separating out the individual value of items in a trade consisting of multiple articles is all part of the tactical assault on the price. The best Agents can instantaneously perform calculations as talks progress, though they are all masters of diverting conversations so as to calculate mental arithmetic before returning to the real thrust of the deal. Striking a transaction on a major trade that nets an income larger than the baseline value is considered a major coup amongst the Merovingians, usually celebrated behind closed doors with a classic vintage of wine. The more profitable the trade, the older the vintage.

MERCHANT SCENARIOS

The system of acquisitions and resources is covered within the *Infinity Corebook* beginning on p. 328. While the rules offer a light and simple means to track Assets and the purchasing of additional gear, some players and GMs may wish to tackle the actual narrative and structure of such purchases in a more realistic, less abstract format. After all, a Merovingian Commercial Agent PC hell-bent on out-profiting their rivals needs a playground to perform in!

PRIOR CONSIDERATIONS

Before setting up a scenario that heavily focusses on trade, the onus is very much on the GM to ensure that it's something their players will both benefit from and enjoy. Note here that "benefit from" doesn't necessarily mean the players will always walk away flush with additional Assets and outstanding bargains; the benefit can just as easily be in the form of personal lessons learned, contacts gained, or information acquired independently of the trade, which may itself just as easily have been a bad experience for the PCs. Of course, if your campaign focusses on a disparate group of Ariadnans seeking to cream profit from the other G-5 nations, then all to the good. There is also nothing wrong with creating short missions as part of a scenario that require the PCs to acquire something rare or exotic, though these should always be related to the larger goal.

SETTING THE SCRIPT

If able to do so, GMs will find an advantage in making notes prior to the scene. The benefit gained from the scenario has already been touched upon, though this might not necessarily be obvious. There are a few key points to establish:

THE AIM

There could be one or several, in a mixture of obvious and hidden goals. Establishing a good price for a product and uncovering the corrupt official benefitting from the previous deal would net two goals in one scenario, for instance, though the PCs might not immediately understand or appreciate the importance of the latter. The aims can be broken down into a checklist along the lines of the benefits mentioned in *Prior Considerations*.

THE CONSEQUENCES

What happens after the conclusion of the scenario? This should also take into account whether the PCs succeed or not. Any potential gain or loss might not also be immediately apparent to the PCs, or may lead to further consequences. The corrupt official mentioned previously may themselves become aware that the PCs are either on to them or undercutting their own profits, which will certainly lead to repercussions.

MOMENTUM

Momentum is a great tool that is readily at hand to increase the rewards for good use of skills and resources. The *Infinity Corebook* provides a number of uses for Momentum within the warfare arena, plus additional options for quantronic and social scenes. With some additional planning, however, this handy tool can provide unique benefits tailored to any scenario, potentially across all three mediums of conflict. In the trade deal/corrupt official scenario mentioned previously, the PCs might be able to spend Momentum on increasing their profit from the venture, potentially accessing new markets if enough is spent. Or they could end up selling their products or services in smaller increments at a greater price, or gain access to off world connections, for instance.

Momentum can also be a requirement to gaining the additional benefits or goals that have been established for a scenario. Surreptitiously learning the name of the corrupt official, for example, will likely involve the use of Momentum. If the PCs realise that there may be potential repercussions over their current deal, buying the NPC trader's silence might also constitute a Momentum spend.

Not everything requires the use of Momentum, but, as previously mentioned, the system provides a valuable means of rewarding good use of skills and subsequent results of rolls. Prior preparation, even just a note or two, will help each scenario to feel unique.

HEAT

The GM's tool to increase the challenge of the scenario on the fly. Much like with Momentum, not every scenario requires or even benefits from a list of unique Heat spends, but key scenes that offer a number of goals and consequences should have options that offer increased difficulty. In a trade scenario, Heat spends can be as immediately obvious in their impact as the GM spending Heat on additional dice during negotiations, which represents the trader digging his heels in over a price. Heat can also be specific to a scenario or NPC; the arrival of a rival trader who proceeds to undercut the PCs might also necessitate a Heat spend. Noting down Heat options for NPCs and scenarios beforehand and making use of them will provide the players with a feeling of increased challenge and diversity, which can be important in a scenario that doesn't focus on adrenaline-infused danger.

COMPLICATIONS

Consequences of successful and unsuccessful trades have already been discussed, but this section relates to a complication in a very immediate sense, i.e. rolling one during a skill test. Noting a few general complications in terms of trade scenarios will help to keep the narrative moving, with some focussed examples helping to supplement the consequences of each individual scenario. For instance, successfully selling one product or service might devalue the next item that the PCs were hoping to sell, or their reputation as tough negotiators precedes them, netting an NPC a bonus in negotiations with them. More immediate complications might involve the trader finding some flaw with the PCs' product, meaning they can still sell it, just not as profitably.

Of course, the GM might simply grab some Heat to add to the pool to fuel some of those unique spends discussed previously.

BUYING IN BULK

The buying in bulk information, p. 330 *Infinity Corebook*, still applies to merchant dealings, although the GM should account for the fact that the scene or campaign is focussed on conducting a profitable deal and adjust the meaning of bulk to suit the situation. GMs can build goals or Momentum requirements into the scenario to accommodate high-difficulty tests.

TRADING PLACES

Bartering and negotiating for equipment, information, or favours can seem restrictive on the surface, as the scenarios focus heavily on the actions of one or two characters. Keeping all of the PCs active to a greater or lesser degree is sound advice for GMs when designing any scenario, which remains no different when considering trade scenes. Make sure the main characters have their moments to shine, but also work the narrative to ensure the other players have input, no matter how minor. If possible, talking through roles – preferably in-game to personalise them, though outside will work just fine – prior to the scenario can serve to provide players with a sense of purpose. Some options to consider follow, though PCs might also consider fulfilling more than one role. There are also many variations on these themes, particularly between the G-5 factions; this should by no means be considered an exhaustive list of responsibilities.

THE FACE

Not necessarily the prettiest member of the group – although it might help in some situations – but definitely the PC who will front negotiations. The face will undertake the bulk of discussions concerning the transaction and will most likely be the PC required to make any rolls relating to this (although they can be assisted by active group members). The PC fulfilling this role can also vary from scenario to scenario; a Merovingian Commercial Agent is likely the most qualified to secure the best rates for a standard Teseum deal, but might not be the go-to for black market negotiations.

THE COORDINATOR

Someone needs to make sure that everyone stays on task and performs their role. The coordinator can sit back – possibly even in another room or building – keep an eye on proceedings, and offer adjustments to team members as the scenario unfolds. The coordinator might also be responsible for any tech on hand, such as comms equipment and quantronic connections. Assistance can be provided by monitoring the other party's reactions or rapidly checking data.

THE MUSCLE
Taking additional security to a deal is never a bad thing. When that security is a hulking mass of muscle that can transform into a gigantic ball of teeth and fur, people tend to take extra notice and care. The muscle might not be there for any other reason but to ensure the safety of the face, but their presence can still have an intimidating impact. Assistance can be provided through subtle intimidation and distraction, though care should usually be taken to avoid being too overt.

THE CHAUFFEUR
Most meetings of trade deals of substance take place away from the streets, possibly even on an orbital or spaceship. The PCs will certainly need some means to get to and from the meeting, particularly for the latter case if the deal turns bad. Having a means of transport on standby for just such an eventuality can be very prudent. A vehicle might even provide a base for the coordinator to operate from. Although it can be difficult to offer direct assistance (unless fulfilling a dual role), chauffeurs rapidly become pivotal to any action that might ensue if negotiations go badly. Physical goods can also remain with the pilot or driver while the transaction is being negotiated, making them directly responsible for its security.

MULTIPLE ARENAS

Infinity caters to three arenas of conflict. The social arena is directly applicable to trade scenarios: after all, negotiations can't take place without some form of dialogue. Warfare and infowar can both have their functions within the trade scenario, though to differing degrees.

WARFARE
Introducing warfare to a trade scenario likely means that a trade has gone south, probably rapidly so. It will also likely mean that the trade is effectively over for now. Reparations might be made after the battle on new terms, but for now, the focus shifts from the social arena to combat. Consider options for switching from warfare to trade if this is something that will engage the players. Examples of how to achieve this include captured objectives (snatching a hostage or vital equipment for negotiation terms) or terms of surrender (both in a winning and losing capacity).

INFOWAR
Despite the capacity for its presence being limited on Dawn, infowar can add a huge amount of variety to a trade deal. The fact that the PCs have to find suitable access to Maya in order to conduct a deal in the first place introduces plenty of opportunity for a variety of scenarios during the lead-up. Avatars, meeting places, security: so many nuances can add infinite depth to a trade meeting. Additionally, various activities related to infowar can be occurring in the background of the trade, such as hacking systems to affect real-time or historical prices, editing quantities, transferring funds, uncovering sensitive material to influence the trader, etc. Both infowar and warfare considerations relate directly back to the team (see *Trading Places*).

PSYWAR
The social arena is the foundation on which trade deals are conducted. Transactions can be conducted by quantronic means, but Merovingians (indeed, most Ariadnans) would prefer to look their counterparts in the eye and gauge physical reactions in the flesh. Social maps can be constructed that relate to the scenario, events, people, and places surrounding it. All the Actions and Reactions presented in the *Infinity Corebook* can be brought into play and put to use, with additional Momentum spends introduced as previously discussed. Some of the methods of interaction also present an opportunity for other team members to become directly involved in the scene; a Caledonian highlander meticulously honing their claymore whilst keeping one eye on the opposing trader throughout negotiations would be hard to ignore, granting at least bonus dice to a test, if not warranting a face-to-face Intimidate test.

SWEET TREATS

As mentioned, scenarios involving trade should focus on the social elements of the system, but GMs can use this opportunity to expand on the rules already presented. An area that can certainly benefit from this is modifiers to social tests, particularly if the PCs work hard to uncover positive effects that can be used to influence their opposite number. If the NPC trader likes a certain flavour of coffee, for instance, providing a pot during negotiations might provide bonus Momentum. Taking this further, offering gratuities in the form of free products or services could increase the amount of Momentum gained or add to any resultant Resolve damage inflicted. An entire tree of modifiers could then be established with which to affect a scenario, providing additional depth and intrigue for engaging trade scenes.

Taking the previous example further, consider a Rodinian trader who rarely leaves her own establishment, has a penchant for Merovingian coffee, and is known to dabble in rare antiquities as a pastime. Meeting her on her own premises sets a neutral tone, providing the current most popular blend of Merovingian coffee might provide a Momentum bonus, and sweeting the deal with an antique pottery set might increase the amount of Resolve damage inflicted. Conversely, forcing her to a meeting outside of her premises might provide additional Heat for the GM but may add Resolve damage as she is already fairly unnerved. The possibilities and variations can be tinkered with to suit each scenario, which will undoubtedly add depth and intrigue to provide an engaging experience for the players.

Of course, the PCs may have to be careful about who they try to positively influence, as some individuals might not take kindly to something that could effectively be termed a bribe; Irmandinhos wouldn't bat an eyelid, but a member of the Cossack Diplomatic Corps wouldn't take too kindly to it... probably.

MERCHANT CAMPAIGNS

Extending trade scenarios further, GMs and players might want to consider running an entire campaign based around the trade cultures of the Human Sphere. There is plenty of information to be mined from this chapter that can be used to make this happen, particularly in an Ariadnan sense, although this can be tailored to other factions with a little effort (see *Interlocking Arenas*, p. 48). Stand-alone merchant scenarios can be fairly easily inserted into standard Bureau Noir campaigns – the default setting for *Infinity* – particularly if information or services are at the heart of the deal. Merchant campaigns, however, will largely be tailored to actively replace the default setting of the game, although the machinations of the Human Sphere and the Wilderness of Mirrors can still have an effect of course.

CAMPAIGN GOALS

As with any campaign, the GM – possibly in concert with the entire group – should establish the ultimate aim of the campaign. Providing the PCs with an overall goal to work towards will help to focus sessions and keep the players working towards a common goal. This could be as simple as establishing a new trade route stretching from Le Douar to Dalnîy, or as complicated and far-reaching as causing the collapse of the Ariadnan Interstellar Commerce Act so as to establish a new empire amongst the ashes of the old.

The types of campaigns mentioned previously provide fixed goals, but some groups might enjoy a more open-ended goal, which can be the case if they don't wish to be tied to one particular planet or faction. A loose goal can be determined – perhaps something as elusive as establishing a new interstellar corporation during the PCs' travels – but the entire campaign can glide along without this ever coming to fruition. Scenarios and missions can still be interlinked to provide continuity, but each session is likely to be much more free-flowing when compared to a campaign with a fixed goal. So long as everyone involved understands which type they are involved with, both campaign styles are fine; the choice remains with the GM and players.

CHOOSING SIDES

In addition to setting the type of campaign to be run, GMs and players might want to establish any limits on the factions involved. Single faction campaigns can be loosely defined by G-5 faction, or more tightly by region within those factions. An Ariadnan campaign, for instance, will cater to PCs hailing from Dawn, while an Ariadnan regional campaign might establish the need for all of the PCs to be of Caledonian descent. These types of choices will help define the type of merchant campaign on offer; an all-Ariadnan merchant campaign could focus on dealings with other G-5 factions, whilst an all-Caledonian campaign could relate to dominating the Teseum markets or establishing alternative incomes for one or more clans. Single faction merchant campaigns can offer a ready means for a common goal.

Multi-faction merchant campaigns are less restrictive for the players when it comes to creating thier characters, but require a little more thought when tying the PCs into a common goal. That said, there's nothing wrong with introducing the odd non-resident into a single faction campaign; plenty of off-worlders get lost in the wilds, particularly if they're running from something, so it's only a short leap of narrative for one of them to turn up in the employ of another member of the group.

EXPANDED ROLES

Several roles and responsibilities were discussed in *Trading Places* under *Merchant Scenarios*, p. 44. These roles and more are still directly relatable to merchant campaigns, though they can be considered on a much grander scale as the campaign evolves.

The face, for instance, might become the director of the group, taking responsibility for deciding which lead to follow towards the next step of the campaign, dealing with authorities and officials along the way, and generally leading the group. The coordinator might become responsible for the groups finances, providing up-to-date information on available credit, the current status of the market, advising on where to go next, and making sure enough resources are on hand. The muscle can readily step into the role of head of security, working with the coordinator to make sure there are enough resources available to ensure the groups' safety, checking routes of travel and destinations for security alerts, and making certain enough heat is being packed to protect everyone. The chauffeur might not only be responsible for getting the PCs from A to B, but can become involved in the larger sense by ensuring that transport is of an adequate size to convey any physical goods, any vehicles are maintained and fit for duty, materials are on hand to conduct repairs, and contingency plans are in place if the worst happens.

As the campaign evolves, so too might these roles, particularly in merchant campaigns that are designed to expand business dealings beyond the boundaries of planets and systems.

THE ECONOMICS OF COMMERCE

A number of other factors will need to be considered in order for a merchant campaign to succeed. Products and services can't just be teleported from one place to another, for instance, and will need to be physically transported. Transportation involves its own cost, which will decrease overall profit but might introduce the opportunity for side revenue – which will then offset some of those costs. The following sections will examine some of the finer details of a merchant campaign with a view to addressing them prior to and during the campaign. A successful merchant understands that driving costs down in a number of areas is key to success and can be as important as any deal itself; negotiating advantageous logistical terms are crucial.

Travel and transport costs are found within the *Infinity Corebook*, p. 396, but these offer standard rates on stable and settled worlds; GMs should feel free to fluctuate these due to factors such as region, planet, and major local events. The costs should also be considered cumulative, so that transporting small goods to the nearest spaceport will incur a certain fee, but an additional payment will be required if the goods are then required to head into space. Small goods can range in size from handheld packages to two-person lift boxes, while large goods consist of the modern equivalent of several pallets of goods.

TRANSPORTATION

To be successful as merchants, the PCs will not only need to move themselves to their destination, but also any goods or wares they are selling. The PCs and their product might have different destinations of course, but the fact remains that they both still need to get to their journey's end. Luckily, there are many modern methods to ensure this happens, most of which – on Ariadna at least – aren't too dissimilar to today's means. Space and weight are still very real considerations.

The following methods of transport offer guidance on the maximum capacities of the space and weight of the goods being transported. In game terms, which need to remain rather abstract (though GMs and players are welcome to add more realism), transportation is offered in units considerate of weight and dimensions. One unit of large cargo in the *Infinity Corebook* equates to approximately 2 cubic metres and 2000 kilograms. The dimensions of small cargo can be considered virtually negligible in comparison, although they still have space requirements and hence a cost in terms of transportation. Moving goods in bulk is undoubtedly much more cost-effective.

Using the units of shipment method, GMs will need to assign a comparative amount of space and weight to any bulk items being transported. The table below offers some guidelines for common items that might need transporting across Dawn in terms of one cargo unit, though the list is by no means exhaustive or explicitly accurate. Each situation and load will need some thought.

CARGO

ITEM	NUMBER PER CARGO UNIT
Reloads	10
Powered Combat Armour	1
Combat Jump Pack	2
Survival Rations	100
Combi Rifle	5

Overland Vehicle: Ranging in size to suit the needs of the goods or services being transported, usually from small vans to large articulated trucks. If the PCs own the vehicle being used for transport, side revenue here is a real possibility – necessity even. Maximum space and weight considerations range from a single unit of cargo in smaller vans, up to thirty units of large cargo in massive lorries. Dangers inherent in this method of transportation – particularly across the surface of Dawn – include banditry, poor weather, and an increased chance of vehicle failure.

Rail: The Transtartaric Railroad is a marvel of retroengineering that criss-crosses the continent of Ariadna and serves as the lifeblood of its people. Merovingians in particular are masters of maximising rail profit by ensuring that freight space is purchased in bulk, with drop-offs and pick-ups of goods along the route ensuring this space is utilised to maximum efficiency. The beauty of rail is the ability to connect directly to shipping ports

BUBBLES AND BOUNDARIES

Part of the beauty of the *Infinity* setting is the diversity on offer, which relates directly to the types of campaigns that can be created. Choosing whether to restrict a campaign to a single planet or multiple systems is, in many ways, related to the question of single faction or multi-faction; a Caledonian clan operating within their own little economic bubble will provide an entirely different style of campaign to sanctioned Commercial Agents jetting across the Human Sphere in search of new profit avenues. That said, a certain amount of fun could be obtained by blending the two – such as dropping the aforementioned Caledonians into a program that begrudgingly sends them to Neoterra in order to learn new trading skills that will put them ahead of a rival clan. Cue mayhem and growing pains!

so that containers can be easily removed or fitted directly from the ships. Shipping containers range in size and capacity and carry important considerations. Both small and large containers can hold fifteen units of large cargo, although this can be increased to thirty-five units for the larger containers so long as the overall weight of the cargo does not increase beyond fifteen units worth of standard cargo (larger containers can only carry as much weight as the smaller, but have a far larger volume, which is mainly due to the weight of the container itself). The railways of Ariadna are much better protected than the roads, considering that each train is itself a rolling tank bristling with defences, though it can be costlier for this very reason.

Sea Freight: Shipping has become much more prevalent on Dawn, with the increased competition helping to reduce overall costs. The fact that shipments can be easily transferred to rail has only served to heighten its allure as a viable means of transporting goods, making large cargo ships heavily laden with containers a frequent sight on the stor-tossed seas of Ariadna. Transportation times are longer than by air, rail, or road, however. Refer to the previous section for units of cargo considerations, as they generally use the same containers as their rail counterparts.

Air Freight: Faster and more reliable – in a planetary sense at least – than its overland counterparts, air freight carries an increased cost per unit of cargo, particularly as less units can typically be carried overall. A large aircraft dedicated purely to air freight might carry in the region of seventy cargo units, but considering that most trains and ships can carry total loads far beyond this, the benefits to speed, reliability and bulk capacity need to be outweighed against each other.

Interstellar Spacecraft: Interstellar transport can be considered in two forms: interplanetary freight and intersystem freight. Interplanetary freight refers to the atmospheric spacecraft that ferry cargo from surface to space, whilst intersystem refers to the orbital spacecraft that ferry passengers and freight between the systems of the Human Sphere (this also includes the Circulars, although they act as docking platforms for smaller vessels). Each vessel should be considered on its own merits in terms of cargo capacity – particularly in terms of interplanetary or intersystem capability – with even the smallest intersystem spacecraft being able to carry one train's worth of cargo, the larger several trains or more.

SIDE REVENUE

Being responsible for the transportation of goods opens up the opportunity for several alternative income streams alongside the main bulk of the cargo, particularly if the PCs outright own the transport. They might want to consider sharing cargo space with other merchants, rent cargo space out (if they own the transport), offer to carry small individual items, or transport a small number of passengers. Relevant paperwork needs to account for this of course, although smuggling contraband and immigrants could make for an interesting campaign and tense encounters.

COOKING THE BOOKS

Merchant campaigns might seem like a whole lot of bookkeeping to a large degree, which is a fair assessment. Merchants need to understand how much of one particular item or service they have available and the costs involved in getting it to its destination – including if they transport it themselves. The abstract system of Assets and acquisitions takes some pain out of the bean counting, but some paperwork will be necessary in this type of campaign, particularly as profits increase and organisations grow. Part of the excitement of the campaign can be garnered from watching value and credit grow through this means

CARGO SPACE

VEHICLE TYPE	CARGO UNITS
Small Van/Arroaz Skimmer/AUV	5
Large Truck/Ore Hauler	30
Small Shipping Container	15
Large Shipping Container	15
Freight Train (approx. 160 wagons)	2400
Cargo Ship (approx. 1200 containers)	180000
Small Interplanetary Vessel	750
Large Interplanetary Vessel	2000
Small Intersystem Vessel	2400+
Large Intersystem Vessel	5000+

EXPENSES

Fuel, food, lost or damaged goods, gratuities, deal sweeteners, and more all serve as expenses that will impact profit. Any merchant worth their Tartarian salt will want to factor in a small percentage on top of a deal to cover such costs.

UNFORESEEABLE LOSS

Markets fluctuate, wars happen, bandits and pirates pillage and raid, trains derail, ships get lost at sea: all unforeseeable events that can severely impact a merchant's plans and profits. Although GMs shouldn't regularly saddle PCs with catastrophic events – they aren't an everyday occurrence – there is a risk of such calamities taking place, particularly across the politically turbulent planet of Dawn and the systems of the Human Sphere. Equally, however, the PCs might stumble across a boon that increases their profit: a salvage claim to an oceangoing or interstellar ship, increase in market value of goods, additional goods reclaimed from bandits, or the discovery of a rich Teseum vein can all serve to boost a merchant's career. Prepopulating a set of random event tables and determining the frequency at which a roll is made can serve to embellish a campaign and provide an element of randomness that can take the game in a direction which might not have been considered, particularly in open-ended campaigns.

INTERLOCKING ARENAS

THE SPHERICAL SPECTRUM

Trade doesn't just take place on Ariadna at the behest of the Merovingians of course. The Human Sphere encompasses several systems, numerous planets, and the vast regions of space between, including the quantronic networks that connect them all together. Not a second goes by without some sort of deal being struck somewhere within the immense entirety of the human-occupied regions of space. Trade is also conducted across many arenas, using a huge number of different mediums. Not all of the possible variations can be covered within the scope of this chapter, but some common themes that might appear regularly across campaigns are discussed here, particularly those that appear within other supplements related to *Infinity*. There is also plenty of opportunity to include aspects of trade discussed within this chapter in various other types of games.

STELLAR ASPIRATIONS

The foundations of interstellar trade are already being laid and negotiated by the Ariadnans – see *Interstellar Transit*, p. 42 – which, by definition, requires some means of stellar travel. Some Commercial Agents have been tasked with purposefully seeking independent traders outside of the normal processes undertaken between the G-5 factions. These types of objective provide an opportunity for truly open-ended campaigns, the entirety of which can ebb and flow based upon the PCs' successes within the negotiating arenas of the spaceports that they choose to hawk their wares.

BOUNDLESS OPPORTUNITY

A merchant campaign that spans the Human Sphere can take place against many backdrops and introduce a wide variety of complications, themes, and goals. Alternatively, it can simply focus on the next best deal. Inventive GMs could look to produce a system of profiteering that incorporates trade values across each region of the Human Sphere, with profit-hungry PCs chasing the best prices between the regions. Many of the aspects of this type of campaign have been previously discussed throughout this chapter. It's worth noting here, however, that there are many sources that can be drawn upon as additional inspiration for this type of game. Some additional work will need to be undertaken in order to adapt them to the rich and unique flavour and politics of the *Infinity* setting, but possibilities include *Firefly* and *The Expanse* (TV series), and the *Elite* video game franchise to name but a few.

ADDITIONAL CONSIDERATIONS

Open-ended campaigns can provide a great test bed to discover exactly what the players enjoy in their games. Trade campaigns that move rapidly from setting to setting provide a huge amount of leeway to simply move on if a scenario or plot hook fails. As with any campaign, however, GMs should be sure they are catering to their players' desires rather than their own.

MERCHANT TYCOONS

Although their cultures have a vastly different outlook, history, and philosophy, direct comparisons can be drawn between key aspects of Haqqislamite and Merovingian reverence for the necessity of trade. Haqqislam, however, dwarfs Merovingia in both overall size and the deep-rooted nature of trade within its society. In addition to gathering great wealth from its trade activities, Merovingia places much honour and privilege on those who succeed in commercial careers. Haqqislam also does the same, of course, though its people additionally build their entire lives around trade and barter; they literally eat, sleep, and socialise in bazaars that continually hum with the songs of merchants. With little alteration other than the considerations discussed within the opening sentence of this paragraph, much of this chapter and more can be applied to campaigns that take place entirely within Haqqislamite space, particularly if they are run under the umbrella of the Merchant Guilds.

A PIRATE'S LIFE FOR THEE

Pirates are a plague on the trade routes of the Human Sphere. For that very reason, they could also provide an interesting spin to a campaign that focusses on trade. The PCs might establish connections that provide details on shipments, or blindly plunder passing starships in the hopes of finding lucrative booty. Avenues to trade their loot will certainly feed back into many aspects of trade campaigns already discussed within this chapter, although with a hefty piratical slant. Pirates don't simply rock up to the nearest caravansarai to carry out trade of course, but they must still find some means to offload their plunder.

The types of goods available for trade within a corsair campaign can also provide a different aspect to commercial campaigns. Trading human flesh, VoodooTech, drugs, or similar highly illegal and dangerous contraband is a whole different kettle of fish compared to shipping rare furs between Dawn and Svalarheima. Campaigns that touch upon these dark aspects of human nature are of a very mature and often uncomfortable theme, however, and may be best left as activities undertaken by less scrupulous, more bloodthirsty outfits, and spoken of with scorn by more honourable pirates, who eagerly slaughter their malicious kin.

THE VALUE OF POLITICS

Votes, political favours, lobby seats, even the mere hint of a potential meeting with a prominent politician all carry their own value. Many of the tools and features of standard trade negotiations can be applied directly to the political arena, where skilled

PLAYTEST TIP

ONE FOR THE TEAM

Not every trade need be profitable. Sometimes, a deal can be accepted for the doors that are opened behind it. Access to new markets, materials, or contacts can all lead to increased profit in the long-term, so long as the merchant can absorb the loss in the short-term of course. GMs can design interlinked scenarios to offer just such opportunities, perhaps including additional Momentum and Heat spends during the initial scenario that present clues and inhibitors leading towards the increased profit opportunities beyond the scene.

negotiation, charisma, and level-headedness can mean the difference between the continuation or rapid end of a politician's career.

A POTENT BREW

Before trade can even begin between two parties, negotiations often take place to establish ground rules for how such trade will take place; consider the Cossack Diplomatic Crops, who – much to the frustration of the Commercial Agents – head up discussions with the other G-5 factions to determine policies before trade can begin. Establishing each party's position is very much a form of haggling, with dire consequences to subsequent trade terms if done incorrectly. Savvy diplomats and politicians draw upon experienced economists and commercial experts to advise them both prior to and during such negotiations. Political campaigns can therefore involve aspects of trade purely in relation to the value of political manoeuvring, or can also suitably offer some hybrid of both politics and commerce.

COLOSSAL IMPLICATIONS

Conducting trade within the political arena also offers the opportunity to impact the campaign and setting on a grand scale. Being part of the team that levers open the door on the Ariadnan Interstellar Commerce Act – thereby flooding the markets of Dawn with mass-produced G-5 alternatives and destabilising the economy – can be something performed within the boundaries of the tools presented here, provided the PCs possess enough political clout and acumen of course. Enacting or thwarting such events, however, would probably best function as the climatic culmination to a campaign, rather than serving as an everyday occurrence for the PCs.

TAGGING ON

TAG campaigns can be fast-paced, brutal affairs that launch the players rapidly from one area of conflict to another. But what about all of the logistical considerations that need to be met between each battlefield? An all-encompassing TAG campaign that considers repairs, maintenance, transport, upgrades, and contracts won't be for everyone, but such games will provide plenty of opportunity to employ trade and negotiation skills. If the PCs form part of a mercenary company, then their reliance on a fair deal is even more critical, as every single ruble counts. From ammunition to new machinery, a wide range of considerations can be dealt with that ensure the smooth running of an outfit, including even contract negotiations and cross-boundary political considerations.

CHAPTER 4

ARIADNA GEAR

Though rarely do they discuss it directly, the Ariadnan colonists' early struggle to survive demonstrates itself in myriad ways in their equipment. Most modern Ariadnan items can trace their lineage back to a piece of *Ariadna*'s settlement gear, and are more durable, simpler, warmer, or easier to repair than their galactic counterparts. Without ALEPH or geists to micro-manage their demotics, they rely on long-wearing natural materials and manual switches instead of smart materials and quantronic commands – most galactic gear seems flimsy and overly complex in comparison.

The recent exposure to the Human Sphere's technology and nations and reconnection with an Earth that's changed significantly since *Ariadna* left Sol is a profound challenge to Ariadnans' way of life, and Hiraeth nostalgia and a focus on cultural heritage is an important counterweight for their identities. Expressing allegiance through aesthetic is crucial in Ariadnan fashion and daily carry, resulting in a widespread sartorial conservatism, particularly in cultural capitols, and that exasperates galactic traders.

Other galactic goods are intensely in demand, and how much of their heritage Ariadnans will exchange for them is a matter of quiet debate. Wares unique to *Dawn*, particularly arms and armour made with Teseum, are difficult for outsiders to acquire, and almost always at higher prices than locals pay. Even locals can expect to pay higher prices outside their home territory, and off-world imports are still relatively rare.

On the other hand, USAriadnan manufacturers' public showrooms can be reached within a few days of overland travel if you'd like to make a purchase in person, widespread Merovingian trade networks ensure a steady circulation of consumer goods, and the relatively unmonitored Caledonian frontier is a smuggler's paradise, particularly for those who'd prefer to avoid ALEPH's oversight. And with a few of the right calls at the right price, you'd be amazed with what a Rodinan chinonivki can conjure on short notice.

GEAR CATALOGUE

Adhesive Shells: Used by Loup-Garou specialists for non-lethal pacification of Dog-Warrior riots, these modified fire shells spray rapid-expanding quick-set foam instead of jellied fuel. The thinner adhesive formulation isn't entirely reliable, so their use is relatively uncommon elsewhere, and even the Loup-Garous often resort to viral "silver bullets" instead. Adhesive Shells add Area (Close), Immobilising, Improvised 1, Nonlethal, and Unsubtle to the shotgun.

Americolt Eagle: Blurring the line between heavy pistol and heavy shotgun, these massive hand-cannons are sidearms for Dogface warriors and the extraordinarily strong. Their overbuilt construction and massive recoil makes firing one a recipe for humiliation and injury if you can't easily wield it one-handed, adding Backlash 1 and +2 complication range for anyone with Brawn 12 or lower. Better to settle for a lighter, weaker, lesser sidearm, and keep your dignity and wrists intact. (Range R/C, 2+5 N damage, Burst 1, Unbalanced, Piercing 1, Non-Hackable, Knockdown, Vicious 1)

Apex Ammunition: Primarily used in portable autocannons, with a propellant blend of rare earths native to Dawn and a Teseum-coated core, Apex ammunition noisily combines the best anti-armour traits of armour piercing and explosive rounds, adding Piercing 2, Unsubtle 2, and Vicious 2 to the weapon, as well as Salvo 2 (Anti-Materiel 2). Kaztec has exclusive rights to make and sell Apex rounds, and continually counters local and galactic espionage into the secrets of their construction, particularly by TVZ.

Ariadnan Heavy Machine Gun: While every faction uses some version of AP HMG with exotic material projectiles, Ariadnans level the technological playing field with carefree bursts of one of the most expensive munitions in the Human Sphere: T2 rounds. The AKNovy Drozhat is the most popular model, though Highlanders swear by the "Kilgour" KGR variant's Teseum barrel-banding to reducing heat-fatigue during sustained full-auto fire. The USARF, on the other hand, relies on the homegrown Americolt RIP-SAW, and controlled bursts. (Range L, 2+6 N damage, Burst 3, 2H/Unw, Spread 1 Unsubtle)

Arroaz Skimmer: Stealthy ground-effect watercraft used by Irmandinho black-market smugglers, arroaz skimmers' self-stabilising wings allow them to "fly" just above the surface of the water once they build up speed. This not only allows them to carry a great deal more contraband farther than ordinary craft, but reduces their sonar profile. Every aspect is designed for stealth – a carefully shaped faceted hull for radar signature, integrated heat sinks for thermal emissions, and both traditional paints and photoreactive coatings for blending almost invisibly into the horizon.

WHAT YOU'LL FIND IN THIS CHAPTER

A catalogue of new weapons, armour, items, and vehicles used by Ariadnans

DAWN-MADE

Their homegrown industries are a source of pride for Ariadnans, particularly weapons and personal vehicles, leading to disappointing sales for megacorp goods except among Merovingians, who are generally broader-minded. Savvy Nomad and Haqqislamite traders form co-op partnerships with local makers to provide materials and design advice, letting the locals do the hands-on work. Goods with the Dawn-Made logo are becoming a staple of caravansarai and Commercial Delegation offerings.

DAILY CARRY

Carrying weapons, particularly firearms, is illegal in Rodina and Merovingia, although there are licenses available for hunting, private security, or for anyone with sufficient bureaucratic pull and resources. Caledonians are permitted to carry weapons with a clan's authorisation, which is easily obtained, particularly for melee weapons. USAriadnans proudly claim their right to carry weapons – it's considered polite to keep them concealed in the cities of the northern states, fashionable to wear several openly in southern ones, and generally in good taste to put them away when visiting friends.

KAZTEC

Научно-производственная корпорация, the scientific and production corporation best known as Kaztec, is the semi-private company in charge of the research and development of new Rodinan weaponry and military technology. Both publically and privately funded, and directly supervised by the Stavka, it has a higher budget and generally superior results to USAriadna's DARPS, ensuring Rodinan dominance.

TVZ

TVZ was founded as the Tartary Research and Production Corporation during the Age of Exploration to create inexpensive shipping containers and railway materials for colonising Tartary and building the Transtartaric Railway. Meant as a private sector competitor for the publicly owned Dynamo-based Dinamotraktorzavod (DTZ) to ensure efficiency, they have been a motivating second-place rival for decades, though DTZ maintains a near-monopoly on Transtartaric and railway manufacturing.

Initial railcar failures against Antipode attacks led Rodinan wags to call them Tartarvagonzavod, or the Tartary Wagon Company, but as the company up-armoured their railway products and became a significant weapons and vehicle manufacturer in their own right, the TVZ name was officially taken on as a point of pride. Their expansion into munitions and materiel manufacturing during the Third Antipode Offensive positioned them as a competitor to Kaztec as well as DTZ, deeply entwined with Kazak military officials and the Federal Service bureaucracy. A potential private-sector threat to Rodina's publicly owned semi-monopolies, TVZ is primed to become a prized megacorp acquisition, or even metastasize into one itself.

ARROAZ SKIMMER

ENCLOSED, HOVER, WATERCRAFT

ATTRIBUTES

Scale	Speed	Brawn
2	4	14 (+3)

DETAILS

Max. Passengers	Impact
4	4+5 N (Knockdown)

Hard Points
Chassis 1, Comms 2, External 1, Internal 1, Motive 1, Weapons 1

DEFENCES

Structure	18	Firewall	10
Armour	3	BTS	1

SPECIAL ABILITIES:

- **Ground-Effect Craft**: The skimmer needs to build speed to take off. If it did not move at least one zone in the previous round, it cannot take advantage of Hover and its speed is reduced to 2.
- **Stealthy Construction**: The skimmer adds +1 Momentum to stealth state tests, and +1 difficulty to Observation tests to detect it.

Ariadnan Utility Vehicle (AUV): Sold in dozens of different makes and models and owned by majority of households, the Ariadnan utility vehicle is a sturdy high-clearance four-wheel drive people – and cargo-mover. AUVs are profoundly inefficient compared to galactic vehicles, and their overbuilt resilience is vestigial on cities' well-maintained roads. But they are a reminder of an era when infrastructure was far less reliable, and strongly tied to Ariadnan ideals of rugged self-sufficiency. In frontier regions they are a practical necessity, especially since they are substantially simpler to repair and maintain than more modern designs.

ARIADNAN UTILITY VEHICLE (AUV)

EXPOSED (+2 N COVER), GROUND, RUGGED, WHEELED

ATTRIBUTES

Scale	Speed	Brawn
2	2	14 (+2)

DETAILS

Max. Passengers	Impact
6	3+7 N (Knockdown)

Hard Points
Chassis 2, Comms 2, External 1, Internal 1, Motive 1, Weapons 1

DEFENCES

Structure	24	Firewall	4
Armour	4	BTS	–

Baba: A long-lasting fever-inducing euphoric, baba (Баба, "grandmother" in Russian), helps counteract the physical and psychological effects of cold exposure, though it leaves the user more vulnerable once it wears off. (Ingested, Instant 1, Day)

- *Special Effect*: Once administered, the user gains a bonus d20 to all Resistance and Discipline tests against exposure to the cold for twelve hours. Once twelve hours are up, they become highly sensitive to temperature for the following four hours, taking double damage from extremes of cold or heat.
- *Addiction*: 1 (6 doses), Compulsion 1
- *Withdrawal*: 2, 2+2 N damage, Harm Effect (user takes double damage from extremes of cold or heat until recovered)

Baba/Yaga: When baba, a long-lasting fever-inducing euphoric, is blended with yaga, a fungal entheogen from the Antipode Wilds, the two have a profound synergistic effect, sending the user on a 1d20-hour trip through their own subconscious. It induces a severe fever and deep immobilising sleep, and waking the user before the trip is complete deals 3+3 N Nonlethal Terrifying 3 damage. (Ingested, Instant 3, Day)

- *Special Effect*: Each hour the user is under, they can make an Intelligence (D0) test, and spend Momentum 1 for 2 to recover Resolve, 3 for 1 to recover a Metanoia, or with GM permission, 6 for 1 to gain or lose a trait. On a complication, take 2+2 N Nonlethal Terrifying 2 damage.

Backwoods ATV: The Frankensteinian love child of a lifted truck, a four-wheeled all-terrain vehicle, and a hydraulics factory, backwoods all-terrain vehicles are designed for travel through the forests and mountains of the Antipode Wilds, where trails are rare and roads even rarer. Each studded tire has an independent transmission and suspension, allowing for intense bouldering and rock-climbing maneuvers, and is on an extensible hydraulic strut that can be pulled close to slip through narrow gaps, or extended to bridge pits.

BACKWOODS ATV

EXPOSED, GROUND, RUGGED, WHEELED

ATTRIBUTES

Scale	Speed	Brawn
1	2	10 (+1)

DETAILS

Max. Passengers	Impact
2	2+5 N (Knockdown)

Hard Points
Chassis 3, Comms 1, External 1, Internal 1, Weapons 2

DEFENCES

Structure	14	Firewall	4
Armour	2	BTS	–

SPECIAL ABILITIES:

- **Spider Crawl**: In the wilds of Dawn, the backwoods ATV can leap over gaps and grind up mountain slopes as if they were driving on level ground. While in the Ariadnan wilderness reduce any difficult or hazardous terrain test by 1 step, This can reduce tests to Difficulty 0.

Bandolier: Pioneered during the Commercial Conflicts, modern bandoliers are a band that goes around the chest, with a series of pouches and stick-pads embedded in a layer that slides independently for quick quiet access, allowing the user to swap between ammo types as a Free Action once a round.

Binoculars: A reliable classic often built into armour, binoculars allow distant objects to be seen more clearly, removing range penalties to observe targets at Long range, but adding +1 difficulty to notice things in the same zone due to reduced peripheral vision.

Cherkesska Armour: The Cossack heavy uniform is lighter and easier to wear than other nations' heavy combat armour thanks to Teseum-heavy manufacture, but provides slightly less head protection in the interest of freer movement. Because Teseum processing is costly and laborious, they are reserved for soldiers of proven worth and the well-connected. Cherkesska incorporate a bandolier around the chest and a Teseum knife at the waist, but resist alteration – Tech tests to alter the armour are at +1 difficulty, and no additional equipment slots can be added.

Chest Mine: Directional anti-personnel weapons attached to vehicles, TAGs, and most notoriously on the front of Buffalo powered armour, chest mines are particularly effective when triggered in concert. They do not add bonus damage from attributes, and cannot be used to attack targets at Medium, Long, or Extreme range, or who are outside the 120° arc they face, but if multiple chest mines are triggered simultaneously, they replace their Area (Close) quality with Indiscriminate (Close), stack qualities as charges do, and deal +2N damage to any targets in Reach. (Range R/C, 2+5N damage, Disposable, Grievous, Area (Close), Piercing 1, Vicious 1, Unsubtle)

Cobra Baton: Collapsible batons initially built by Bracco Limited for their own private security's use, cobra batons quickly became popular with the non-descript government agencies Bracco worked with, and are now a sizable portion of their business. (Melee, 1+4N damage, 1H, Knockdown, Stun, Subtle 2, Vicious 1)

Cod: Slang for any one of hundreds of protein-rich dietary powders and chalky drinks used by weightlifters and fitness fanatics, "cod" supplements are often adulterated by unscrupulous Submondo dealers to maximise profits, so allergic reactions are common.

If one dose is taken daily for a month in combination with regular intense exercise, they allow the user to increase their Brawn as if it was 1N ranking lower. If an Effect is rolled, the user has a negative reaction to the cod brand's fillers and impurities, and takes a Wound – that brand will have no further beneficial effect for them, and they must find a new brand. Cod is not a substitute for ordinary nutrition, and if used as one, inflicts a Wound every week.

D.E.P.: Always popular with guerrillas and irregulars looking for inexpensive anti-tank power, particularly on *Dawn*, the D.E.P. is a lightweight single-shot *Corregidor*-kitbashed Panzerfaust variant. Whether Descanse En Paz – "Rest In Peace" – refers to user or target depends on accuracy. Each D.E.P. contains 1 Reload, and after use, the weapon is empty and cannot be used until reloaded. Disassembling the weapon to reload it requires a Tech (D1) test as a Standard Action. **(**Range L**,** 2+5N damage, 2H, Munition, Needle)

Digicloak (Environment): Thanks to a ruthless evolutionary competition between Antipode packs and *stanitsa* scouts, Ariadnan camouflage is remarkably advanced despite their technological handicaps, resulting in the digicloaks relied on by military snipers, pickets, and scouts. Each is a thin cloak of digital-ink panels specialised to work in a particular environment, displaying textures to match nearby terrain. Mountain, forest, and jungle texture libraries are most common, but all are difficult to obtain outside of military requisitions.

A digicloak counts as a kit for face-to-face Stealth tests made against targets at Medium range or farther, granting 1 bonus Momentum, so long as the wearer is prone. If the wearer is not *revealed* – even if *detected* – the cloak provides +2N Cover Soak against ranged attacks.

Dog-Bowl Armour: Customised sports padding reinforced with Teseum, Dog-Bowl armour is a player's only protection against their opponents' tackles, fists, teeth, claws, and even the ball itself. Besides the ball and their own fists, teeth, and claws, that is. The recent addition of helmet-mounted recorders allows fans to get even closer to Dog-Bowl's pulse-pounding action and no-holds-barred brutality. Usually worn under a jersey, they are also powder-coated in team colors for when the jersey is inevitably ripped to shreds.

Dog-Bowl Jersey X: Dog-Bowl jerseys are lightweight shirts worn over Dog-Bowl armour to show which team a player is on, and replicas are worn by fans to show their allegiance to a team or favorite player. Designs vary, but always include the player's name and team number, and often add team sponsors' logos and the player's personalised slogan or symbol. They provide no protection, but are hard

POD TATTOOS

Arroaz is slang for a swift young dolphin, and discreet dolphin tattoos with a design shared by the crew of a long-running arroaz skimmer is sign of an unbreakable bond among Irmandinho, and a way to prove one's history if questioned. Incorporating Helot cultural imagery is a recent trend, leading to sporadic violent conflicts with Libertos.

VEHICLE OWNERSHIP

Ariadna is a vehicle-dependent society – infrastructure is still irregular, so most Ariadnans have driver's licenses and either own or share a vehicle. Among Nomads, only those who serve in the military or work in construction would know how to drive, since most of their transportation is handled by trains, towlines, slideways, and shuttles. PanOceania and Yu Jing have shared automated vehicles throughout their cities as part of their public transportation services, accessed by paying a monthly fee. Haqqislam is a mix of all of the above, as Bourak has highly developed cities and habitats, as well as areas still under active colonisation.

CLAN COD

A joke that's taken on a life of its own, Clan Cod is an imaginary clan all gym rats, bodybuilders, and exercise obsessives that use cod are supposedly members of. After over a hundred years of over-the-top memes, slogans, tattoos, jokes, and annual competitions related to mashups of fish, fishing, fitness, and religion surrounding "The Lord Cod", it's still going strong, transcending national, ethnic, and racial boundaries, snagging the swole in its vast sinewy nautical net. It's a fairly Dogface – and Helot-friendly subculture, and many Dog-Bowl and Scuball players sport prominent "dogfish", "get hooked!", or "c-wulf" tattoos.

DOG-BOWL RIVALS

While the top-dog teams are different every year, rivalries can transcend seasons and last for decades, triggered by an event that creates bad blood, then reinforced with repeated close or contested losses. Some notorious rivalries include the "green war" between the Scots Greens and Firbolg of Cailleach, the Riverside Alpha Dogs and the Newport Krakens "five foot <expletive>", and the Picts of Scone and the Tsitadel Sentinels yearly "spike game". Hooligans loyal to rival teams often riot after especially tense games and attack the opposing team's neighborhoods, sparking Dog-Warrior riots

CURRICULA CONUNDRUMS

Until recently, fusebox curricula were managed by a nominally pan-national council, dominated by the Merovingian Ministère de l'Éducation Nationale due to their long tradition of trade caravan tutors and fusebox manufacture. Now, along with a small swarm of O-12 Ariadnan Educational Commission bureaucrats, they have the difficult task of incorporating several hundred years of galactic educational and technological advancement into their lesson plans without outraging their students' parents. While there have always been slight cultural variations to maximise sales, retrofitting multiple educational systems on the fly is a delicate matter, and a flashpoint for culture shock.

to completely destroy – jerseys worn during games are signed and sold to fans afterward.

They are rated and priced by quality and authenticity: 1 for ordinary jerseys sold in stores or at games, 2 for exact replicas or special editions, and 3 for certified signed jerseys worn through an actual game that made it out in wearable shape. Wearing one grants X bonus Momentum on Lifestyle and Persuade tests with a fan of the same team or X-1 bonus Momentum with most Dog-Bowl fans, but gives no benefits and adds +X difficulty to those tests with passionate fans of the team's hated rivals.

Dueling Bracers: While Caledonian duelists train and spar in lightweight imported Yu Jingese fencing suits that track movement and impacts, they officially duel in only a kilt, Teseum-reinforced bracers, and sandals, as both a show of bravery and Hiraeth affectation. Though the contest is traditional, innovative fighting techniques are welcomed, and modern duelists use their bracers not only defensively, but as another set of striking edges. When worn as a set and used by someone practiced in their use, they provide 2N Armour Soak to the wearer's arms, and add 1+1N damage, Parry 1, and Vicious 1 to Unarmed Strikes.

Eagle Ammunition: This USAriadnan ammunition relies on an unusually large explosive charge to accelerate a Teseum-tipped armour-penetrating projectile, all in a cartridge small enough for use in Americolt Eagle hand-cannons. It can be fired by lesser heavy pistols, but the recoil is so severe that it adds Backlash 1 and +2 complication range to the weapon for anyone with Brawn 12 or lower. Eagle ammo adds Piercing 3 and Unsubtle to the weapon.

E/Mauler: E/Maulers are E/M pulse mines, equipped with a motion detector and IFF linked to a stealthy single-use pulse emitter. The design is a Nomad patent, but Ariadna bought an ample supply of them during the Commercial Conflicts – the leftovers are relatively cheap, with the right contacts. While non-hackable versions are profoundly illegal elsewhere, enforcement is relatively lax on *Dawn* since so few Ariadnans have Cubes. **(**Mine, 2+5N damage, 1H, Breaker, Comms or Non-Hackable, Disposable, E/M, Indiscriminate (Close), Piercing 2, Unsubtle)

Fusebox: A generic term named for the tutor tablets (детонаторчик Russian "little detonator" or "tiny fusebox") carried on Dawn, these brightly colored soft-case tablets contain interactive lessons for a complete primary childhood education, as well as limited secondary education tracks, along with the basics of Ariadna's most commonly spoken languages. Often the only educational materials available on the frontier during colonisation, they allowed even inexperienced teachers to give their charges a solid educational grounding, and its characters and themes are a nostalgic pan-cultural touchpoint between Ariadnans. Modern versions receive regular updates from dNet, and are often cracked to access illicit content from Arachne nodes by enterprising students.

Using a fusebox halves the XP costs for the first ranks of Education Focus and Expertise, and the extensive interrelations, reinforcement, and rigorous evaluations between lessons also halve the XP cost of Disciplined Student if both ranks were learned using the fusebox. Additionally, it reduces the cost of learning Ariadnan languages – English (Scots or American), French, or Russian (Kazak) – to 30 XP each, although the speaker will have a limited vocabulary until they spend time around fluent speakers.

Heavy Shotgun: A scaled-up boarding shotgun commonly mounted on vehicles or used as an integrated weapon for Remotes such as Sputniks or Bulleteers elsewhere in the Human Sphere, heavy shotguns are a favourite close-quarters weapon for Wulver and Dogface troops. Technically portable artillery, only individuals with remarkable strength or servosystems can absorb their extreme recoil – add Backlash 3 and +3 complication range to the weapon if used by anyone with Brawn 13 or lower unless mounted on a vehicle, TAG, or emplacement. (Range C, 2+6N damage, Burst 1, 2H/Mounted, Knockdown)

- *Normal Shells Mode (Primary)*: Area (Close), Spread 1
- *AP Slugs Mode (Secondary)*: Piercing 3

Hopak Ammunition: By lacing its rocketry and armour-penetrating warheads with Teseum, this Kaztec-developed artillery munition incorporates a guidance package without compromising ballistics, payload, or armour penetration. Hopak rockets can only be fired from a Massive or Mounted weapon, and reduce its Burst to 1, but add Area (Close), Grievous, Guided, and Piercing 2. When used in Urugan MRL launchers, they add an additional mode, but remove Non-Hackable.

- *Hopak Guided Mode*: Area (Close), Grievous, Guided, Piercing 2

Katyusha Ammunition: Katyusha (Катюша, Russian diminutive form of Katherine) rocket warheads are packed with dozens of DA bomblets. Dispersed above the target in mid-air, they arm during freefall via a simple mechanical orientation system, saturating the target area with a physically and psychologically overwhelming barrage. The recent addition of compact bomblet guidance packages allows improved accuracy, though it exposes launchers to quantronic attack. They can only be fired from a Massive or Mounted weapon, and reduce that weapon's Burst to 1, but add Area (Close), Guided, Spread 2, Unsubtle, Terrifying 2, and Vicious 2. When used in Urugan MRL launchers, they add an additional mode, but remove Non-Hackable.

- *Katyusha Guided Mode*: Area (Close), Guided, Spread 2, Terrifying 2, Unsubtle 2, Vicious 2

Long Jehans: Popularised by Commercial Agent Jehan Chastel, and supposedly named after a French wolf-hunting ancestor, these sets of warm and comfortable long underwear (and their many, many counterfeits) have a lining of silver-infused synthetic zeolite and activated carbon that mitigates odors. So long as they are washed at least once a week, all attempts to track the wearer by scent are at +1 difficulty, even against trackers with Keen Senses (Smell) such as Antipodes.

***Métros* Armour**: The Troupes Métropolitaines de la Défense Nationale, commonly known as Métros, are militias that serve as guardians of Merovingian trade infrastructure, and as the backbone of the FRRM. In times of peace they are a national police force, but in times of war become fierce guerrilla fighters – their armour is reversible to conceal insignia, and designed to fit easily under clothing if needed. Targets are often unaware they are surrounded by Métros until it's already too late.

Molotok: The Ariadnan molotok (молоток, Russian for "hammer") is a mid-range machine gun akin to the spitfire that uses lightweight armour piercing rounds for a faster fire rate. Ideal for close quarters and urban combat, its compact construction is popular with front-line paratroopers and motorcycle scouts, and with Bratva gangsters for hits on armoured targets. (Range M, 1+5 N damage, Burst 3, 2H, Spread 2, Unsubtle)

Mormaer Armour: Ostentatious use of Teseum is a sign of wealth and power in Caledonia, and mormaer armour is the absolute pinnacle, a walking boast, made of plates of enough pure Teseum to represent most of a minor clans' entire hoard or a significant investment from a major one. This construction allows protection equivalent to heavy combat armour without the usual cumbersome bulk, and, when worn by the aristocracy and distinguished elite of Caledonian troops, provides +2 Morale Soak from the pride of being chosen to wear it.

Official Vehicle: Bland bureaucratese for Federal Service cars used – theoretically – exclusively for state business, these TVZ-made sedans are a common perk for Chinonivki (Russian for bureaucrat, see *Infinity Corebook*, p. 154–156) who have clawed their way up the Table of Ranks. Whisper quiet, luxuriously appointed, E/M sealed, and subtly up-armoured, their most important perk is the blue micro-LED strips that outline the car's bodywork. Once those lights are turned on and flashing, an official vehicle has absolute right of way, can disobey traffic laws as needed, and cannot be stopped or searched by law enforcement. Despite sporadic protests and scandals, they remain a tangible reminder of Federal Service power, and a motivating prize for ambitious Chinonivki.

OFFICIAL VECHICLE

EXPOSED (+4 N COVER), GROUND, WHEELED

ATTRIBUTES

Scale	Speed	Brawn
1	3	13 (+1)

DETAILS

Max. Passengers	Impact
5	2+6 N (Knockdown)
Hard Points	
Chassis 2, Comms 2, External 1, Internal 2	

DEFENCES

Structure	16	Firewall	8
Armour	4	BTS	4

SPECIAL ABILITIES:

- **Blue Lights**: Once its warning lights are turned on and flashing, the vehicle has absolute right of way, can disobey traffic laws as needed, and cannot be stopped or searched by law enforcement. All other Rodinan vehicles will attempt to get out of the way.

Ojotnik: Ojotniks are military-grade Ariadnan big-game hunting rifles – more potent but slower than conventional assault rifles, the ojotnik's true edge comes from its Teseum ammunition's fearsome armour-piercing capabilities. With lightweight stocks made from native hardwoods, Teseum-coated rifling, and the best scopes available, ojotniks are hand-crafted heirlooms, passed between generations from master marksmen to their prized pupils. Their rarity makes them a status symbol and a point of pride for Cossack Spetsnaz Scouts, each of whom bears a personalised ojotnik. (Range M, 1+6 N damage, Burst 2, Unwieldy, Unforgiving 3)

Ore Hauler: Gargantuan dump trucks used primarily to transport Teseum-bearing ore to processing plants, ore haulers slowly evolved from ordinary cargo trucks into their current form in response to predation by human bandits and Antipode raiders. These huge trucks are propelled by powerful fuel-guzzling engines that allow them to outpace slower-moving threats, are armoured to ensure delivery, and carry squads of well-paid and well-armed guards for additional protection.

MOTHER TRUCKERS

Ore haulers are also used to ship USARF provisions from main operations bases to advanced posts in the AEZ during the winter months, when air delivery is impossible. The Mother Truckers logistic regiment call these routes Dead Drops – if you don't make it in under twenty-four hours, the odds of returning home alive drop quickly. Intense cold, unpredictable blizzards and avalanches, Antipode ambushes, and bandit raids mean any ride could be the last, so the Truckers and their escorts keep the gas pedal down, don't let up until they reach the end of the line, and drink hard 'til the next Drop.

COMMON HAULERS

The Nova Industries Gichimakwa (Ojibwe for "Big Bear") and Starling Flatboat are the most popular ore haulers for USAriadna freight, while Caledonians endlessly debate the merits of the Silurian Draigsman, the Wodhela Wagoneer, and the Luchta Lugger. The AngUS Big Jack, everyone agrees, is rolling garbage ever since they switched to cheaper drive-engines – three axles just mean more maintenance.

WORKING ANIMALS

For examples of companion animals suitable for more dangerous work, see Guard Dogs *Infinity* Corebook, p. 341, or Riding Horses, *Infinity* Corebook, p. 489.

DÉJÀ BREW

A bitter equivalent made from local plants was popular initially after Ariadna's arrival, but was almost completely eclipsed by transplanted terrestrial Leadplant, which thrived in Tartary soil and had a pleasant taste when prepared Lakota-style. The sudden availability of dozens of galactic teas has only intensified the addiction. Yu Jingese varieties are popular, but tea from Earth acquired legendary traits over long decades of deprivation, and hosting "tastings" is popular among well-connected Caledonian and Rodinan elites.

USAriadnans claim to not notice any difference in taste between galactic coffee beans and those grown in local greenhouses, and stick with the varieties they've relied on for decades. But Merovingians, while characteristically choosy about their coffee, have enthusiastically embraced a handful of NeoTerran brands, thanks in part to devoted hypercorp marketing campaigns.

ORE HAULER

EXPOSED (+3 N COVER), GROUND, HANDS, RUGGED, WHEELED

ATTRIBUTES		
Scale	Speed	Brawn
3	3	16 (+3)

DETAILS	
Max. Passengers	Impact
2/8	5+7 N (Knockdown)
Hard Points	
Chassis 4, Comms 1, External 1, Internal 2, Weapons 4	

DEFENCES			
Structure	24	Firewall	4
Armour	4	BTS	1

SPECIAL ABILITIES:

- **Rolling Fortress**: The cabin for an ore hauler only has room for a pilot and engineer, but there are cramped gun turret compartments for an additional six guards around the vehicle, and crawlways and ladders and bulkheads throughout, allowing defenders to benefit from +3 N cover even when fighting inside the hauler.

Pet X (tiny/small/large): Primarily home companions, pets are small and largely inoffensive animals. While other factions' demogrant apartments rarely allow small or large pets, pets of every size are a valuable source of companionship and relaxation even for the poorest Ariadnans, granting a bonus d20 on Discipline tests made to recover Resolve when nearby. Pets cannot be used in combat – they aren't large enough or dangerous enough to do more than provide a brief distraction, and tend to flee or hide at the first sign of violence. Those large enough to be useful in dangerous situations are classified as working animals.

Pets come in three categories: tiny, small and large. Tiny pets can live on the user or in a small portable habitat, and grant no other benefits, but are generally cheaper and easier to keep. Large pets take more time and effort, but can potentially provide useful benefits at the GM's discretion (for example, a dog could grant bonus Momentum on its owner's Observation tests).

Pets also come in a variety of rarities: 1 for animals commonly used as pets in the area without any particular pedigree or traits, 2 for animals rarely sold as pets or common ones with a specific pedigree or trait, and 3 for dangerous or exotic animals from specific regions of distant planets, or with extremely rare traits.

Photoreactive Coating: Photoreactive coatings incorporate high-resolution e-inks that respond to the presence, absence, and colour of light, to mimic their surroundings. Slogans and obscenities in deliberately glitched coatings scrawled onto clothing are popular with rebellious Ariadnan teens in Mat', Burgo, and particularly Poictesme. While not the most effective personal camouflage, and incompatible with other camo gear, it's relatively easy to apply, and better than going without, allowing the wearer to reroll a single d20 when attempting a Stealth test. If the user takes physical damage from a weapon with the Incendiary quality, the coating automatically suffers a Fault, and is disabled until repaired.

Portable Autocannon: By eliminating or simplifying recoil-suppression and ammo-feed systems, and using only crude optical sights, Ariadnan technicians create compact, lightweight versions of weapons used by primitive armoured vehicles when Ariadna first left Earth. Firing Kaztec-manufactured Apex rounds, the portable autocannon gives Kazak Tankhunters an undeniable punch even against modern ground units. (Range L, 1+6 N damage, Burst 2, Non-Hackable, Unwieldy)

Portable Rescue Supply Kit: A compact case carried by every member of the 112 Emergency Service, portable rescue supply kits contain rope, a grappling hook, a fire extinguisher, basic medical supplies, a crowbar, nylex bags that can quickly be filled with dirt for improvised barriers, and a variety of other tools and supplies. The case counts as a Medikit for emergency medical care and triage purposes, and a Survival Kit for a particular environment. Alternatively, a Tech (D2) test can be convert one into a Part or Pick resource.

Rebreather: Masks connected to a supply of 3 Oxygen Loads and designed to recycle exhaled air to prolong it, rebreathers provide 1 BTS when used. It takes a minute to don a rebreather, as the bulky and complex equipment takes some effort to fit properly.

Rucksack X: An easy way to safely carry a large number of items, rucksacks are reinforced lockable bags worn on the carrier's back, secured via straps over their shoulders. Modern materials allow additional pouches to be affixed anywhere on the bag for balance and organisation. For the paranoid customer, integrated locational beacons, biometric locks, or selectively adhesive security strips can all be added for a modest fee. The Merovingian trader's faithful friend, Thievery tests to steal belongings placed in a rucksack are at +X difficulty. Rucksacks can be purchased with a rating of 1–3.

Samovar: A samovar (Russian: самовар, literally "self-boiler") is a metal container traditionally used to heat and boil water for strong tea throughout Eurasia. A compact collapsible version with a built-in heating element and long-lasting battery was created for the *Ariadna*, and the joke goes that unity lasted as long as the tea stores did. Copies are common throughout Ariadnan territory – Rodinans use it to make strong concentrated *zavarka*, Caledonians favour smooth weak tea at strictly observed teatime. Similarly while Merovingian hospitality welcomes guests and customers with strong hot coffee, USAriadnans tend towards the classic Americano coffee served communally amongst friends and co-workers.

Sgian Dubh: The sgian-dubh (Scottish Gaelic for "covert knife") is a small, single-edged knife worn as part of traditional Caledonian Highland dress along with a kilt and mid-calf stockings. When worn openly, it is placed with the handle visible at the top of the stocking nearest the wearer's dominant hand. Otherwise, it is designed to be easily concealed and drawn, ensuring the wearer has a weapon at hand if attacked. Sgian-dubh are incredibly common in Caledonia, and sold in a variety of styles, including blackened blades common among Submondo thugs and dealers, ornate and antler-handled pieces favored by clan elites, and the simple sturdy versions worn by honest folk. (Melee, 1+3N damage, 1H, Concealed 2, Non-Hackable, Subtle 2, Unforgiving 1)

Silver Bullets: Specifically formulated for use against Antipodes and their Dogface and Wulver descendants, this viral ammo is used by Loup-Garous special action units when lethal force is required. Dog Nation Dogface-rights activists had it banned by the Concilium Convention, but thanks to DNAriadnan lobbying and deep-seated prejudice, the Merovingian parliament is not so easily swayed. Silver Bullets provide Biotech, Grievous, Knockdown, and Toxic 3 against Antipodes, Dogfaces, or Wulvers, but only Biotech against all other targets.

T2 Boarding Shotgun: Caledonian forces often use locally made T2 Shells in place of slugs. The weapon requires subtle modification to maximise the ammo's effect, a process perfected in the AKNovy Uzhas. Other manufacturers' shotguns suffer catastrophic jams or barrel degradation after repeated T2 firings, making AKNovy's technique a much sought-after trade secret. T2 boarding shotguns are MULTI [Medium] weapons, but use Normal Shells and T2 Shells instead of Standard or Special ammunition. (Range C, 1+5N damage, Burst 1, 2H, Knockdown, Medium MULTI)

- *Normal Shells Mode (Primary)*: Area (Close), Spread 1
- *T2 Slugs Mode (Secondary)*: Anti-Materiel 2, Piercing 3, Vicious 2

T2 Slugs: Like Armour Piercing Slugs, T2 slug cartridges are mostly carefully arranged accelerants designed to project a solid metal dart to punch through armoured targets. Unlike them, however, T2 slug darts are made of solid Teseum, with stabilising wings that shred materials at the point of impact. T2 slugs add Anti-Materiel 2, Piercing 3, and Vicious 2 to the shotgun.

Tactical Webbing: A system of selectively adhesive belts, braces, and straps to attach equipment to for quick access, tactical webbing allows an attached item to be drawn as a Free Action once a round. However, Thievery tests to steal attached items are at −1 difficulty, and the webbing is unmistakably military gear.

Teseum Claws: Antipode raiders and warriors use Teseum-laced claws to eviscerate heavily armoured opponents, including each another's hides in inter-tribal warfare. Details about the ritual binding of Teseum to claws are obscure, but researchers believe that the process is permanent, and all three members of a trinary undergo the process during the same day-long period. Less publicised is that the process was rare before humanity came to Dawn. (Melee, 1+3N damage, Piercing 2, Subtle 1, Vicious 2)

Teseum Claymore: A two-handed Caledonian classic, the Teseum-edged claymore (from claidheamh-mòr, "great sword") is a deadly and reliable infantry weapon, pride of the mantelpiece for many a Highlander veteran, and devastating even against heavily armoured targets in the hands of a skilled duelist. Each is a masterwork of blacksmithing tradition and Teseum-shaping craft, and storied blades are passed down within clans for generations – even new Teseum claymores are eye-wateringly expensive for outsiders. (Melee, 2+5N damage, 2H, Grievous, Non-Hackable, Parry 2, Piercing 2, Vicious 2)

Teseum Hatchet: A civilian one-handed hand axe popular with frontier hunters and farmers, Teseum hatchets saw bloody use during the Commercial Conflicts, becoming prized memorabilia for mercenaries who raided outlying communities. While still a common piece of useful and long-lasting if somewhat expensive kit, a galactic carrying one on

MACROFEIDH ANTLERS

Lords of the tundra and 2.5 meters high at the shoulder, Megaloceros ariadniensis (see p. 93) are gigantic deer found throughout the forests of Ariadna. A well-formed set of antlers from a mature male Macrofeidh are iconic decor for hunting halls and pubs, particularly in Tartary, where they are largest and most aggressive.

Since they are grown slowly over decades rather than regrown annually as males' are, the antlers of female deer are smaller and denser, making them even more valuable. A doe will often shatter her antlers in her death throes, so hunting them is a fool's errand – the wise keep their distance, and wait for the antlers to naturally shed. Properly treated, their dense patterning, comforting heft, and rough grippy surface make them an ideal if extremely expensive material for knife handles, pistol grips, and other craftwork. A knife or otherone-handed weapon with a Macrofeidh antler handle or grip adds 5 to the base cost, but the wielder is immune to any attempt to forcibly disarm them of the weapon or otherwise knock it from their hands as if they had the Strong Grip talent.

BUCKSHEE TESEUM

Derived from an ancient army term for off-the-record gear, "buckshee" is Submondo slang for fake, adulterated, or otherwise illicitly obtained Teseum. Since openly worn Teseum is a show of wealth, lesser materials plated with Teseum or difficult to spot imitations are an easy way for individuals, or even entire clans, to keep up appearances on a budget.

Wildcat prospectors on the frontier, expert forgers in the cities, and cunning thieves and smugglers in the mines ensure there's always Teseum of dubious provenance to be had, and fat bribes for officials willing to look the other way. Calling someone's Teseum wares or weapons buckshee or "chalky" – after an old easily spotted method – is a quick way to start a fight, and profoundly humiliating if you can prove it.

TESEUM WEAR

While each Ariadnan nation has a currency, Teseum is the true signifier of wealth. Worn openly and ostentatiously as solid torcs, rings, necklaces, or armbands in Caledonia, it is also more subtly displayed as earrings, seals, and necklace crosses among Kazaks, inlaid on flasks, cigarette cases, and drinking vessels in Merovingia, and used extensively as a clothing accent in USAriadna. Buttons, bolo ties, hat badges, or any of a dozen other accessories or decorations can be made of Teseum to demonstrate wealth, and when given as a gift, as a clear sign of friendship and trust.

Any time a character would gain 1 or more Assets from an Ariadnan source they are on friendly terms with, they can instead choose to gain an equal amount of Teseum Wear jewelry or other accessories, negotiated with the GM. With the right contacts or skills, it can be convertedinto Teseum-reliant weapons, armour, or ammunition later, provided half the item's cost is paid for with Teseum Wear.

the frontier, particularly if they have a martial look, is on a short trip to a shallow grave. (Melee, 1+3 N damage, 2H, Grievous, Non-Hackable, Piercing 2, Subtle 1, Thrown, Vicious 1)

Teseum Knife: As invaluable for frontier survival as in a knife fight, Teseum knives hold an edge longer, fly farther, slice deeper, and punch in harder than any ordinary blade. Elite Ariadnan troops, such as Kazak Spetsnaz parachutists, Highlander S.A.S., and USAMC Devil Dogs, receive inscribed Teseum knives on graduation from training. Hardcases have their own similar, if more intense, "graduation" ceremonies. Unlike other Teseum weapons, Teseum knives are relatively affordable to off-world buyers. (Melee, 1+4 N damage, 1H, Concealed 1, Non-Hackable, Piercing 2, Subtle 2, Thrown, Unforgiving 2)

Tracking Collar: Used to monitor the location of pets, working animals, or captured and tagged wildlife, this collar pings a local satellite network – such as Roving Star – every five minutes, or on-demand with a Hacking (D2) test. Once affixed, it is nearly impossible for the animal to remove, requiring an Athletics (D3) or Brawn (D4) test to escape. Trakstar TC collars are the dominant brand on Dawn, thanks to early adoption by New Southern Fleet scientists based in Dalnîy, and implanted versions are used by Antipode handlers to track escaped charges.

Trail Bike: A rural teenage favorite for doing stunts and racing on backwoods trails, these cut-down motorcycles have reinforced suspensions for massive jumps and cornering at high speeds. Though under-armoured compared to ordinary motorcycles, their simple construction makes them easy to repair. Popular models include the TVZ Mishka, the Harry-Davis Philly, the Husq FCM 371-T, and the Cerif 460 – despite marketing claims, they all have near-identical performance.

TRAIL BIKE

EXPOSED, GROUND, RUGGED, SINGLE-SEAT, WHEELED

ATTRIBUTES		
Scale	Speed	Brawn
0	3	8

DETAILS	
Max. Passengers	Impact
1	1+4 N (Knockdown)
Hard Points	
Chassis 1, Comms 1, External 1, Motive 1	

DEFENCES			
Structure	8	Firewall	4
Armour	1	BTS	0

SPECIAL ABILITIES:

- **Reinforced Suspension**: As a Reaction when falling, the rider can make a Pilot (D1) or Acrobatics (D2) test to halve any damage from a fall.

Traktor Mul: About the size of a small car, these crude remotes are driven with a dedicated control device, but can do basic wayfinding on their own.

Often used for materiel transport or as a mobile artillery platform, their narrow profile, fuel-efficient engines, and maneuverable tank treads are well-adapted for rapid movement through *Dawn's* dense forests and steep mountains.

Since they are specifically designed for it, actions taken using remote control only suffer +2 complication range if the user is at Extreme range from the traktor. However, their lack of a true LAI means that unless remotely controlled, they can only move – or attack if equipped with a weapon and cannot take more complicated actions.

TROOPER

TRAKTOR MUL

ATTRIBUTES

AGI	AWA	BRW	COO	INT	PER	WIL
8	9	12 (+2)	10	7	5	5

FIELDS OF EXPERTISE

Combat	+1	–	Movement	+2	+2	Social	–	–
Fortitude	–	–	Senses	+1	–	Technical	–	–

DEFENCES

Firewall	4	Resolve	4	Structure	8
Security	1	Morale	–	Armour	2

GEAR: Binoculars, Recorder

SPECIAL ABILITIES

- **Common Special Abilities**: Inured to Disease, Poison, and Vacuum; Superhuman Brawn 2
- **Stable**: A low center of gravity and dynamic tread system grants the mul a bonus d20 to Athletics Reactions or tests to avoid being knocked prone.
- **Dual Socket Mounts**: Attaching a single Mounted weapon to the mul replaces one of its manipulator arms and unbalances it, adding +1 difficulty to Agility tests. If two are added, it balances, but the mul is unable to take actions that require arms or hands.

Uragan Multiple Rocket Launcher: The Uragan (Ураган, or "Hurricane" in Russian) is an inexpensive multi-launcher artillery weapon designed for counter-battery tactics and anti-tank direct fire. Archaic, unhackable, reliable, and usually mounted in pairs on traktor muls or other unarmoured mobile platforms, each MRL cluster comes with an integrated self-loading system for sustained barrages. They can also be used in combination with advanced hopak and katyusha guided rockets, but lose Non-Hackable when they do so. (Range M, 1+5 N damage, Burst 3, Mounted, Non-Hackable, Unsubtle 2)

- *Airburst Mode*: Area (Close), Grievous, Piercing 2, Speculative Fire
- *Direct Fire Mode*: Grievous, Piercing 2, Vicious 2
- *Hopak Guided Mode*: Area (Close), Grievous, Guided, Piercing 2
- *Katyusha Guided Mode*: Area (Close), Guided, Spread 2, Terrifying 2, Unsubtle 2, Vicious 2

USARF Fighting Uniform [Environment]: The USARF fighting uniform uses photoreactive e-inks alongside extracts from the local maycust plant for terrain-customised camouflage patterns, adding concealment to USAriadnan light combat armour. Common patterns include Winter Sun for snowy conditions, Sandstorm for southern desert environments, and Forestland for the dense forests of the Ariadna Exclusion Zone.

Though incompatible with other kinds of camo, they are quite effective in their target environment, counting as a kit for face-to-face Stealth tests made against targets at Medium range or farther and granting a bonus Momentum to successful

Buying In Bulk – see *Infinity Corebook*, p. 330

MRCY & CO.

MRCY & Company is a clothing manufacturer founded by 1st Ranger Division veterans Moses Renen and Camilla Youphes to make the tough long-wearing apparel they missed from Earth – jeans, boots, work pants – and that Dawn's frontier demanded. While many companies have attempted to supplant them in the decades since, their goods remain icons of USAriadnan culture and staples of frontier fashion, particularly among hardcases.

The founders' history also led to less-publicised work: military contracts. Several veterans they served with became influential researchers in DARPS, resulting in a steady sideline in bespoke apparel for special forces and intelligence agents. While the USARF fighting uniform is their first public military contract, make no mistake: they've been putting the "industrial" in military-industrial complex for over a century.

face-to-face Stealth tests. A DARPS innovation now mass-produced by MRCY & Co. and popular with off-world mercenaries, they are available in bulk to galactic buyers – difficulty penalties due to buying them in bulk are reduced by –1 difficulty.

USAriadnan Entrenching Tool – see *Infinity Corebook*, p. 385

USAriadnan Entrenching Tool, Custom X: Some colonists and wanderers aren't satisfied with stamped steel and plain wood. No, they need a little more in their E-tool, and expert crafters throughout USAriadna are happy to oblige. By replacing the handle with exotic hardwoods from deep within the Antipode Wilds or even modern smart materials, replacing the folding spade with one made of carbon steel or even Teseum, and adding sharpened, spiked, or serrated edges, they transform a simple military tool into a functional work of art.

Custom entrenching tools can be purchased with a rating of 1–3, addsing Armoured X and Piercing X, reducing the penalty to use it as an improvised weapon by – X complication range (ordinarily +3), and allowing the user to ignore the first X complications generated while using the tool for X Heat each.

Yaga: Yaga is an entheogen and depressant made from a rare fungus found in the Antipode Wilds, and favoured by Antipodes for concluding Blood Tree rituals. It induces mild synesthetic hallucinations and relaxing sensations for 1d20 hours, and then an immediate deep sleep for an equal amount of time. (Ingested, Instant 3, Day)

- *Special Effect*: Each hour the user is under yaga's effects, they heal 2 Resolve. Every ten hours, they also heal a Metanoia.
  - *Addiction*: 1 (12 doses), Compulsion 1
  - *Withdrawal*: 1, 3+3 N damage, Harm Effect (must make a Willpower (D2) test to sleep)

BUFFALO POWERED ARMOUR

Worn by 10th Heavy Rangers Battalion Blackjacks, Buffalo powered armour is the result of the USAriadnan DARPS' most ambitious and successful project to date. Fielded the instant they passed testing, they are a crucial Dawn-built response to galactic powered armour and TAGs, and in combination with the 10th's skill and toughness, rapidly earned a fearsome reputation during the Commercial Conflicts. The archaic technical solutions, basic radios, and crude servo-designs involved allow incredible endurance in the field, and are a source of fascination, even awe, for galactic analysts and paleoengineers. The armour currently comes with standard built-in weapons, as well as one of two heavy weapon loadouts: swapping out one loadout for the other takes a day and a Tech (D2) test.

STANDARD WEAPONRY:

- **Chest Mine (×2)**: Range R/C, 2+5 damage, Disposable, Grievous, Area (Close), Piercing 1, Vicious 1, Unsubtle
- **Heavy Pistol**: Range R/C, 2+4 damage, Unforgiving 1, Unsubtle
- **Teseum Chopper**: Melee, Piercing 4, Vicious 2

LOADOUT ALPHA:

- **AP HMG**: Range L, 2+6 damage, Burst 3, Piercing 2, Spread 1, Unsubtle
- **D.E.P**: Range L, 2+5 damage, Burst 1, Munition, Piercing 2, Spread 1, Unsubtle, Vicious 2

LOADOUT BRAVO:

- **SMG Pod**: Range C, 1+5 damage, Burst 2, Spread 1, contains 4 Reloads
- **T2 Sniper Rifle**: Range L, 1+6 damage, Burst 3, Unwieldy, Anti-Materiel 2, Piercing 2, Unforgiving 2, Vicious 2

SPECIAL ABILITIES:

- **Ambulatory Tank**: The armour has Armour Soak as listed, Structure score of 8, can take up to four Faults before being disabled, and absorbs damage in place of the wearer until disabled – the wearer takes any excess damage not absorbed by the armour when that occurs.
- **Heavyweight**: Buffalo powered armour's bulky lo-tech components and servos make the armour almost as large as a Gecko TAG, and add +2 difficulty to Agility-based skill tests. Additionally, moving to a point within Medium range is a Standard rather than Minor Action.
- **Lo-Tech Revenant**: With a Tech (D1) test as a Standard Action by the wearer, or if disabled by taking four Faults, the suit's archaic redundancies cannibalise components to keep it functioning long after modern equipment would collapse. This can only be done once, reduces its Armour Soak by 1 for all hit locations, reduces its Structure by 4, its Faults by two, its BTS to 0, and adds +1 complication range to all subsequent tests in the armour, but heals all of the suit's Structure damage and Faults.

"THE WINNING HAND"

Named for the ace of spades they leave on the corpses of their enemies, or the tactical black colour of Buffalo armour test models, or the original Earth military unit, or perhaps after their commander Lieutenant Colonel Michael Cortado's fondness for gambling, the Blackjacks of the 10th Heavy Rangers Battalion were carefully selected for a combination of toughness, technical ability, piloting skill, physical fitness, and capacity for brutality – they take no prisoners. Whatever their name's origins, their results against radically higher-tech foes during the Commercial Conflicts quickly silenced critics of the Blackjack program's expenses, and they are a key element of the USARF's and Ariadnan Joint Command's defence strategy.

AMMUNITION TABLE

NAME	CATEGORY	QUALITIES ADDED TO WEAPON	RESTRICTION	RELOAD COST	TARIFF
Adhesive Shells	Shell	Area (Close), Immobilising, Improvised 1, Nonlethal, Unsubtle	1	3+2	T2[1]
Apex	Heavy	Piercing 2, Salvo 2 (Anti-Materiel 2), Unsubtle 2, Vicious 2	3 (Rodina 1)	4+3	T2[2]
Eagle	Special*	Piercing 3, Unsubtle	3 (USAriadna 1)	4+1	T2[2]
Silver Bullets	Special*	Biotech / Biotech, Grievous, Knockdown, Toxic 3 against Antipodes, Dogfaces, Wulvers	3 (Merovingia 1, Ariadna 2)	3+3	T2[1]
T2 Slugs	Shell	Anti-Materiel 2, Piercing 3, Vicious 2	4 (Ariadna 3)	4+4	T3[2]

ARMOUR TABLE

ARMOUR	ARMOUR SOAK HEAD	TORSO	ARM	LEG	BTS	QUALITIES	RESTRICTION	COST	TARIFF	MAINTENANCE
Buffalo Powered Armour	4/3	5/4	3/2	3/2	3/0	Exoskeleton 3, Heavy Armour, Non-Hackable, Self-Repairing[1]	5	12+23	T3[1]	1
Cherkesska	2	4	3	3	1	Bandolier, Teseum Knife, Non-hackable, hard to alter	3 (Rodina 2)	13+3	T3[1]	1
Dog-Bowl Armour	2	2	1	1	0	Non-Hackable	2 (Ariadna 1)	8+3	T2	1
Dueling Bracers	0	0	2	0	0	enhances Unarmed Strikes, Non-hackable	3 (Caledonia 2)	8+2 (per pair)	T4[1]	–
Métros Armour	0	2	1	1	0	Hidden Armour 1	2 (Merovingia 1)	7+1	T2[1]	–
Mormaer Armour	3	4	3	3	1	+2 Morale (Caledonia), Non-hackable	4 (Caledonia 3)	14+4	T4[1]	1
USARF Fighting Uniform	1	2	1	1	0	enhances Stealth, Non-hackable	2 (USAriadna 1)	7+2	T2	–

Banned by the Concilium Convention.
* Ammunition has special effect or requirements. See description.

[1] No Tariff in Merovingian territory, or from Merovingian traders.
[2] No Tariff in Ariadna.

MELEE WEAPONS TABLE

NAME	DAMAGE	SIZE	QUALITIES	RESTRICTION	COST	TARIFF
Cobra Baton	1+4N	1H	Knockdown, Stun, Subtle 2, Vicious 1	2	5+2N	T2
Dueling Bracers	Special	n/a	Adds 1+1N, Parry 1, and Vicious 1 to unarmed damage	3 (Caledonia 2)	8+2N (per pair)	T4[1]
Sgian Dubh	1+3N	1H	Concealed 2, Non-Hackable, Subtle 2, Unforgiving 1	2 (Caledonia 1)	3+1N	–
Teseum Claws	1+3N	1H	Piercing 2, Subtle 1, Vicious 2	Antipodes only	–	–
Teseum Claymore	2+5N	2H	Grievous, Non-Hackable, Parry 2, Piercing 2, Vicious 2	4 (Caledonia 2, Ariadna 3)	10+2N	T4[1]
Teseum Hatchet	1+3N	1H	Grievous, Non-Hackable, Piercing 2, Subtle 1, Thrown, Vicious 1	3 (Caledonia 1, Ariadna 2)	4+2N	T4[1]
Teseum Knife	1+4N	1H	Concealed 1, Non-Hackable, Piercing 2, Subtle 2, Thrown, Unforgiving 2	2 (Ariadna 1)	5+2N	–

EXPLOSIVES TABLE

EXPLOSIVE	CATEGORY	DAMAGE[1]	SIZE	QUALITIES	RESTRICTION	COST (PER 3)	TARIFF
E/Mauler, Hackable	Mine	2+5N	1H	Breaker, Comms, Disposable, E/M, Indiscriminate (Close), Piercing 2, Unsubtle	2 (Ariadna 1)	5+2N	T2[1]
E/Mauler, Non-Hackable	Mine	2+5N	1H	Breaker, Disposable, E/M, Indiscriminate (Close), Piercing 2, Non-Hackable, Unsubtle	3 (Ariadna 1)	5+3N	T4[1]

RANGED WEAPONS TABLE

NAME	RANGE	DAMAGE	BURST	SIZE	AMMO	QUALITIES	RESTRICTION	COST	TARIFF
Americolt Eagle	R/C	2+5N	1	Unb*	Normal, Eagle	Knockdown, Non-Hackable, Piercing 1, Vicious 1	1 (USAriadna 0)	5+3N	T2
Ariadnan HMG	L	2+6N	3	Unw	T2	Spread 1, Unsubtle	3 (Ariadna 2)	9+4N	T1
Chest Mine	R/C[1]	2+5N	1	Mounted	–	Disposable, Grievous, Area (Close), Piercing 1, Vicious 1, Unsubtle	3 (Ariadna 2, USAriadna 1)	6+3N per 3	T1
D.E.P.	L	2+5N	1	2H	Needle	Munition*, Unsubtle	2 (Ariadna 1, Nomads 1)	5+1N	T2
Heavy Shotgun	C	2+6N	1	2H*/ Mounted	Normal Shells / AP Slugs	Knockdown	3	9+1N	T1
MK12 Rifle	M	2+5N	3	2H	H-12	Salvo (Knockdown)	3	7+3N	T2
H-12 Pisotl	C/M	2+5N	1	2H	H-12	Salvo (Knockdown)	4	6+3N	T2
Molotok	M	1+5N	3	2H	AP	Spread 2, Unsubtle	2	7+2N	T1
Ojotnik	M	1+6N	2	Unw	AP	Unforgiving 3	5 (Rodina 2, Ariadna 4)	10+3N	T3
Portable Autocannon	L	1+6N	2	Unw	Apex	Non-Hackable	3 (Rodina 2)	9+4N	T2
T2 Boarding Shotgun	C	1+5N	1	2H	Normal Shells/ T2 Slugs	Knockdown, Medium MULTI	3 (Ariadna 2)	8+1N	T1
Uragan MRL	M	1+5N	3	Mounted	Normal, Hopak, Katyusha	Non-Hackable, Unsubtle 2	3 (Rodina 2)	9+3N	T3

REMOTES TABLE

REMOTE	RESTRICTION	COST	TARIFF	MAINTENANCE
Traktor Mul	3 (Ariadna 2)	8+3N	T2[1]	1

* See weapon entry.
[1] No Tariff in Ariadna.

VEHICLE COSTS TABLE

NAME	SCALE	SPEED	STRENGTH	ARMOUR	BTS	IMPACT	RESTRICTION	COST	TARIFF
Ariadnan Utility Vehicle	2	2	14 (+2)	4	0	3+7Ⓝ	1	10+1Ⓝ	T2
Arroaz Skimmer	2	4	14 (+3)	3	1	4+5Ⓝ	3 (Merovingia 2)	12+4Ⓝ	T2[1]
Backwoods ATV	1	2	10 (+1)	2	0	2+5Ⓝ	2	11+3Ⓝ	T1[1]
Official Vehicle	1	3	13 (+1)	4	4	2+6Ⓝ	5 (Rodina 3)	2+3Ⓝ	T6
Ore Hauler	3	3	16 (+3)	4	1	5+7Ⓝ	2	14+4Ⓝ	T1[1]
Trail Bike	0	3	8	1	0	1+4Ⓝ	1	7+2Ⓝ	–

TOOLS TABLE

TOOL	QUALITIES	RESTRICTION	COST	TARIFF	MAINTENANCE
Bandolier	Non-Hackable	–	4+1Ⓝ	-	-
Binoculars	Non-Hackable	–	3+1Ⓝ	-	-
Digicloak (Environment)	Non-Hackable, Fragile	3	6+3Ⓝ	T3	-
Dog-Bowl Jersey X	Non-Hackable, Armoured 2	X	3X + XⓃ	T(X)	-
Fusebox	Comms	1	4+1Ⓝ	-	1
Long Jehans	See entry, Hidden Armour 1	1	4+2Ⓝ	-	-
Pet X (tiny/small/large)	Non-Hackable	X	2X +XⓃ	-	X-1 (Minimum 0) / X / X+1
Photoreactive Coating	NFB	1	5+4Ⓝ	-	-
Portable Rescue Supply Kit	–	2	5+5Ⓝ	-	-
Rebreather	–	1	5+2Ⓝ	-	-
Rucksack X	Comms, Locational Beacon at rating 2 or 3	1	6 + XⓃ	T(X)	-
Samovar	Non-Hackable	0	4+1Ⓝ	-	0
Traktor Mul Control Device	Comms	1	4+2Ⓝ	1	-
Tactical Webbing	Non-Hackable	1	5+1Ⓝ	T1	-
Tracking Collar	Comms	1	4+1Ⓝ	-	-
USAriadnan Entrenching Tool, Custom X	Armoured X, Piercing X, –X complication range, ignore first X complications when using it for X heat each	X-1, X for non-USAriadnans	(2+X) + (2+X)Ⓝ	T(X-1)	-

[1] No Tariff in Ariadna.

DRUGS TABLE

DRUG	RESTRICTION	COST	TARIFF
Baba	2	4+4Ⓝ	T1
Baba/Yaga	3 (Antipode Wilds 1)	9+3Ⓝ	T1
Cod	1	4+4Ⓝ per month	T1
Yaga	2	5+5Ⓝ	T2

CHAPTER 5

ARIADNAN CHARACTERS

Coming of age on *Dawn* is many things, but rarely is it easy or uneventful. In a world where technological advancements have made wonders like Cubes commonplace, in Ariadna, such devices are incredibly rare. Even urban centres like Mat' or Mariannebourg would be considered rustic by most denizens of the Human Sphere and life in more remote regions would seem unconscionably harsh.

Even so, Ariadnans don't think of themselves as disadvantaged *per se*; they hold the opinion that the rest of the Human Sphere wouldn't last a day on their world. A harsh crucible to be sure, but the tough-as-nails, self-reliant Ariadnans wouldn't have it any other way. For their part, Ariadnans simply do what they have for generations: endure.

Ariadnan characters can be created using the variant rules in this chapter, rather than those in the *Infinity Corebook*. If doing so, the entries presented here supersede their counterparts in the corebook.

PLAYTEST NOTE

EXPANDED TABLES

With some of the tables (such as Rodinan/Tartarian) their names don't quite line up with their counterparts in the corebook. Just remember: it's an expansion. The first word is the one you need to line up.

DECISION ONE: BIRTH HOST

Determining Alien Heritage: Roll 1d20. On a roll of 19 or 20, your character belongs to an alien species. (This means that you're Dog-Blooded; see p. 78.) If you roll an alien heritage, you can instead choose to spend 1 Life Point to be human.

CUBELESS

Unless specifically stated otherwise, Ariadnan characters do not begin play with Cubes.

Alien Host: Each alien species or non-human type has a template. Apply the species' attribute modifiers to both your attributes and the host section of your character sheet. Make note of any special abilities possessed by the species.

Alien species also have a Life Point cost. You can choose to pay this cost in order to simply choose the species, but the cost must be paid even if you randomly roll into it. (If the cost cannot be paid, the character is considered human.)

DECISION THREE: EXPANDED HOMELANDS

While off-worlders may think of Ariadnans as a homogenous group, to the Ariadnan nations, there exist countless differences. After determining your region by rolling on the *Ariadna Homeland Table* (p. 43, *Infinity Corebook*), add your attributes and skill as normally, then roll on the associated *Homeland Table* to determine your precise region, and what language(s) you speak.

DECISION SEVEN: ADOLESCENT EVENT

Compared to other factions, Ariadnans have several disadvantages, but their hostile environment toughens them up, and while they have lower earnings and less gear, their event tables are more likely to provide a favourable outcome.

Characters in the Ariadna faction roll on the *Ariadna Faction Adolescent Event Table*. If the character's heritage and faction are different, then they may choose to roll on either faction's unique table on a roll of 1–3.

CALEDONIAN HOMELAND TABLE

D20	REGION	LANGUAGE
1–4	Cailleach	Russian (Kazak) or Antipode Creole (Snarl) (choose one) and English (Scots)
5–6	Calonack	English (Scots) [1]
7–8	Coille Laith	English (Scots) [1]
9–10	Dál Riada	English (Scots) [1]
11–12	Inverloch	English (Scots) [1]
13–16	Scone	Russian (Kazak) or French (choose one) and English (Scots) [1]
17–18	Skara Brae	Russian (Kazak) and English (Scots)
19–20	Tuathcruithne	Antipode Creole (Snarl) and English (Scots)

MEROVINGIAN HOMELAND TABLE

D20	REGION	LANGUAGE
1-4	Auron	English (American) or Russian (Kazak) (choose one) and French [1]
5-8	Le Douar	English (American) or Russian (Kazak) (choose one) and French [1]
9-13	Mariannebourg	French [1]
14-16	Poictesme	English (Scots) and French
17-18	Lafayette	English and French
19-20	Dauphin	French1

RODINAN/TARTARIAN HOMELAND TABLE

D20	REGION	LANGUAGE
1-2	Dynamo	Russian (Kazak) [1]
3-4	Gök-Burgo	Russian (Kazak) [1]
5-7	Mat'	English or French (choose one) and Russian (Kazak)
8-9	Novocherkassk	Russian (Kazak) [1]
10-12	*Stanitsas*	Russian (Kazak)
13-14	Castropol (Tartary)	Russian (Kazak) [1]
15-16	Dalnîy (Tartary)	Russian (Kazak) [1]
17-18	Ovsyanka (Tartary)	English, French, or Yujingyu (choose one) and Russian (Kazak)
19-20	Tsitadel (Tartary)	Russian (Kazak) [1]

USARIADNAN HOMELAND TABLE

D20	REGION	LANGUAGE
1-2	MountZion-The Wall	English (American) [1]
3-5	Jackson	English (American)
6-8	Jefferson	Russian (Kazak) and English (American)
9-11	Lincoln	French and English (American)
12-14	Kennedy	English (American) [1]
15-17	Roosevelt	English (American) [1]
18-20	Washington	English (American) [1]

ANTIPODEAN WILDS/OUTLANDS/ HOMELAND TABLE

D20	REGION	LANGUAGE
1-7	Ariadna Exclusion Zone	English, French, or Russian (choose one) [1]
8-14	The South Mirror	English, French, or Russian (choose one) [1]
15-19	Tartary Outlands	Russian (Kazak) [1]
20	Antipodean Wilds2	English, Russian, or French (choose one)

[1] Roll again on the *Ariadna Homeland Table* to determine another language you're fluent with. If you roll a result you already know, you learn no new languages.

[2] You grew up in – or at least near – Antipodean tribal lands. Roll on the *Antipodean Tribe Table* (p. 81) to determine whose lands you lived near. Gain the entry's language in addition to the one you chose here.

DECISION EIGHT: CAREERS

Dawn is a harsh mistress, but in her crucible, Ariadnans find great strength. Compared to other Lifepaths, Ariadnan careers offer lower earnings and less gear; but there's a flip side. As with Decision Seven, beneficial options are more frequent than in other factions' Lifepaths.

Ariadnan characters roll on the *Basic Career Table* as normally, can spend 1 Life Point to pick a career from the *Basic Career Table*, or spend 1 Life Point to roll on the *Ariadna Faction Career Table*. Additionally, characters in the Ariadna faction roll on the *Ariadna Faction Career Event Table*. If the character's heritage and faction are different, then they may choose to roll on either faction's unique table on a roll of 1–3.

ARIADNA FACTION ADOLESCENT EVENT TABLE

D6	CAREER
1–3	Ariadna Adolescent Event Table
4	Adolescent Event Table A[1]
5	Adolescent Event Table B[1]
6	Adolescent Event Table C[1]

[1] *Infinity Corebook*, p. 49–52

ARIADNA FACTION CAREER EVENT TABLE

D6	CAREER
1–3	Ariadna Career Event Table
4	Adolescent Event Table A1
5	Adolescent Event Table B1
6	Adolescent Event Table C1

[1] *Infinity Corebook*, p. 56–58

ARIADNA FACTION CAREER TABLE

D20	CAREER
1	Special Forces[1]
2	Intelligence Operative[1]
3	Frontiersman
4	Assault Pack Controller[1,2]
5	Sports Personality[1]
6	Paratrooper[1]
7	112 Emergency Responder[2]
8	Bratva Gangster[2]
9	Caledonian Noble[3]
10	Claymore Duellist[2]
11	Free Miner
12	Frontier Doctor
13	Hardcase[2]
14	Irmandinhos Smuggler[2]
15	Loup-Garou[2]
16	Merovingian Commercial Agent[3]
17	Militia Member
18	Spetsnaz[3]
19–20	Roll on *Faction Table* of your choice

[1] Career from *Infinity Corebook*.

[2] Career has a prerequisite of belonging to this faction. You can't hazard this career unless you're of the matching faction. If you roll into this career, you automatically fail your defection check. You can override these limitations by spending 1 Life Point (in which case you were somehow undercover while working the career).

[3] Career has a prerequisite of Ariadnan heritage, and the appropriate homeland; without those two factors, you can't hazard this career. If you roll into this career, you automatically fail your defection check. You can override these limitations by spending 1 Life Point (in which case you were somehow undercover while working the career).

ARIADNA ADOLESCENT EVENT TABLE

D20	ADOLESCENT EVENT	SUGGESTED CHARACTER TRAIT	OPTIONAL EFFECT
1	A surprise Antipode attack nearly claimed your life – until you picked up a weapon and fought back.	Survivor	Gain 1 rank in either Ballistics or Close Combat.
2	You were stranded on the frontier for a solid month with no aid. By the time they found you, you'd already identified which mushrooms were poisonous – the hard way.	Grizzled	Gain 1 rank in Survival, but suffer +1 complication range on Resistance tests to resist poison.
3	A dying soldier entrusted you with their unfinished business.	Weight of the World	Gain 1 rank in Discipline.
4	When the dust settled, you were the only one left alive. How? And why?	Sole Survivor	Gain 1 rank in Survival, but reduce Earnings by 1 (minimum 0).
5	You suffered a terrible childhood accident.	Disabled	All movement-related skill tests suffer +1 difficulty, but you have gained a strong will; reduce the difficulty of all Discipline tests by 1 (to a minimum of 1).
6	You got involved in underground fight clubs at an early age.	Street Fighter	Gain 1 rank in Close Combat, but gain a 1 Asset debt representing medical bills.
7	You were stranded in the wilderness for an extended time.	Raised in a Barn	Gain 1 rank in either Animal Handling or Survival, but add +1 to the complication range on Personality-based tests.
8	Facing the consequences of crimes you most assuredly did commit, someone offered to make it all go away. Did you let them? If so, what was the cost?	It Takes One to Know One	Either spend 1d6 years in jail before starting your first career, and gain a Criminal Record (see p. 54, *Infinity Corebook*) – or gain a debt of 1+5 N Assets, and 1 rank of Thievery.
9	You found success as part of a Hiraeth culture musical act. You handled the instant celebrity as well as can be expected – that is to say, poorly. You're often recognised in the street; not just in Ariadna, but across the Human Sphere.	Rockstar	Choose a drug from the *Infinity Corebook* (p. 348) – you begin play at that drug's addiction threshold, and with 1+3 N doses in your possession. Additionally, reduce the difficulty of all Lifestyle tests by 1 (to a minimum of 0).
10	Trapped in a dire situation, you didn't see a way out – until the 112 rescued you. You've been enamoured with them ever since.	Spirit of the 112	Gain +1 rank in Medicine, and you may choose 112 Emergency Responder as your first career.
11	You spent some time in the Helios orbitals – it didn't suit you at all.	Astrophobia	Increase the complication range of Extraplanetary tests by 1.
12	An accident left you needing cybernetic replacements; but the local clinic had to make do with what was on hand. Your Augmentation has some quirks, but you've learned how to squeeze the most out of it.	Cybered-Up	You have a cybernetic arm or leg (*Infinity Corebook*, p. 346: Basic Limb Replacement). Increase the Maintenance cost by +1, but add 1 bonus Momentum on successful tests made with the limb.
13	True or not, your family is believed to have betrayed Ariadna during the Commercial Conflicts. Now that you've come of age, that stigma is yours to bear.	Infamous Lineage	Social skill tests with fellow Ariadnans suffer a +2 complication range.
14	By yourself, or as part of Dog Nation, Caledonian Independence, or something more sinister – you raged against the system.	Rebel	Gain +1 Morale Soak against authority figures.
15	You were entrusted with a weapon that's had real use. It's seen better days, but you know you can rely on it.	Heirloom Weapon	When using this weapon, you may roll an additional 1 N, but you suffer +1 complication range.
16	You got burned once. You vowed not to let it happen twice.	Sardonic	Gain +1 rank in Discipline, but suffer +3 complication range on all social skill tests related to positive or pleasant interactions.
17	You were fortunate enough to get a real, Ariadnan weapon at an early age; nothing else feels quite right in your hands.	Brand Loyalist	Acquire one of the following: Americolt Eagle, Ojotnik, or Teseum hatchet. Suffer +1 complication range when using other weapons.
18	An early event left you with a taste for adventure.	Pioneer Spirit	Add +1 Resolve.
19	You were awoken in the middle of the night and told to pack your things. Two days later, your old home was a scorch mark, and you were on a new planet.	Paranoid	You defect to a new faction. Roll on the Faction Table (*Infinity Corebook*, p. 41) to determine your new allegiance. You may roll on your new faction's career table for your first career at no cost.
20	You should have died, but you didn't. Plenty of Ariadnans don't believe in luck. But maybe it believes in you.	Lucky	Gain +1 Infinity Point refresh (maximum 4).

ARIADNA CAREER EVENT TABLE

D20	CAREER EVENT	GAME EFFECT
1	Your work carries you to a different Ariadnan nation. Why did that go as well – or as poorly – as it did?	Choose a different homeland. Gain a character trait describing your new status.
2	Bureau Toth brings you in for questioning. What do they want to know? They let you go, but under what condition?	Gain Trait: On the Watchlist.
3	An Antipode attack demolishes your place of business, leaving it in shambles.	Gain Trait: Harried. In addition, you may not repeat or extend this career unless you lose 1 Earnings.
4	When everything went to hell, through sheer stubbornness, you somehow kept it together.	Gain Trait: Ariadnan Grit.
5	While out hiking, you stumble onto some interesting ruins.	Gain Trait: Amateur Archaeologist.
6	Your employer is incredibly enthusiastic for an off-world technological solution. How does it end in disaster? And why does it leave you suspicious of advanced technology?	Gain Trait: Luddite.
7	You are the "lucky winner" of a transfer to the front line.	Gain a character trait describing your unfortunate experience.
8	You save a tourist from a horrible fate.	Gain an ally in a random faction.
9	You find yourself caught in between a Dog Nation protest and police forces. Why do people think you put the protesters "in their place?" And what did you actually mean to do?	Gain Trait: Wolfsbane. In addition, your new reputation precedes you; gain an additional point of Momentum on Leadership tests.
10	You agree to let some Nomad "friends" install a Cube for you. This goes shockingly well.	Gain a Cube.
11	You agree to let some Nomad "friends" install a Cube for you Unsurprisingly, this ends poorly.	Gain a Cube, but your system's a little more vulnerable: all infowar attacks deal you an extra 1 [N] damage.
12	You grow close to a Dog-Bowl player. What's the nature of your relationship?	Gain a trait describing your new contact.
13	Somehow, you find yourself in a duel. What brought this on? And what did it cost to succeed?	Gain a character trait describing your scars, physical or otherwise, from the encounter.
14	Someone you were close to dies in an attack. Who was behind it? And what do you plan to do about it?	Roll on the *Faction Table* (*Infinity Corebook*, p. 41), and gain a trait describing your relationship with said faction. If you roll Ariadna, roll again on the *USAriadnan Homeland Table* (p. 65) to determine their homeland.
15	You foiled an act of galactic sabotage.	Gain Trait: Patriot. Additionally, gain +1 Earnings for your act of balance sheet-friendly heroism.
16	A disaster occurs; you grit your teeth and keep going.	Gain Trait: True Grit. Gain 1 Life Point.
17	You are scouted by an unlikely employer.	You may hazard your next career, even if you don't meet the faction or homeland prerequisite.
18	You are fired. What did you do, and why was it worth it?	You are fired (*Infinity Corebook*, p. 54). Gain an appropriate trait. If your character is unemployed or has the Scavenger career reroll this result.
19	You were killed, fighting for off-world employers. At least, that's the official story – only you know what really happened.	Your character died, and was resurrected (*Infinity Corebook*, p. 54). In addition, gain a trait describing the aftermath of the mysterious event. With the GM's permission you may defect to another faction
20	You've got the Devil's Own Luck. Interesting times ahead.	Roll again three times on the *Career Event Table* for this career phase. (When spending a Life Point to choose a specific event, you may not choose this result. If you roll duplicate events, it means some similar event has occurred. If you roll the Devil's Own Luck again, add additional rolls.)

CAREER PROFILE

112 EMERGENCY RESPONDER

It's said that in Ariadna, there are three callings that never rest; drinking, debauchery, and the 112 Emergency Services. While the first two are debatable, the third is not: the 112 are always on-duty, patrolling the borders and byways twenty-five hours a day, seven days a week. Stormy weather, natural disasters, Antipode attacks – whatever the conditions, whatever the danger, it doesn't matter – when distress signals go up, the 112 head out. In the remote reaches of Ariadna, they're not just first responders; they're often the only responders. As such, they train not just as field medics and firefighters, but as trackers, engineers, and soldiers. Sometimes, saving lives means splinting a broken bone, or repairing a busted generator. Sometimes it means cracking heads. But whatever the need, when the call goes out, the 112 answer.

ATTRIBUTES

AGI	AWA	BRW	COO	INT	PER	WIL
+1	+2	+1	+1	+2	+1	+2

SKILLS

Mandatory	Discipline	Medicine	Tech
Elective	Close Combat	Psychology	Survival

EARNINGS

1 + 2Ⓝ

GEAR: MediKit (with 5 Serum), Powered Multitool, Merovingian Survival Gear, Survivial Rations (×4), Teseum Hatchet

CAREER PROFILE

ASSAULT PACK CONTROLLER

Assault Pack Controllers guide mind-controlled Antipodes into battle. The fierce lupine natives of Ariadna possess heightened senses and ferocious strength. A Controller must lead these creatures, biochemically manipulated to be pliable and obedient, with equally fierce determination. Assault Pack Controllers use their bestial troops to break through enemy lines and shatter their resolve. Life as a Controller means harsh training and rigorous discipline to carry the strength and presence of an alpha. Controllers face danger every day that they lead their packs, from the savagery of the Antipodes themselves to the missions that require an Assault Pack. Because a Controller must be strong, ruthless, and driven, few forces are more feared on the battlefield than an Assault Pack. Many Controllers form close bonds with their Antipodes.

ATTRIBUTES

AGI	AWA	BRW	COO	INT	PER	WIL
+1	+2	–	+2	+2	+2	+1

SKILLS

Mandatory	Athletics	Animal Handling	Stealth
Elective	Close Combat	Survival	Ballistics

EARNINGS

2+1Ⓝ

GEAR: Antipode Control Device, Teseum Chopper, Pheromone Dispenser

SPECIAL: Prerequisite (Ariadna Faction)

CAREER PROFILE

CALEDONIAN NOBLE

The Caledonian clans boast a form of government unique in the Human Sphere, and their nobility form its proud, honour-bound heart. Caledonian nobles work among their people; they hear their concerns, champion their causes, and fight their battles. If the clan chief is governor, judge, and warlord, they're still one person. Rather than try to be everywhere at once, their additional nobles provide the legislative, judicial, and administrative apparatus. Usually originating from the chief's family and friends, capable Highlanders occasionally find themselves elevated to the position; and of course, anyone can challenge an existing noble for their title. Loathe to show any signs of weakness, nobles have learned to throw their weight around. Clad in heavy Tesum jewellery – torcs, rings, necklaces and the like – they eschew subtlety, preferring strong, decisive action to lengthy deliberation.

ATTRIBUTES

AGI	AWA	BRW	COO	INT	PER	WIL
+1	+1	+1	+1	+1	+3	+1

SKILLS

Mandatory	Command	Lifestyle	Persuade
Elective	Analysis	Animal Handling	Close Combat

EARNINGS

2 + 4Ⓝ

GEAR: Armoured Clothing (Kilt or Arisaid), Sgian Dubh (ceremonial Teseum chopper)

SPECIAL: Requires a homeland in Caledonia

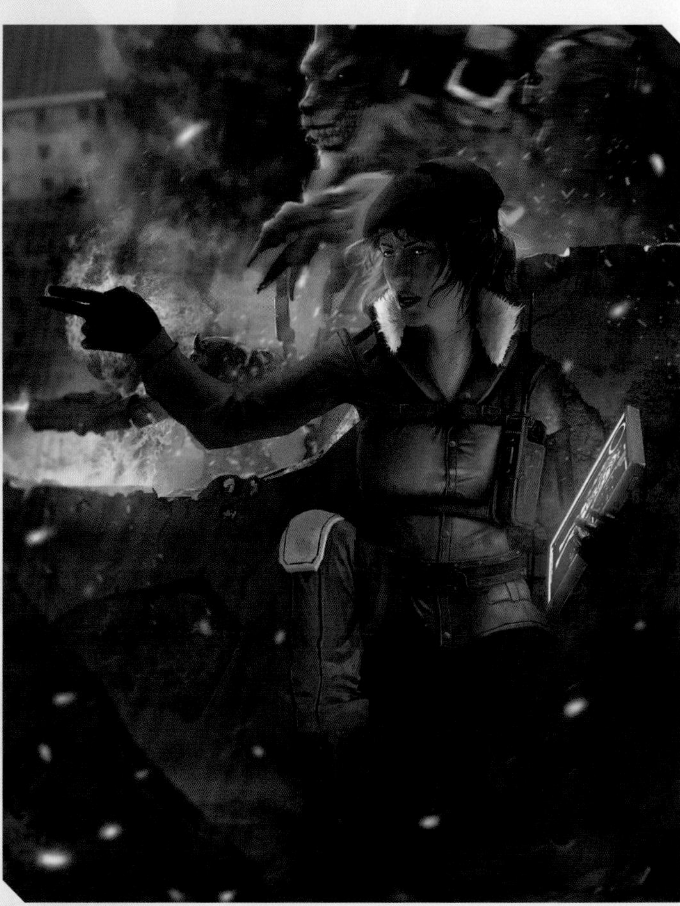

CAREER PROFILE

BRATVA GANGSTER

Every society has its criminals. Every underworld, its kingpins. In Rodina, that's the Bratva – and they know it. Even though their style evokes the trappings of Russian mafioso from Earth, the Bratva aren't an import; they're a fully homegrown enterprise. An empire built from scratch and tailored to the harsh realities of life on Dawn, the Bratva are possessed of a uniquely Rodinan form of pragmatism. Every mafia family employs fronts, but the Bratva treat these polite fictions as what they are: a necessary cost of doing business. This leads to their remarkably integrated, unapologetic place in Ariadnan society. From tattooed underlings in tracksuits to the semi-legitimate "shipping professionals" that make up their lieutenants, their grim practicality is a constant, subtle presence in major cities.

ATTRIBUTES						
AGI	AWA	BRW	COO	INT	PER	WIL
+1	+2	+2	+2	–	+1	+2

SKILLS			
Mandatory	Close Combat	Resistance	Thievery
Elective	Ballistics	persuade	Survival

EARNINGS
1 + 2Ⓝ

GEAR: Armoured Clothing, Fake ID 1, Heavy Pistol (with 2 Standard Reloads), Wurari (2 doses)

SPECIAL: Requires a homeland in Rodina or Tartary

CAREER PROFILE

CLAYMORE DUELLIST

In a society where duels are an acceptable means of resolving disputes, it pays to have a dedicated expert on your side. And while Caledonians respect anyone who can fight their own battles, there's also a great deal to be said for inspiring loyalty in capable warriors. Sometimes serving as bodyguards, but never far from their liege's side, a professional duellist hones their craft to a keen edge through an intense training regimen and a tireless thirst for competition. Of course, such capable warriors do more than just settle disputes; when the Highlands are in danger, duellists are often the first to leap to its defence, claymores held high.

ATTRIBUTES						
AGI	AWA	BRW	COO	INT	PER	WIL
+2	+1	+3	+1	–	–	+2

SKILLS			
Mandatory	Acrobatics	Close Combat	Discipline
Elective	Atheletics	Close Combat	Observation

EARNINGS
0 + 4Ⓝ

GEAR: Light Combat Armour, Teseum Claymore

CAREER PROFILE

FREE MINER

Teseum is the wealth of *Dawn*, but it doesn't grow on trees; it's hewed from stone through sheer grit, determination, and stubbornness. In the absence of sophisticated mining tools, early Ariadnans learned to make do with what was available, and that attitude persists among its miners today. While every nation employs dedicated teams, most Teseum mining is handled through independent contractors. These "free miners" are paragons of the Ariadnan spirit; heading off into dangerous territory, with only their wits and their grit, forcibly extracting their fortune out of some of the hardest, most unforgiving terrain anywhere in the Human Sphere. From the mountains of Caledonia to the hills of Tartary, their adventures aren't always profitable, but few lives are as self-reliant.

ATTRIBUTES						
AGI	AWA	BRW	COO	INT	PER	WIL
+1	+1	+2	+1	+1	–	+3

SKILLS			
Mandatory	Resistance	Survival	Tech
Elective	Atheltics	Pilot	Spacecraft

EARNINGS
0 + 6Ⓝ

GEAR: Bottled Water, D-Charges (×2), Custom 1 USAriadnan Entrenching Tool, XO Suit

CAREER PROFILE

FRONTIER DOCTOR

Far from the cushy accoutrements of a private practice, the security of a major hospital, or even the relative stability of a wartime medical facility, the life of a frontier doctor is chaotic, but satisfying, and rarely dull. Often the only person with medical training – or an advanced education of any sort – as far as the eye can see, a frontier doctor can treat snakebites one day, tend to sick cattle the next, and deliver a bouncing baby Dogface the day after that. Not for the faint of heart, or the weak of stomach, frontier doctors take pride in looking after their communities. After all, if they don't, it's unlikely anyone else will.

ATTRIBUTES						
AGI	AWA	BRW	COO	INT	PER	WIL
+1	+2	+2	+1	+2	–	+2

SKILLS			
Mandatory	Analysis	Animal Handling	Medicine
Elective	Education	Medicine	Survival

EARNINGS
2 + 1Ⓝ

GEAR: Ballistic Vest, Basic Medical Supplies, MediKit, USAriadnan Entrenching Tool

CAREER PROFILE

FRONTIERSMAN

The men and women of the frontier explore the little-known regions of human space. They are the first to expand the maps, eager to set foot on new ground and stake a claim in humanity's interstellar expansion. These rugged folk brave environmental dangers, unknown flora and fauna, and set up trading posts in seldom-travelled regions. A frontiersman is skilled at hunting, gathering supplies, and often in working with technology out away from urban centres, with little to no technical support. Frontiersmen prospect for resources, like the rare and valuable Teseum, or rare herbs and wildlife with properties useful to the medical industry. Some are criminals fleeing the reach of the law by living on the frontier, and others are bounty hunters sent to hunt down those who would otherwise escape justice.

ATTRIBUTES						
AGI	AWA	BRW	COO	INT	PER	WIL
+2	+2	+1	+1	+2	–	+2

SKILLS			
Mandatory	Survival	Animal Handling	Resistance
Elective	Discipline	Athletics	Thievery

EARNINGS
1+1Ⓝ

GEAR: Survival Rations (×6), Survival Kit, Axe or Powered Multitool

CAREER PROFILE

HARDCASE

USAriadna's southern border is sparsely populated, plenty dangerous, and unforgiving by any standard. A desolate place to be sure, but the refuge of choice for the rough souls collectively known as hardcases. A term with its roots in the American Old West, hardcases are a different breed – rough as rawhide, and tough as Teseum nails – but to the homesteaders of the southern border, they're heroes. Between the smugglers, bandits, and Antipode raids, life on the frontier is incredibly dangerous and when the nearest major city is hundreds of kilometres away, law is what you can make it. But whether they're veterans, adventurous frontier folk, or just someone looking to forget the past, when things are at their worst, hardcases step into the void as grievous angels in Stetson hats and leather dusters, dispensing frontier justice with hardly a word.

ATTRIBUTES						
AGI	AWA	BRW	COO	INT	PER	WIL
+1	+2	+2	+2	–	+1	+2

SKILLS			
Mandatory	Ballistics	Observation	Survival
Elective	Analysis	Animal Handling	Pilot

EARNINGS
1 + 2Ⓝ

GEAR: Americolt Eagle (with 1 Standard Reload and 1 Eagle reload), Bandolier, Binoculars, Long Modcoat (Leather Duster)

SPECIAL: Requires a homeland in USAriadna and most are from the south.

CAREER PROFILE

INTELLIGENCE OPERATIVE

The tense state of conflict in the Human Sphere means every agency looks for an edge over its competitors. Intelligence Operatives conduct corporate espionage, deep-cover spy missions, acts of sabotage, and other acts which risk their life and limb for agencies that would disavow any knowledge of, or connection to, their operations. An Intelligence Operative is quick-witted, highly disciplined, and often alone in a place surrounded by enemies unaware of the traitor in their midst. They trade in secrets – information that can turn the tide of small-scale conflicts, like raids on secret warehouses holding valuable experimental gear or data – and they can influence the large-scale skirmishes that take place between rival nations. The intelligence an operative collects can cause wars or end them with equal facility.

ATTRIBUTES						
AGI	AWA	BRW	COO	INT	PER	WIL
+1	+3	–	+2	+2	+1	+1

SKILLS			
Mandatory	Observation	Stealth	Analysis
Elective	Hacking	Education	Thievery

EARNINGS
3+1Ⓝ

GEAR: Fake ID 2, AP Pistol (with 4 Reloads), Breaking & Entering Kit, Recorder

CAREER PROFILE

IRMANDINHOS SMUGGLERS

Castropol has long been home to all manner of interesting, often underhand, dealings. Founded by a group of Galician biologists from the Ariadna, early settlers used their oceanographic research vessels to requisition and transport items for Ariadna's nascent black market. Today, members of the Brotherhood of Waterborne Surveillance Volunteers – the Irmandinhos – act as a shock force, run supplies to remote locations, and continue smuggling. New recruits learn to scavenging, repair, and engage in short-range combat tactics alongside Irmandade veterans. With Galician essentially a dead language outside their own, they can ensure secrecy that can't be hacked. They're a mainstay of the Ariadnan army and remain in contact with intelligence services from across the Human Sphere, though it's unknown to what end.

ATTRIBUTES

AGI	AWA	BRW	COO	INT	PER	WIL
+2	+1	+2	+1	+2	+1	+1

SKILLS

Mandatory	Close Combat	Pilot	Tech
Elective	Observation	Stealth	Thievery

EARNINGS: 1 + 4N

GEAR: Binoculars, Chain Rifle (with 4 Standard Reloads), Knife, Light Shotgun (with 1 T2 Reload), or Americolt Eagle (choose one), Smoke Grenades (×2)

SPECIAL: Gain language: Galician.

CAREER PROFILE

LOUP-GAROUS

Regardless of position on the civil rights issues, a rampaging mass of tooth, claw, and muscle in the throes of a blood-thirsty fury is a danger to everyone, including themselves. Rather than trust Dog-Blooded to police themselves, the Federation created the Loup-Garous. A joint task force, the Loup-Garous receive the best training and equipment to provide every possible advantage in containing Dogface, Wulver, and Antipode threats. In the aftermath of riots that culminated in the brutal apprehension and killing of a (later exonerated) Dogface, the organisation is hastily reforming to shed its shady past. Able to rapidly assess threats, and versed in multiple de-escalation methods, modern Loup-Garous units eschew violent solutions whenever possible. When that isn't an option, however, they strike with blinding precision, disabling their targets before matters get out of hand.

ATTRIBUTES

AGI	AWA	BRW	COO	INT	PER	WIL
+1	+2	+1	+3	–	+1	+1

SKILLS

Mandatory	Analysis	Close Combat	Athletics
Elective	Ballistics	Observation	Psychology

EARNINGS: 1 + 4N

GEAR: Boarding Shotgun (with 3 Adhesive Shell Reloads, and 1 Silver Bullet Reload), Medium Combat Armour, Tactical Webbing

CAREER PROFILE

MILITIA MEMBER

It's sometimes said that every Ariadnan is a soldier. And while that's not technically true, it's easy to see how it looks that way, given the prevalence of militias – both volunteer and drafted – dotting the landscape. Much of Rodina mandates a term of service for citizens – equal parts education, training, and patrol – while USAriadna takes pride in its multiple volunteer armies; and in Caledonia, it's less an official designation, and more something one does when needed. However they come to be, militias are diverse by nature, as well as necessity: on any given day, they may be called upon to provide scouting, fire support, field medicine, or just drive a truck. And while they might (and often do) complain, most Ariadna Militia veterans are intensely proud of their service. They know that freedom isn't free; they enjoy making their enemies foot the bill.

ATTRIBUTES

AGI	AWA	BRW	COO	INT	PER	WIL
+2	+2	+1	+2	–	+1	+2

SKILLS

Mandatory	Ballistics	Close Combat	Observation
Elective	Medicine	Piloting	Stealth

EARNINGS: 0 + 2N

GEAR: Armoured Clothing, Painkillers (×1), Rifle, Custom 1 USAriadnan Entrenching Tool

CAREER PROFILE

MEROVINGIAN COMMERCIAL AGENT

Take one part explorer, two parts merchant, and mix in roving traders, spies, and con artists to taste. Add a dash of exploration, and season with an adventurous spirit, and you've got the recipe for a Merovingian Commercial Agent. If the cities are Merovingia's heart, and the trade caravans her arteries, Commercial Agents are her blood, and her sweat and tears as well. Trained in a variety of disciplines, and often a primary interaction point between Ariadna and galactics, a Commercial Agent has to be ready for absolutely anything. If they seem arrogant, it's because confidence is their best weapon. If they seem uncaring, it's because neutrality is their sworn duty. And if they keep one hand on their wallet, and another on their weapon? It's because they've learned the hard way that not every partner can be trusted.

ATTRIBUTES

AGI	AWA	BRW	COO	INT	PER	WIL
+1	+1	–	+1	+2	+3	+1

SKILLS

Mandatory	Education	Lifestyle	Persuade
Elective	Hacking	Lifestyle	Stealth

EARNINGS: 2 + 2N

GEAR: Fusebox, Negotiator's Suite, Pistol, Rucksack

SPECIAL: Requires a homeland in Merovingia

CAREER PROFILE

PARATROOPER

In the advanced warfare of the Human Sphere, Paratroopers drop onto planets and battlefields inaccessible by land. These brave men and women parachute into hostile territory, using high-tech glider suits and stealth chutes to slip past enemy defences. Air support is key to victory in the countless conflicts that grip the Human Sphere, and airborne soldiers engage in dynamic operations all across space. Paratroopers often adopt a "live fast" motto, jumping out of the sky and into combat for a living. This can give them a reputation for wild behaviour, but Paratroopers are every bit as disciplined as their fellow soldiers. A Paratrooper character often finds themselves far behind enemy lines, facing challenges that less elite soldiers could only imagine.

ATTRIBUTES

AGI	AWA	BRW	COO	INT	PER	WIL
+2	+2	+2	+1	+1	–	+2

SKILLS

Mandatory	Survival	Athletics	Ballistics
Elective	Close Combat	Pilot	Discipline

EARNINGS: 2+1(N)

GEAR: Combat Jump Pack, Medium Combat Armour, Combi Rifle (with 4 Standard Reloads)

CAREER PROFILE

SPECIAL FORCES

The most elite soldiers in the Human Sphere carry out spec ops missions across known – and even unknown – space. Special Forces units operate in covert mission of international warfare, hunting war criminals, striking critical assets, and fading before anyone can blame their employers. These elite units also carry out the most difficult ops in the war for Paradiso, harassing the Combined Army, rescuing allies trapped behind enemy lines, and neutralising elite enemy opposition. Governments deploy Special Forces when discretion is needed – all too common in the shadow warfare of the G5 nations – and when regular mercs or law enforcement are inadequate. A Special Forces soldier receives the finest training equipment, and most important missions, demanding more from themselves than their own people do.

ATTRIBUTES

AGI	AWA	BRW	COO	INT	PER	WIL
+2	+2	+2	+1	+1	–	+2

SKILLS

Mandatory	Survival	Resistance	Ballistics
Elective	Close Combat	Hacking	Discipline

EARNINGS: 2+1(N)

GEAR: Medium Combat Armour, Combi Rifle or AP Rifle (with 5 Standard Reloads), Climbing Plus or Combat Jump Pack, Garrotte

CAREER PROFILE

SPORTS PERSONALITY

Sporting events are a time-honoured tradition of competition between cities, countries, even whole worlds. The greatest sports stars are legends, heroes to their people, larger than life. They possess a sway and a swagger that few political leaders can match, all stemming from their ability to perform incredible athletic feats. With the advances in genetic engineering, wetware implants, and cybernetics, professional athletes boast physiques and abilities the common person can only imagine. A Sports Personality could be a rising star of Dog-Bowl or the Aristeia! Underground. Champions of these bone-breaking contests and professional duels can rise from humble roots to touch immortal fame. Sports Personalities can bear the colours and face of a nation, quest only for the next adrenaline rush, or hunt for personal glory.

ATTRIBUTES

AGI	AWA	BRW	COO	INT	PER	WIL
+2	+2	+1	–	+1	+2	+2

SKILLS

Mandatory	Athletics	Persuade	Close Combat
Elective	Acrobatics	Athletics	Ballistics

EARNINGS: 1+3(N)

GEAR: Biografted Attribute Augmention 2 or Super-Jump, Uniform

CAREER PROFILE

SPETSNAZ

Dubbed "The Walking Death" by the River Tribe during the First Antipode Offensive, most people have different names for the Spetsnaz, and few are flattering. Heirs to the most underhanded and brutal tactics of the Russian Special Forces, their techniques have been honed by years of Cossack discipline, and the harsh, unforgiving teacher that is the planet *Dawn*. Their boot camp is founded on one simple principle: rather than stretch the limits of human endurance, they flatly deny the existence of such limits, and push forward. Paragons of the Rodinan virtue of "work hard/play hard," these soldiers are an unholy terror whether you encounter them in the training yard, the saloon, or the battlefield. But when Ariadna needs defending, there is no better barbed-wire fence than this caustic group of troublemakers.

ATTRIBUTES

AGI	AWA	BRW	COO	INT	PER	WIL
+2	+1	+2	+2	+1	–	+2

SKILLS

Mandatory	Ballisctis	Close Combat	Resitance
Elective	Discipline	Stealth	Thievery

EARNINGS: 0 + 4(N)

GEAR: Boarding Shotgun, Combat Jump Pack, Heavy Combat Armour, Tactical Webbing

SPECIAL: Requires a homeland in Rodina

CHAPTER 6

ANTIPODES AND KIN

Perhaps the most notable thing on *Dawn* is not its Teseum, but rather, the Antipodes and their "relatives" known as Dogfaces and Wulvers. If *Dawn* is a wild, savage place, no one embodies those traits quite like the Dog-Blooded.

ANTIPODES

The original inhabitants of *Dawn*, these canid predators have been loathe to release their claim on the planet. While both sides of the conflict produce the occasional stubborn, brave soul intent on diplomacy, years of conflict – and both sides' contentious internal politics – make any sort of truce a seemingly impossible goal. Defined by their hostility to a group they didn't invite, the Antipodes endure, much the same way that they always have; through grit, toughness, and a stubborn refusal to die.

Ironically, the very traits that Ariadnans take pride in themselves.

ANTIPODE NAMES

An "individual" Antipode is the product of their trinary; named for deeds, reputation, or regional features, Antipode names are as varied as the trinaries who bear them. A single Antipode usually doesn't merit a name apart from their trinary; any identification is purely practical, such as Lightfoot Third, or Smallest Razor Fang. The one exception is when an Antipode who's lost their trinary is integrated into a new one; they keep a compound of their former name as a distinction, and to honour the fallen. Ariadnan soldiers have long learned to dread compound names like Swift Stride Heartfang, or Falling Star Addertongue.

ANTIPODE TRIBES

Because of the risk involved, no serious effort has been made to catalogue the various Antipode tribes in some time. However, between military intelligence, historians, and the occasional scholar with wanton disregard for their own safety, Ariadna maintains a passable understanding of their neighbours.

Bitter Leaves: The tale of Amanda Greene and Gentle Leaf still holds a great deal of weight, not only among Ariadnan anthropologists, but among Antipodes as well. Whether or not Gentle Leaf's memory line passed to the Bitter Leaves or not is a hotly contested issue – even among the tribe – but nevertheless, they hold two truths to be unassailable. First, that even though it was one brief instance, co-existence with humanity is technically possible.

And secondly, that humanity employs betrayal, deceit, and trickery as their primary means of interaction which must never be forgotten.

Bringers-of-Peace: Recently formed by the unprecedented alliance between Long Shadow's Night Stalkers and Deep Voice's Ironblood Tribe, resulting in the single largest Antipode warband in history, massing on Caledonia's northern border. Their aim is simple: an end to the conflict with Ariadna, once and for all.

Long Shadow posited that there would never be peace as long as the Ariadnan military remained, while Deep Voice reasoned that Dogfaces and Wulvers might prove more amenable to co-existence. As it turns out, their conclusions weren't mutually exclusive. Today, the Bringers stage large-scale assaults, deep into Caledonian territory, destroying military infrastructure, and spreading the cuckoo virus with abandon.

Their methods are brutal, efficient, and decidedly thorough.

Gentle Embrace of the Sagacious Progenitors: Some concepts just don't translate cleanly; this is assuredly one. For starters, the "Gentle Embrace" is usually anything but. For creatures with rending claws, no embrace can ever be truly without injury; the implication is that the wounds they inflict are mild, and born of compassion. Similarly, the "Sagacious Progenitors" are the mythic ancients of the Antipode race, a trinary said to be born from the very sun – a belief that finds little traction outside the tribe, where animism and Blood Tree worship are the dominant forms of spirituality – implying that the "embrace" is guided by holy authority.

A better translation would be "Tribe that will torture you – out of love – until you become wise, guided by the authority vested in them by gods you don't believe in" – but at some point, enough is enough. Religious zealots to the last, they are simultaneously among the most gregarious, and most frightening of all the Antipodean tribes – even to their own kind.

Ice Fangs: Known for their distinctive bluish-white fur – when they're not photoreactively blending, that is – this elusive, aggressive tribe makes their home in the mountain regions east of Le Douar, giving the Merovingian patrols – who call them *Crocs de Glace* – all they can handle and then some. Notoriously reclusive, even by Antipode standards, likely due to their close proximity to the White Knives.

River Tribe: Humanity's first contact with an alien species was a complete disaster, and a source of strife to this day. The River Tribe is based out of Coldspring, to the east of the USAriadna Revere Line and even the massive Fort Apache hasn't quelled the threat, so much as contained it. For now.

Given the dogged persistence of its primary memory lines, the River Tribe isn't righting past wrongs; to them, the wounds inflicted during the First Antipode Offensive are real, present, and fresh. And they need to be repaid in kind.

White Knives: While little is known about their reasoning, no tribe is more likely to engage in combat with their fellow Antipodes. Devout Blood Tree worshippers, they strike when it suits them, offering no explanation. Nestled in the southwestern corner of the spinal mountains, they are a constant source of terror for Merovingia, USAriadna, as well as their fellow Antipodes.

SOUTHERN TRIBES

Dawn's southern subcontinent is one of the Human Sphere's last great frontiers: wild, uncharted, and virtually unsettled.

That is not the same thing as being uninhabited.

Home to dozens of nomadic Antipode tribes, while they focus on the fertile lands between southern Rodina and the Lost Sea, their presence is felt across the entire subcontinent. With an even stronger focus on hunting than their den-dwelling counterparts in the north and east, the Southern Tribes represent a particular expression of Antipode ideals: wild, free, and entirely untethered. Unfortunately, their interactions with humanity have been less than friendly.

While some believe that establishing Ariadna divided the Antipodes, the arrival of humanity simply reinforced an existing truth: the culturally, biologically, and geographically distinct Southern Tribes had become their own people. Their wide-ranging travels left them lean and wiry compared to their northern counterparts, and the comparatively homogeneous terrain they covered left them even less inclined towards bipedal stances.

Their *laissez-faire* hunting culture means that any sedentary being is considered fair game. Cattle, humans, even den-dwelling Antipodes are all – quite literally – on the table. Needless to say, this hasn't endeared them to their neighbours.

OMERZENIYE

Everyone knows that the humans are unique in the way they interact with the Antipodes to breed Dogfaces. All other lifeforms are either immune to

OTHER KNOWN ANTIPODE TRIBES

3-Winged Moth Tribe: The closest the Antipodes have to scientists, the Moths' curiosity tends to express itself primarily by kidnapping subjects and exposing them to various stimuli. This can be as benign as learning what mushrooms make humans sick, to studying mind-shock through vivisection.

Broken Plains Tribe: The location of the original Broken Plains has been lost to history, but that doesn't stop this tribe from searching for it.

Death Claws: Physically larger than most, and savage even by Antipode standards.

Long Talons: Warmongering tribe led by Sharp Knife, fond of deep incursions into Ariadnan territory.

OMERZENIYE

While it's true that most Ariadnan creatures are immune to the virus, there are occasional hybrids that not only survive birth, but the inevitable abandonment of their parents afterwards. They'd be rare – less than one creature in 10,000 survives the cuckoo virus in utero, and most of those perish as prey to Antipodean hunters. So if any survive to encounter the characters, they're bound to be incredibly hardy, vicious, and large hulking monstrosities built for conflict.

The following template can be applied to any Ariadnan creature as a unique threat. Bears and Elks are the most common animals to use as a baseline:

Omerzeniye: Add the following special abilities: Superhuman Agility +1, Superhuman Brawn +2, as well as the Thick-Skinned, Monstrous, and Super-Jump abilities from Antipodes (p. 79). If the creature was not a Nemesis, you may treat it as such for the purposes of wounds and deriving stress tracks.

"We do not get scared. We do not surrender. And we cannot be domesticated."

-John "Vanya" Rotten, Wulver and leader of the Dog Nation movement

METISY

From the Russian Метисы, meaning "mongrel", "half-blood", or "crossbreed" "metisy" was one of the many derogatory terms hurled at early Dogfaces and Wulvers. It has since been reclaimed by those communities; most famously by Dog Nation leader John "Vanya" Rotten in his "Equality or Death" speech. While many find the term unacceptable – even within the Dog Nation movement – Rotten and his followers have adhered to the term, perhaps because of its divisive nature.

the virus or react so badly that their offspring fail to gestate or emerge as terrible gasping things that simply don't have the capacity for life.

But if one life form can breed monsters, why not others?

Tales of Омерзение (Omerzeniye) – AKA Bukavac, Chupacabra, Jackalope, or whatever ancient cryptid is in fashion this week – litter the journals and audio logs of the deranged, isolated, and above all bored settlers of *Dawn*. Old Rodinan soldiers each have their own story, where a long-dead platoon leader came face to face with "a thing" of meat and claws that hunted man, bear, and Antipode alike. These tales are told with bravado by most, a glorious ghost story to amuse and inspire caution in new recruits. In the wilds, Antipode hunters follow these rumours, searching for proof that has yet to emerge. In all likelihood, there is no such creature. Perhaps the Antipodes ensure these supposed monsters simply vanish into the woods.

Or perhaps it is something else entirely.

WULVERS AND DOGFACES—THE DOG-BLOODED

Born into a world that fears and hates them, for events that transpired before they were even born, humans that carry Antipode traits face an uphill battle for every scrap of respect that they earn.

DOGFACES

Homo sapiens lupus – more commonly known by their sobriquet Dogfaces – are strangers in their own lands. Every doorjamb, taxi, and restaurant table is a stinging reminder that the world they inhabit was simply not built for them. Clothes, transportation, lodging – acquiring the basic necessities of life is a constant challenge.

Career options for a Dogface are sparse. While the military always has room, not every Dogface relishes the notion of fighting alongside people who hate and fear them, to protect people who hate and fear them, only to come back from the front to find that – surprise, surprise – the hatred and fear are just as strong as ever. Still, military life is often more appealing than the alternatives: Submondo enforcers, stadium security, or a glorified piece of construction equipment at the docks. Woe to the Dogface who would prefer a vocation where violence isn't part of the equation.

And of course, once the blood fury hits, there's no such thing.

WULVERS

If Dogfaces have it tough, *Homo sapiens lupus mulus* – Wulvers – make their lives look like a holiday. Larger than most humans, and even most Dogfaces, a Wulver's life is a constant stream of awkward compromises. Even the rare place of business that caters to Dogfaces will be hard-pressed to meet a Wulver's needs, and that's when they're trying; most simply never make the effort. A minority within a minority, the comparatively small number of Wulvers means that in addition to fear, bigotry, and mistrust, most people have never seen your kind before so good luck finding clothes that fit.

While Dogfaces are remarkably human-looking until they shift forms,

Wulvers have the worst of both worlds. While Wulvers are compact in comparison to a Dog-Warrior, they're still incredibly dense with bone and musculature, furry, and possessed of prominent canines protruding past their powerful jaws. To be a Wulver is to live in a world perpetually too big or too small, which never quite knows what to do with you.

DOG-BOWL

Ariadnans tend to be fanatically competitive and nowhere is that more evident than in their abiding love for local Dog-Bowl teams.

THE GAME

Modern Dog-Bowl is big business, but the game owes its roots to the streets of Ariadna's ghettos. "Street scrimmage" is the basic game, still played by kids in alleyways as well as professionals. Teams of five square off in an amalgamation of American football, rugby, basketball, and a bloody street fight. Off-world scholars have even noted similarities to the ancient Mesoamerican ball game, but a simple explanation is likely: Dog-Bowl was played with the people, tools, and spaces available. And its unique gameplay bears that heritage like a badge of honour.

The rules are loose, the action fast-paced, and the dynamic play is much greater than the sum of its parts. Matches are high-scoring, hard-hitting affairs, and the combination of possession-based tactics and frenetic action has proven a hit with audiences across *Dawn*. And with most games now streaming on Maya and Arachne, the rest of the Human Sphere is fast learning what Ariadnans already know: there's nothing quite like a good Dog-Bowl match.

FULL SCRUM

A variant on the street scrimmage rules, full scrums are used in tournament play, to settle overtime between professional squads, and for special exhibitions. Featuring twenty-one players per side, and three balls in simultaneous play, a full scrum can make nuclear fusion seem tame by comparison.

While difficult for all but the most die-hard fan to keep up with, the ensuing chaos has proven surprisingly popular on foreign dataspheres; both on the Arachne darknet, where Bakunians appreciate the controlled anarchy, and ironically on Maya – where the sport has a loyal underground following.

DOG-BOWL STADIUMS

One of the things that makes Dog-Bowl so unique is its signature three-lane arena. Frustrated by limiting their games to a single street, athletic Dogface youths incorporated the alleyways between avenues to expand the field of play. The game quickly adapted to the divided field, which has become largely formalised as a main lane with two side lanes (although a dual-lane variant remains popular in Caledonia).

The buildings which separate the lanes of play remain an important part of the professional game, although these structures have become increasingly abstract in form. A stadium's "buildings" are one part obstruction, one part climbing wall, and one part art sculpture, with different stadiums offering vastly altered play. In addition to separating lanes, they add an exciting element of verticality to the game, capturing the high ground in Dog-Bowl is not only entertaining, but it provides a powerful tactical edge.

The stadiums themselves are typically modular affairs; in addition to Dog-Bowl matches, they can change configurations to host concerts, political speakers, or conventions at a moment's notice.

DOG-BOWL PLAYERS

One of the most notable aspects of professional Dog-Bowl is not the game itself, but rather, its impact on society. While human history is replete with bigotry that made exception for athletes, there's still no denying the impact that Dog-Bowl's popularity has had on the day-to-day life of Dogfaces and Wulvers. A Dog-Bowl team means big money, but to field a team, you need players. For the first time in their lives, Dogfaces and Wulvers found themselves in unfamiliar territory:

They were wanted.

DOG NATION

"Equality or death." Lately, it's been too much of the latter, with precious little of the former.

Before the Commercial Conflicts threw everything into disarray, John "Vanya" Rotten had become something of a cultural phenomenon; his charismatic speeches and logic-based tirades capturing the imagination of the average Ariadnan. Twenty years later, Rotten is a grizzled veteran of numerous conflicts; though he's lost count of which scars are from defending Ariadna on the front lines, and which are from hate crimes. No longer the patriotic idealist from his youth, time has installed in Rotten a cynical pragmatism; a trait now reflected in the larger movement.

Other notable Dog Nation members include:

Brooklyn Carver: A pacifistic, mediagenic Wulver who runs her popular dNet podcast "A Wolf Among Sheep" from her sheep farm in Tara, Carver is determined to charm the wider world into accepting metisy. While her sheep seem mildly terrified, they're at least well-behaved.

Donnel McIntyre: A radical activist who some see as the heir to Rotten's legacy, McIntyre is constantly working angles with galactic powers, leaving senior members of the movement unsure if he can tell a good deal from a bad one.

Oksana Ivanova: A minor fitness celebrity, Ivanova is a competitive weightlifter and supplement enthusiast. After footage of her casually tossing weights through a wall in a blood fury went viral, she thought her career was over. Instead, a major Cod chain licensed the footage, turning her into a Maya novelty overnight.

Mikhail Mogila: Formerly the bassist for sludgecore band Bloodfeast, Mogila is a consistently violent – but not yet lethal – protester. The current record holder for residency in the greatest number of Ariadnan prisons in one calendar year (twenty-one), many wonder when – not if – he'll be locked up for good.

1 HEAT

A Wulver's exceptional bulk inadvertently causes significant property damage.

OPTIONAL RULE: BLOOD FURY

In *Infinity*, characters have a great deal of personal agency; whatever their instincts might be telling them, the choice of how to act is ultimately theirs. That doesn't mean you have to make it easy on them.

As a standard complication, the GM may declare that an Antipode, Dogface, or Wulver is suffering from the blood fury condition. When in a blood fury, the character takes 1+X[N] Resolve damage (wherein X is the amount of Heat spent to trigger the complication, or 2 if it was the result of rolling a 20) per round. This condition lasts until:

The conclusion of the current scene.

The character makes a successful Absterge action against a Challenging (D2) test.

The character charges at the source of their rage, attacking it. The character immediately recovers all resolve.

THE DAWN CUP

With a gruelling schedule that encompasses three-quarters of the year, the unofficial Ariadnan pastime culminates in the Five Nations Championship, a round-robin tournament between the teams of Caledonia, Merovingia, USAriadna, Mat', and Tartary. Easily the biggest spectacle of the year, the tournament is starting to become a reliable source of foreign capital both from the occasional tourist and from Maya sales. Whether Dog-Bowl ever gains more than a cult following has yet to be seen.

OPTIONAL RULE: LONE WOLVES

At the GM's discretion, if there is only one Antipode PC in the group, the cost of an Antipode fireteam can be reduced to +3 Life Points, bringing the total cost of playing an Antipode down to 5 Life Points.

OPTIONAL RULE: INDIVIDUAL FIRETEAMS

Groups with two or more Antipode PCs may each want their own fireteams. In this case, each Antipode character may pay an additional 4 Life Points each (two for each Antipode Companion) to gain their own fireteam(s).

OPTIONAL RULE: K-9 UNITS

With GM permission, upon taking the Assault Pack Controller or Devil Dog careers, players may purchase Antipode NPC companions with Life Points.

SPLIT FOCUS

Whether a single NPC or a fireteam, friendly Antipode NPCs can't normally act in the same round as the player characters. However, spending an Infinity Point can absolutely allow the trinary to split its focus in this fashion, if only for a moment.

NEW TRINARIES

If a member of a trinary dies, the remaining member(s) enter mind-shock; the only way to resolve this is to integrate a new Antipode to the trinary. A difficult, multi-phasic process involving auditory, pheromonal, and visual signalling via chameleonic fur patches. To integrate the new member, the would-be trinary must make a Psychology (D1) test (6 Momentum, 3 failures) to incorporate the new member.

DOG-BLOODED CHARACTERS

Dogface and Wulver characters who failed to fully integrate into Ariadnan society can be created using the variant rules in this chapter, rather than those in the *Infinity Corebook*, or the variant rules for Ariadnan characters on p. 64. Antipode characters present a unique situation, and must be created with these Lifepath options.

ANTIPODE CHARACTERS

The original inhabitants of *Dawn*, and still some of its most fearsome, playing Antipodes presents a special challenge. Not simply because they're a traditional antagonist of the setting, nor their rarity outside of *Dawn's* wilderness, and not even because there are no recorded instances of an Antipode ever leaving *Dawn*. All these play a role, but the main impediment to Antipode characters is the very same factor that confused the original Ariadnans: typically speaking, they don't come as individuals, but groups.

Antipodes rely on other Antipodes, not just to accomplish tasks, but for their very sapience. This presents a challenge for groups with fewer than three Antipode PCs. In these cases, the characters are accompanied by a number of trinary companions. These NPCs join the characters on their adventures, providing support, assistance, and of course, the remaining elements of their personality. This can take several different forms.

ANTIPODE FIRETEAM (+4 LIFE POINTS)

The character is joined by two NPCs (use the stats for Antipode Warriors, *Infinity Corebook,* p. 462), who create a fireteam with the character, as per the Antipode's trinary mind. This is the default assumption for Antipode PCs, and the only option for groups with a single Antipode PC.

SINGLE NPC (+2 LIFE POINTS)

Groups with two Antipode PCs have the option of completing their trinary with one NPC (use the stats for Antipode Warriors, *Infinity Corebook,* p. 462). This presents a unique roleplaying challenge, as the two players – along with the NPC – create a single personality between the three of them.

ANTIPODE PLAYER CHARACTERS

If there are three or more Antipode characters in the group, no additional NPCs are required. Though again, Antipode players have the option of purchasing additional NPCs for +2 Life Points each.

WULVERS AND DOGFACES

For Dogface characters, use the stats from the *Infinity Corebook* (pg. 41); for Wulvers, use the stats provided in this chapter.

DECISION ONE: BIRTH HOST

Dog-Blooded characters roll on the *Dog-Blooded Host Table* to determine whether they're a Dogface, Wulver, or Antipode.

DOG-BLOODED HOST TABLE

D20	HOST
1–12	Dogface
13–17	Wulver
18–20	Antipode

DECISION TWO: FACTION AND HERITAGE

Whether Dogface, Wulver, or Antipode, all Dog-Blooded characters have origins on the planet *Dawn*. After rolling on the *Dog-Blooded Host Table*, characters are assumed to be from Ariadna. No further roll is necessary, simply note your heritage and faction, add your faction skills, and proceed to Decision Three as normal.

DECISION THREE: HOMELAND

Antipode characters roll on the *Antipodean Tribe* table. If the tribe is in a different region than your heritage, assume your pack migrates at this time. For other Ariadnan characters residing in the Antipodean Wilds, this is the tribe whose territory you're nearest to. Good luck.

ANTIPODE

ATTRIBUTES

AGILITY	+2	AWARENESS	+1	BRAWN	+2	COORDINATION	–1
INTELLIGENCE	–2	PERSONALITY	–2	WILLPOWER	–		

Claws: Melee, 1+2Ⓝ damage, Subtle 1, Vicious 1

Scent: Antipodes have an extraordinary sense of smell. When making an Observation test or any other skill test in which scent would play a factor, they gain +2d20.

Thick-Skinned: Antipodes have +2 Vigour soak.

Monstrous: While not as bulky as a Dog-Warrior, Antipodes are still massive creatures. Increase the difficulty of tests where great size or weight would be problematic by one step. Monstrous creatures are not required to brace Unwieldy weapons, and can use two-handed weapons in one hand without difficulty or penalty. They may spend 1 Momentum to add Knockdown to all of their melee attacks for a turn.

Super-Jump: The Antipode gains 1 rank in the Catfall talent. They can also vault over obstacles up to their height without penalty. This also reduces the difficulty of skill tests to move through difficult terrain by one step.

Primal Technology: Antipodes use muscle-powered weapons exclusively. When operating technology more advanced than a bow (such as a grenade, commlog, or motorcycle), the difficulty of the test increases by +1, and the complication range increases by +5.

Pack Mentality: Antipodes naturally cooperate. They add +1d20 when part of a fireteam containing only Antipodes. These Antipode-only fireteams may take reactions, but all share the leader's stress tracks.

Trinary Mind: The Antipode's intelligence is distributed across three or more individuals. If the members of a trinary are ever farther than Medium range from each other, they all suffer +1 difficulty to all tests. If this persists for more than one scene, or if a member of the trinary dies, the Antipodes each enter mind-shock, suffering an additional +1 difficulty to all tests. These effects stack.

Additionally, for each scene that passes with fewer than three Antipodes in a trinary, the remaining members suffer an additional instance of the Fatigued condition, though neither rest nor recovery actions will remove it. The only solution is to incorporate a new member.

Quantronically Inert: An Antipode's mind is distributed across an organic network, leaving them incompatible with most quantronic technologies. An Antipode does not have a Firewall rating, does not create a geist in Decision Nine, and cannot use cybernetic augmentations. Silk augmentations are possible, but difficult and entirely experimental: increase the cost by 2Ⓝ, +2 Restriction, +T2.

Lifepath Special Rules: In Decision Two, an Antipode belongs to the Ariadna faction even if "Defection" was rolled; on their own, Antipodes have no way to travel off-world.

Life Point Cost: 2 Life Points per Antipode. No Antipode exists in a vacuum; at least two other Antipodes are needed to create a trinary (see *Antipode Characters*, p. 78).

DOGFACE

ATTRIBUTES

AGILITY	–	AWARENESS	–	BRAWN	–	COORDINATION	–
INTELLIGENCE	–	PERSONALITY	–	WILLPOWER	–		

Claws: Melee, 1+2 N damage, Subtle 1, Vicious 1
Scent: Dogfaces have an extraordinary sense of smell. When making an Observation test or any other skill test in which scent would play a factor, the Dogface gains +2d20.
Transform: When a Dogface suffers a Wound, they must succeed on a Discipline (D1) test. On a failure, they transform into their Dog-Warrior form. The Dogface can choose to voluntarily fail this check (although this does not count as a failsafe test). When in Dogface form, they gain the following traits:

- +2 Brawn, +2 Agility
- +1 soak against attacks dealing Vigour damage
- Transformation while wearing human-sized armour inflicts 2+3 N damage and will render the armour in need of repair. (See Dogface Armour, *Infinity* Corebook.)
- Upon transformation, immediately recover all Vigour.
- Gain the character trait Dog-Warrior.
- **Monstrous**: A Dog-Warrior has considerable bulk and mass. Increase the difficulty of tests where great size or weight would be problematic by one step. Monstrous creatures are not required to brace Unwieldy weapons and can use two-handed weapons in one hand without difficulty or penalty. They may spend 1 Momentum to add Knockdown to all of their melee attacks for a turn.
- **Snarling Beast**: All Personality-based tests that are not based on intimidation are made at +2 difficulty. This penalty does not apply to other Dogface characters.
- **Super-Jump**: The Dog-Warrior gains one rank in the Catfall talent. They can also vault over obstacles up to their height without penalty. This also reduces the difficulty of skill tests to move through difficult terrain by one step.
- **Fatigue**: At the end of the current encounter or scene, the Dogface returns to their normal form and suffers from the Fatigued condition.

Lifepath Special Rules: In Decision Two, unless you roll "Defection" you belong to the Ariadna faction. (If you roll "Defection", roll again twice normally: It's possible you're the incredibly rare Dogface who was born somewhere other than Dawn.)
Life Point Cost: 3

WULVERS

ATTRIBUTES

AGILITY	+1	AWARENESS	+1	BRAWN	+1	COORDINATION	–1
INTELLIGENCE	–	PERSONALITY	–1	WILLPOWER	–1		

Claws: Melee, 1+1 N damage, Subtle 1, Vicious 1
Scent: Wulvers have an extraordinary sense of smell. When making an Observation test or any other skill test in which scent would play a factor, they gain +2d20.
Naturally Tough: Wulvers have +2 Vigour.
Monstrous: While not as massive as a dog-warrior, Wulvers are still incredibly dense with bone and musculature. Increase the difficulty of tests where great size or weight would be problematic by one step. Monstrous creatures are not required to brace Unwieldy weapons, and can use two-handed weapons in one hand without difficulty or penalty. They may spend 1 Momentum to add Knockdown to all of their melee attacks for a turn.
Furious: While they're no Dogfaces, a Wulver's rage is easily triggered compared to a human's. They suffer a +1 complication range to all skill tests, and an additional +2 to all Personality-based tests that are not based on intimidation.
Super-Jump: The Wulver gains one rank in the Catfall talent. They can also vault over obstacles up to their height without penalty. This also reduces the difficulty of skill tests to move through difficult terrain by one step.
Odd Fit: Almost nothing is tailored to fit Wulvers. When purchasing gear meant to be worn, such as armour, add +1 to the item's restriction and tariff rating. Gear that is not acquired in this fashion causes the Wulver to suffer a +1 complication range to all skill tests. Tailoring gear to fit the character requires a Tech (D3) test (4 Momentum, 2 failures).
Lifepath Special Rules: In Decision Two, unless "Defection" was rolled, the Wulver belongs to the Ariadna faction. (If "Defection" is rolled, roll again twice normally: it's possible to be the incredibly rare Wulver who was born somewhere other than Dawn.)
Life Point Cost: 3

DECISION FOUR: STATUS

Antipode characters grow up in entirely different situations than humans, Dogfaces, or Wulvers so they roll on the *Tribal Status Table* and *Den Environment Table*.

DECISION FIVE: YOUTH EVENTS

Growing up on *Dawn* is difficult enough. Now imagine what that's like when everyone's afraid of you. The looming spectre of prejudice, constant threats of violence, and the day-to-day struggles just to meet basic needs, and if that wasn't enough, there's still the challenges that every other Ariadnan faces. Still, mixed-race families are no less loving than any other kind and *Dawn* is nothing if not a place of opportunity.

For Antipodes, the transition from cubhood into adolescence is more than just learning to hunt, craft, and track; it's a process of awakening to sapience itself.

DECISION SIX: EDUCATION

When it comes to education, Antipode characters do things a little differently. Even if a human school were – by some terrible decision – to admit an Antipode, their minds aren't fully cognizant yet, to say nothing of the need for a trinary.

Instead, Antipode youths are guided into rough categories of training, based on what aptitude they've shown up to that point. They shadow adults in the tribe, learning through kinesics, osmosis, participation, and observation. Young Antipodes don't gain any equipment in this process, but the knowledge passed on will last them a lifetime.

Note: Antipode characters who paid the full 6 Life Points in Decision One must choose the Born Wild education. Other Dogface or Wulver characters must use a human education table as directed by their Gamesmaster.

ANTIPODEAN TRIBE TABLE

D20	REGION	LANGUAGE	ATTRIBUTE	ATTRIBUTE	SKILL
1-2	Bitter Leaves	Snarl*	Personality	Agility	Animal Handling
3-6	Bringers-of-Peace	Snarl, Antipode Creole	Brawn	Agility	Close Combat
7-8	Gentle Embrace of the Sagacious Progenitors	Snarl	Willpower	Agility	Analysis
9-10	Ice Fangs	Snarl	Brawn	Agility	Stealth
11-14	River Tribe	Snarl*	Brawn	Agility	Observation
15-16	White Knives	Snarl	Willpower	Agility	Stealth
17	3-Winged Moth Tribe	Snarl*	Intelligence	Agility	Analysis
18	Broken Plains Tribe	Snarl, Antipode Creole	Awareness	Agility	Observation
19	Death Claws	Snarl	Brawn	Agility	Resistance
20	Long Talons	Snarl*	Brawn	Agility	Survival

TRIBAL STATUS TABLE

2D6	TRIBAL FAVOUR	ATTRIBUTE	EARNINGS
2	Scavengers	Awareness	0
3-5	Members	Awareness	1
6-8	Trusted	Brawn	2
9-10	Valued	Agility	2
11	Favoured	Personality	2
12	Warlords	Willpower	3

DEN ENVIRONMENT TABLE

D6	ENVIRONMENT	ATTRIBUTE	SKILL
1	Happy Home	Personality	Animal Handling
2	Violent	Brawn	Acrobatics
3	Border Life	Brawn	Resistance
4	Rebellious	Awareness	Stealth
5	Regimented	Agility	Discipline
6	Shamanistic	Intelligence	Analysis

ANTIPODE YOUTH EVENT TABLE

D20	EVENT TYPE	1	2	3	4	5	6
1–2	Survived	an Antipode assault	a wild animal attack	getting stranded	a natural disaster	a border skirmish	severe drought/ famine
3–4	Survived	kidnapping	sabotage	violent riots	an accident	a shooting	a Submondo raid
5–6	Witnessed	perjury	a murder	an assassination	political corruption	a violent crime	long-term abuse
7–8	Witnessed	betrayal	bigotry	an Antipode attack	hypocrisy	selfless bravery	heroic sacrifice
9–10	Involved in	a cover-up	smuggling	amateur Dog-Bowl	Dog Nation protests	charity work	gang activity
11–12	Discovered	religion	scientific curiosity	artistic talent	sexual attraction	a dead body	archaeological ruins
13	Family Change	parent (re)marries	parent(s) disappear	parent(s) killed	parent walks out	parent(s) incarcerated	parent(s) sent to front
14	Family Change	Wulver sibling born	Dogface sibling born	adopted sibling	1+8N new siblings	Divorce	Moved to new nation
15	Succumbed to	galactic propaganda	toxic nationalism	despair	mental illness	peer pressure	loneliness
17	Social Contacts	made a friend in opposite social class	gained mentor (roll on *Ariadna Homeland Table*)	gained contact (roll on *Ariadna Homeland Table*)	gained galactic contact (roll on *Faction Table*)	gained Submondo contact	gained Mercenary contact
18	Entrusted With	an heirloom	a commendation	a task	a legacy	a secret	a Cube
19	Special	gained a 1 Asset debt	gained 1 Asset	gained a Cube – no strings	gained a Cube – strings	gained a 3N Asset debt	gained a 5N Asset debt
19	Special	learned a galactic language	learned an Ariadnan language	gained blackmail on another faction	gained blackmail on Ariadnans	debilitating condition	Vigour poison 1+5N
20	Reroll Twice and Combine Results						

SPECIAL YOUTH EVENTS

Acquired By X: Whether by kidnapping, rescue, or other means, you spent some time as a ward of the listed faction until you escaped. Learn one language spoken by that faction, and gain a contact – either enemy or ally – in the faction.

Debilitating Condition: Whether by genetics, illness, or injury, you suffer from a condition that seriously hampers your mobility. Increase the difficulty of all movement-related tests by one step. A cure is possible, but it's expensive and will cost 4+6N Assets.

Gain X Asset(s): You've gained X additional Asset(s). Add any Assets gained this way add to your total Assets at the end of character creation.

Gain a 1 Asset Debt: You owe someone a debt worth 1 Asset.

Gained a Cube – No Strings: You are one of the rare Ariadnans – and even rarer Dogfaces or Wulvers – outfitted with a Cube. How did this happen, and why are there no strings attached?

Gained a Cube – Strings: You are one of the rare Ariadnans – and even rarer Dogfaces or Wulvers – outfitted with a Cube. How did this happen, and how are you expected to pay this back?

Gain an XN Asset Debt: As above, except that the debt is worth XN Assets. Note: if the number of Effects rolled is greater than the total debt, then you instead gain the Assets, rather than owing them.

Gained Blackmail on Another Faction: You have obtained proof that a person or organisation has committed misdeeds against another. Roll twice on the *Faction Table* (*Infinity Corebook,* p. 41) to determine which factions the two parties belong to. Either side will grant a favour in exchange for the evidence.

Gained Blackmail on Ariadnans: You have obtained proof that your fellow Ariadnans – either a person or organisation – has committed misdeeds against another. Roll once on the *Ariadna Homeland Table* (*Infinity Corebook,* p. 43), and once on the *Faction Table* (*Infinity Corebook,* p. 41) to determine the guilty and injured parties, respectively. Either side will grant a favour in exchange for the evidence.

Learned an Off-world Language: Roll once on the *Random Languages Table* (*Infinity Corebook,* p. 45). If you already speak the language, roll again.

Learned an Ariadnan Language: Roll once on the *Ariadna Homeland Table* (*Infinity Corebook,* p. 43). If you already speak the language, roll again.

Vigour Poison X: Natural or manufactured, you were badly poisoned, and your body never fully recovered. Suffer the Fatigued condition, and reduce your Vigour by X, to a minimum of 6. A cure exists, but it's expensive and will cost 4+4N Assets to acquire. The experience may have an upside: increase your Resolve by +1 for every Effect rolled. Even if cured, the changes to Vigour and (if applicable) Resolve will remain.

ANTIPODE ADOLESCENT EVENT TABLE

D20	ADOLESCENT EVENT	SUGGESTED CHARACTER TRAIT	OPTIONAL EFFECT
1	You contracted a strange human disease. While it does nothing to Antipodes, you're highly infectious to humans.	Plague Rat	When attacking a human target, your claws gain the Biotech quality.
2	Antipode mental structures are resistant to change, but yours proves especially stubborn.	Traditionalist	The XP cost of purchasing skills or talents you don't already have a rank in is increased by +200 XP.
3	Your trinary coalesces well, warts and all.	Stubborn	Double the XP cost of gaining or removing character traits.
4	You are kidnapped, and experimented on. While the process is unpleasant, your insides are downright Silken.	Test Subject	You may ignore the cost increase for Silk augmentations.
5	Another member of your trinary suffered a traumatic head injury.	Fuzzy Link	Reduce Personality by 1, but gain 1 rank of training in Discipline.
6	You suffered a traumatic head injury.	Slow Thoughts	Reduce Intelligence by 1, but gain 1 rank of training in Discipline.
7	You contracted a strange human disease, wreaking havoc on your nervous system. It doesn't seem to be infectious…yet.	Sickly	Reduce an attribute of your choice by 1 rank.
8	The rest of your trinary is killed by Ariadnans. You were accepted into a new one, but you'll always bear the scars of the old.	Vengeful	Reduce Personality by 1, but gain 1 rank each in Close Combat and Survival.
9	You have a violent reaction to some human chemicals; it seems like you're allergic to everything.	Allergies	Resistance tests for substances are one difficulty higher.
10	Your trinary tried some human drugs. While no one died, valuable lessons were learned this day.	Bad Reactions	Artificial stimulants inflict 1+2 [N] Vigour damage to you, but otherwise work normally.
11	You fought alongside a legendary warlord.	Warlike	Increase your Vigour and Resolve by 1.
12	On a raid, your trinary manages to infect a human woman with the cuckoo virus. She's after blood and so is her family.	Deadly Enemies	Increase your resolve by 1.
13	You spend most of your formative years hunting; sneaking up on you is difficult.	Hair-Trigger	You gain +2d20 to surprise tests.
14	One of your parents showed up at the head of an Ariadnan Assault Pack	Traitor's Blood	Reduce your Resolve by 1.
15	You get your hands on some human technology. After a lot of trial and error, you think you've got it figured out. Mostly.	Dangerously Curious	Choose one category of modern gear (vehicles, firearms, etc.). You do not suffer increased difficulty when using items of that type.
16	Deep into human territory, you evaded patrols for months at a time.	Overconfident	Gain 1 rank in Stealth.
17	Your trinary cultivated a relationship with some typically dangerous wildlife.	Overly Trusting	Gain 1 rank in Animal Handling.
18	The humans never spotted you, but you weren't there to hunt. Just… to watch.	Easily Fascinated	Gain 1 rank in Psychology.
19	While out scouting, your pack was wiped out. Your trinary is all that remains.	Sole Survivors	Increase your Resolve by 3, and gain an Ariadnan enemy.
20	Your trinary link is violently severed. While in mind-shock, you're taken in by a group of humans who nurse you back to health, though their reasons are hardly benevolent.	Slave	You must take Assault Pack Member as your first career.

DOGFACE/WULVER ADOLESCENT EVENT TABLE			
D20	ADOLESCENT EVENT	SUGGESTED CHARACTER TRAIT	OPTIONAL EFFECT
1	Determined to show there's no correlation between the cuckoo virus and intelligence, a scientist takes you on as their intern.	Reckless Curiosity	Gain 1 rank in Science.
2	You contracted an alien disease, but suffered no consequences yourself. The same cannot be said for your peers.	Alien Typhoid	Gain Special Ability: Inured to Disease.
3	You ran away, opting for frontier life.	Lone Wolf	Reduce your Earnings by 1.
4	You were killed in the prime of your youth, bravely defending Ariadna from galactic antagonists. At least, that's the official story – you're still very much alive. What happened? Why the ruse?	Non-Entity	Gain one level of Social Status, and a debt worth 5 Assets. You may change your faction to O-12 at this time.
5	You inadvertently destroyed a storefront.	Bull in a China Shop	Gain a debt worth 7 Assets.
6	The Loup-Garous are hunting you. What do they think you did? And did you?	Hunted	Reduce Social Status by 1.
7	Your transport wrecked, leaving you stranded on the frontier. If not for the timely intervention of a Forest Ranger, you surely would have died out there.	Snakebitten	Gain +1 rank in Survival, and you may choose Forest Ranger as your first career.
8	Your first Dog Nation rally ended in a riot, and with you spending the night in jail. Did you do what they said you did? And did you ever go back?	Rabble-Rouser	Gain a debt worth 1 Asset, and you may choose Dog Nation Activist as your first career.
9	You spent your summer working at a career fair for young Ariadnans. You got along better than anyone anticipated.	Backroom Politicker	During Decision Eight, you may hazard one career from the *Ariadna Faction Career Table* at –1 difficulty.
10	You didn't do it. But you saw who did. What did you wind up doing time for? And what became of the true culprit?	The Usual Suspect	Spend 1d6 years in jail before starting your first career. Gain a Criminal Record (*Infinity Corebook*, p. 52).
11	You killed someone. How did it happen, and why did you do it? And what caused you to be set free?	Cold-Blooded Killer	Spend 2d6 years in jail before starting your first career. Gain a Criminal Record (*Infinity Corebook*, p. 52). You can switch to the Submondo faction at this time.
12	You went to space. It was… breathtaking.	Restless	Gain 1 rank in Extraplanetary.
13	Even with the massive time handicap, you still won the Mat' Triathlon.	Relentless	Gain 1 rank in Athletics.
14	An Antipode appeared outside your window one night. Before he was gunned down, you knew: he was your "father", in a sense. Trying to kill you was his last action.	Between Two Worlds	Reduce your Resolve by 1.
15	You were a local Dog-Bowl legend and there was talk about going pro. Did you? Or did something happen to keep you out?	Showboat	Gain 1 rank in Acrobatics, and you may choose Dog-Bowl Player as your first career.
16	Your jaw grows in a little too well. You don't look any more fearsome, but your speech is sometimes hard to understand.	Monstrous	Increase the difficulty of all Personality-based tests that are not based on intimidation by 1.
17	You experimented with some new drugs; this was an objectively terrible idea. The damage was permanent, but at least you made some new friends.	Burnout	Reduce Intelligence by 1. You may choose Volk as your first career.
18	Fed up with life, society, and Ariadna itself, you walked into the Antipodean Wilds. Why? And how did you survive?	Savage	Gain 1 rank in Survival.
19	During an Antipode attack, instead of protecting you, the local militia gunned you down without warning. You – and everyone else – assumed that you were dead. Instead, you woke up in a strange place. It was then that your family came clean.	Turncoat	You defect to a new faction. Roll on the *Faction Table* (*InfinityCorebook*, p. 41) to determine your new allegiance. You may roll on your new faction's career table for your first career at no cost.
20	You should have died; but you didn't. Dog-Blooded usually have rotten luck. Maybe you're the exception. Maybe not.	Strange Luck	Gain +1 Infinity Point refresh (maximum 4).

DECISION EIGHT: CAREERS

When creating your character, you can choose to select the Scavenger career to gain 1 Life Point. (You can gain a maximum of 2 Life Points in this way. You do not gain the Life Point if you are forced to become a Scavenger by a random roll, event, or hazard test.)

Dogfaces and Wulvers roll on the *Dogface/Wulver Career Table*. If you roll a career you don't meet the prerequisites for, roll again until you generate a result you can use. Unlike hazarding another faction's career, there's no good way for a Dogface to pass as a Wulver.

ANTIPODE CAREER TABLE

D20	CAREER
1–3	Scavenger
4–8	Antipode Warlord
9–12	Assault Pack Member
13–16	Forest Ranger
17–20	Raider

DOGFACE/WULVER CAREER TABLE

D20	CAREER
1–3	Scavenger
4–5	Assault Pack Leader[1]
6–7	Dog-Bowl Player
8–9	Dog Nation Activist
10–11	Forest Ranger
12–14	Dog-Blooded Irregular
15–16	Raider
17–18	Volk
19–20	Wulver Shock Troop[2]

[1] Career from *Infinity Corebook*, p. 59.

[2] Career has a prerequisite of being a Wulver; Dogfaces can't hazard this career. If you roll into this career, you automatically fail your defection check. You can override these limitations by spending 1 Life Point (in which case circumstances dictated you joining the unit while working the career).

Dogface and Wulver characters roll on the *Dog-Blooded Career Event Table*. Antipode characters face unique circumstances than the rest of the Human Sphere; they always roll on the *Antipode Career Event Table*.

DOG-BLOODED CAREER EVENT TABLE

D6	CAREER
1–3	Dogface/Wulver Career Event Table
4	Career Event Table A1
5	Career Event Table B1
6	Career Event Table C1

[1] *Infinity Corebook*, p. 56–58

ANTIPODE CAREER EVENT TABLE

D20	CAREER EVENT	GAME EFFECT
1	Your trinary link is violently severed. While in mind-shock, you're taken in by a group of humans who nurse you back to health, though their reasons are hardly benevolent.	tYou must take Assault Pack Member as your next career.
2	You are injured in an Ariadnan hunting accident. How did this happen? And what became of the hunter who shot you?	Roll a random body location. You have a gunshot wound there that has not healed well. Gain Trait: Old Wound.
3	You've been singled out as a problem by a group intent on solving you.	Gain Trait: Priority Target.
4	A Rodinan strike force deploys makeshift biological weapons at you. You survive, but it's difficult to think straight.	Reduce your Intelligence by 1 rank.
5	A USAriadnan strike force shells your den. You make it out alive, but your hearing is permanently damaged.	Increase the difficulty of all Observation tests based on hearing by +1.
6	A Merovingian strike force attacks with experimental tranquilisers. You survive, but you're still a little drowsy.	Gain Trait: Sleepy. Increase the difficulty of Surprise tests by +1.
7	A Caledonian strike force attacks and it's a bloody mess.	Gain Trait: Scarred.
8	You accidentally save a tourist from a horrible fate. Little did you know, they were Mayacasting at the time.	Gain Trait: Entirely Misunderstood.
9	You encounter another tribe's shaman, and something just clicks. Do you convert? And what article of faith spoke to you?	Gain a character trait describing your religion or spiritual experience.
10	Outside of your trinary, no one knows what you did. What did you do?	Gain Trait: Paranoid.
11	You encounter a Dogface in battle and they feel impossibly familiar.	Gain Trait: Vengeful Progeny.
12	You solved a puzzle that stumped your peers.	Gain the Analysis talent: Pattern Recognition, or another Analysis talent you meet the prerequisites for.
13	You survive a terrible accident, but you're not quite the same afterwards.	Reduce your Agility, Brawn, or Coordination by 1.
14	They say you can't teach an old dog new tricks but you learn one anyway.	Gain 1 rank of training in a skill you currently have no training in.
15	You survive a terrible accident… barely.	Reduce your Vigour by 2.
16	You easily survive a terrible accident and now you feel invincible.	Gain Trait: Overconfident.
17	You discover a human language that actually works for you.	Learn a new language of your choice.
18	After what you did, your pack could no longer stomach the sight of you.	You are Fired (*Infinity Corebook*, p. 54). Gain an appropriate trait.
19	After what happened, the rest of the pack thinks you're cursed; they might not be wrong.	Reduce your Infinity Point refresh rate by 1 (minimum 0).
20	It seems you're destined for greatness. What comes next may not be pleasant, but it will at least be interesting.	Roll again three times on the *Career Event Table* for this career phase. (When spending a Life Point to choose a specific event, you may not choose this result. If you roll duplicate events, it means some similar event has occurred. If you roll a 20 again, add additional rolls.

DOGFACE/WULVER CAREER EVENT TABLE

D20	CAREER EVENT	GAME EFFECT
1	Your work carries you to a different Ariadnan nation. Why did that go as well – or as poorly – as it did?	Choose a nation besides your own. Gain a character trait describing your relationship with them.
2	You and an off-worlder discover a shared interest, and bond immediately.	Gain an ally. Roll on the *Faction Table* (*Infinity Corebook*, p. 41) to determine their faction.
3	You catch your superior embezzling. You are fired the next morning.	You are Fired (*Infinity Corebook*, p. 54). Gain an appropriate character trait.
4	Some people have good luck. Others have bad luck. You, it seems, have luck.	Gain 1 Life Point, but increase your complication range by +1 on action scene skill tests.
5	Your co-workers routinely decide to dump their work on you. To their surprise, you handle it with ease.	Gain 1 rank of training in the elective skill you didn't select for this career.
6	Despite being cut-off for weeks, you endure whatever the storm throws at you.	Gain the Resistance talent Sturdy, or another Resistance talent you meet the prerequisites for.
7	Your whirlwind romance turns out to be part of a galactic spy's mission.	Gain a contact in another faction.
8	You save a tourist from a horrible fate. Little did you know, they were Mayacasting at the time.	Gain Trait: Unlikely Hero.
9	You encounter a galactic missionary, and something just clicks. Do you convert? And what article of faith spoke to you?	Gain a character trait describing your religion or spiritual experience.
10	A distant relative passes, bequeathing you their treasures – some of which are even interesting – and their debts.	Gain 10 doses of painkillers, 2 tiny pets, a USAriadnan Entrenching tool, Teseum worth 2 Assests, and debts worth 5 Assets.
11	Desperate to prove yourself, you turn to stimulants to help you keep the pace. It works – sort of – but the cost is real.	You can reduce the difficulty of hazarding your next career by 1. Also, choose a drug from the *Infinity Corebook* (p. 348) – you begin play at that drug's addiction threshold.
12	You come home one night, and your partner is gone, leaving no notice, and taking their belongings with them.	Gain a character trait describing your new situation, and what led to it.
13	You survive a terrible accident, but you can't get it out of your head.	Reduce your Resolve by 2.
14	They say you can't teach an old dog new tricks but you learn one anyway.	Gain 1 rank of training in a skill you currently have no training in.
15	You survive a terrible accident... barely.	Reduce your Vigour by 2.
16	You are fired. What did you do?	You are Fired (*Infinity Corebook*, p. 54).
17	You discover a language that's far easier to speak.	Learn a new language of your choice.
18	You are fired for no apparent reason and local news coverage is surprisingly sympathetic.	You are Fired (*Infinity Corebook*, p. 54). Gain an appropriate character trait, and you may reduce the difficulty of hazarding your next career by 1.
19	You survive a terrible accident, but you're not quite the same afterwards.	Reduce three attributes of your choice by 1 each.
20	You've got the Devil's Own Luck. Interesting times ahead.	Roll again three times on the Career Event Tables for this career phase. (When spending a Life Point to choose a specific event, you may not choose this result. If you roll duplicate events, it means some similar event has occurred. If you roll the Devil's Own Luck again, add additional rolls.

CAREER PROFILE

SCAVENGER

Finding employment can be difficult for anyone. But when you're a hulking mass of muscle, hated and feared by most of the population, it can be a waking nightmare. Demogrants don't apply to the Dog-Blooded. Most get by through a mix of hunting, foraging, and salvage. At least, when they're not fighting off the latest big shot drunk, evading hostile DNAriadnans, or slowly killing themselves with vodka and bitterness. For their part, Antipode trinaries cut off from their packs are no less dangerous for their desperation; like a racoon with Teseum-laced claws, they take what they can get, but getting in their way is unwise.

ATTRIBUTES

AGI	AWA	BRW	COO	INT	PER	WIL
+2	+2	+2	+1	+1	–	+2

SKILLS

Mandatory	Close Combat	Survival	–
Elective	Any 1 Other	Any 1 Other	–

EARNINGS: 0 + 2N (Max 0)

GEAR: None

CAREER PROFILE

ASSAULT PACK MEMBER

Slavery. There's really no other way to put it; at least, not at first. Biochemically shackled and leashed to the will of their would-be conquerors, to be an Assault Pack Member is to be an unwilling fist: a mind-controlled weapon, wielded as the master sees fit. And yet, once that initial breaking period is passed, the equation becomes much more complicated. For every tale of Assault Packs tearing their Controllers to shreds, there's another of an injured handler being dragged back to base by a lone, protective Antipode. For every enemy drugged and mind-controlled, there's an orphan cub who was taken in, now fighting to protect the only family they've ever known. But past the propaganda, an Assault Pack remains a living, breathing, act of violence upon free will… and anything else foolish enough to get in its way.

ATTRIBUTES

AGI	AWA	BRW	COO	INT	PER	WIL
+3	+2	+3	+2	–	–	–

SKILLS

Mandatory	Acrobatics	Close Combat	Observation
Elective	Animal Handling	Stealth	Survival

EARNINGS: 0 + 4N (Max 0)

GEAR: Antipode Control Cranial Implant, Teseum Claws

SPECIAL: This career is only open to Antipode characters.

CAREER PROFILE

ANTIPODE WARLORD

Long Shadow. Sharp Knife. Names that strike fear into anyone who knows them, and lives to tell the tale; which isn't many. To be an Antipode warlord is to face down a technologically superior interloper, and to stand your ground. To look at a changing world, and defiantly bellow, "No. You change." Often mistaken for chiefs or tribal elders, warlords often have little to do with decision-making; unless of course, those decisions take place on a battlefield. Warlords are chosen by a combination of consensus, combat prowess, and the most prized and rare trait among Antipode, the ability to stare down a growling, hungry pack of killers, and command them to follow you. Anyone who can pull that off, the reasoning goes, can face a human army without any trouble.

ATTRIBUTES

AGI	AWA	BRW	COO	INT	PER	WIL
+2	+2	+2	+1	–	+2	+1

SKILLS

Mandatory	Close Combat	Command	Stealth
Elective	Acrobatics	Animal Handling	Survival

EARNINGS: 0 + 2N

GEAR: Knife, Tactical Bow (with 2 AP Arrow Reloads), Wolfshot (×3)

SPECIAL: This career is only open to Antipode Characters.

CAREER PROFILE

DOG-BLOODED IRREGULARS

Most would be hard-pressed to call any unit incorporating Dog-Warriors and Wulvers "regular" as the presence of these preternaturally strong troops allows for atypical tactical options, even by the standards of irregular military units. From Caledonia's Cameronian Regiment – berserkers who injure themselves to enter the battle in Dog-Warrior form – to USAriadnan Devil Dogs Marines, to Rodina's catch-as-catch-can assignment of their primarily Kazak Dog-Warriors, tearing into the enemy with Teseum-laced claws, if you can fight, there's no shortage of opportunities in the Ariadnan armed forces. And whether the brass likes it or not, there's no denying that a blood fury is like unleashed hell on a battlefield. Regardless of their classification, Irregulars are trained to fight, defend their homes, and ultimately, kill their enemies. It's also important to avoid being killed themselves but those lessons come with time and experience. Or not.

ATTRIBUTES

AGI	AWA	BRW	COO	INT	PER	WIL
+2	+1	+2	+2	+1	+1	+1

SKILLS

Mandatory	Ballisctis	Close Combat	Resitance
Elective	Acrobatics	Athletics	Stealth

EARNINGS: 1 + 1N

GEAR: Chain Rifle (×2), Smoke Grenade (×2)

SPECIAL: This career is not available to Antipode characters.

CAREER PROFILE

DOG NATION ACTIVIST

"Equality or Death! This is the voice of the metisy! The voice that cannot be silenced! The shout that cannot be ignored! The roaring cry of the Dog Nation!" It's been years since John "Vanya" Rotten uttered those words; and while it seemed like things were getting better, many Dogfaces and Wulvers feel that it's been two steps forward, two steps back. The Dog Nation isn't in the business of waiting for the world to come around; its members want real change, and they're willing to take action to get it. If that means protests, rallies, and civil disobedience, so be it. And for some, if that means stepping outside the boundaries of the law, that's fine; they consider any damage they cause to be a drop in the bucket when compared to everything they've been through.

ATTRIBUTES

AGI	AWA	BRW	COO	INT	PER	WIL
+1	+1	+1	–	+1	+2	+3

SKILLS

Mandatory	Education	Persuade	Tech
Elective	Hacking	Stealth	Thievery

EARNINGS: 1 + 2N

GEAR: Digicloak (Urban), Fusebox, Rebreather, Recorder (×2)

SPECIAL: This career is not available to Antipode characters.

DOG-WARRIOR REGIMENTS

While they may seem alike to an outside observer – indistinguishable masses of tooth, fur, and violence – there are several key differences between different Dog-Warrior regiments. When working the Dog-Blooded Irregulars career, you may select your regiment from the list below, and use its elective skills and gear in place of the standard.

REGIMENT	ELECTIVE SKILLS	GEAR
Cameronian	Athletics, Close Combat, Resistance	Chain Rifle, Claymore, Grenade, Smoke Grenade
Kazak Dog-Warrior	Acrobatics, Discipline, Stealth	Chain Rifle (×2), Smoke Grenade (×3), Teseum Claws
Devil Dogs Marines	Animal Handling, Resistance, Stealth	Boarding Shotgun, Custom-Tailored Medium Combat Armour, Smoke Grenades (×2) (With the GM's permission, upon taking the Devil Dog career, you may purchase Antipode NPCs for 2 Life Points apiece (p. XX).)

CAREER PROFILE

DOG-BOWL PLAYER

In a world of mistrust, fear, and outright hatred, it's nice to be cheered. It's even better to be cheered while the same qualities that mark them an outcast, propel them to indescribable feats of athleticism. In the streets, the risk of a blood fury causes police to profile them, and parents to hide their children; but in the game, that same fury carries them to glorious victory, amidst thunderous applause. To be a Dog-Bowl player is to live in a pocket of adoration amidst a sea of trouble and the salary's nice. Unfortunately, athletic careers tend not to last all that long. Injury, scandal, the real or perceived effects of aging: any and all of these factors can cause the whole thing to come crashing down. But while it lasts, there's nothing quite like it.

ATTRIBUTES

AGI	AWA	BRW	COO	INT	PER	WIL
+2	–	+3	+1	–	+2	+1

SKILLS

Mandatory	Acrobatics	Athletics	Close Combat
Elective	Acrobatics	Animal Handling	Survival

EARNINGS: 1 + 5N

GEAR: Cod (×3), Dog-Bowl Armour, Recorder

SPECIAL: This career is not available to Antipode characters.

CAREER PROFILE

FOREST RANGER

One of the few career paths that actively recruits Dogfaces and Wulvers, Forest Rangers – or simply "Wardens" in Caledonia – fill a unique niche in Ariadnan society. Even in the Antipodean Wilds, having a lone trinary keep tabs on the territory isn't an uncommon occurrence. Less focused on conservational efforts or cracking down on poachers, Rangers cover wide stretches of wild territory, mapping, cataloguing, and marking changes in the natural ecosystem. Maintaining roads, outposts, and waystations is a constant task and given the large distances between many Ariadnan cities, they also provide guidance, support, and the occasional rescue to travellers. While not soldiers per se, the Wilds are far from safe, so while some Rangers certainly know how to fight, every Ranger learns how to avoid one.

ATTRIBUTES

AGI	AWA	BRW	COO	INT	PER	WIL
+1	+3	+2	+1	+1	–	+1

SKILLS

Mandatory	Medicine	Stealth	Survival
Elective	Animal Handling	Atheletics	Survival

EARNINGS: 1 + 3N

GEAR: Knife, Nav Suite (Forest), Survival Kit (Forest), Tracking Collar, USAriadnan Entrenching Tool, Custom 1

SPECIAL: Antipode characters do not acquire the Nav Suite, Survival Kit, or Tracking Collar.

CAREER PROFILE

RAIDER

From the Dogface desperados of the USAriadnan frontier, to pirates harrying remote *stanitsas,* to the Antipode raiding groups that provide a constant source of terror to frontier folk, Raiders all have one thing in common; they take what they want, using lethal force if necessary. Or sometimes, just if they're bored enough. Between the threats of Antipodes, wild animals, attacks by galactics, and the planet itself, there's no shortage of opportunities for raiding in Ariadna. Unlike Submondo, who generally have an organisational structure, Raiders are wildcards in the truest sense: accountable to nobody but themselves, and one step ahead of what passes for law on the frontier. It is a life that few choose outright, but one that many find themselves particularly well-suited to.

ATTRIBUTES

AGI	AWA	BRW	COO	INT	PER	WIL
+1	+1	+3	+2	–	+1	+1

SKILLS

Mandatory	Ballistics	Close Combat	Thievery
Elective	Pilot	Survival	Stealth

EARNINGS

0 + 4Ⓝ

GEAR: Surge (×1), Teseum Chopper

SPECIAL: Criminal career.

CAREER PROFILE

VOLK

"Pay up, or I throw you to the wolves." Whoever first had the idea is lost to time, but where most Ariadnans saw a problem, the Bratva saw an opportunity. Many Dogfaces are societal cast-offs, who can also casually destroy a motorcycle with their bare hands. The gangsters sensed an opportunity, and began recruiting Dogfaces as cheap muscle. Nowadays, the term "Volk" (from the Russian волк, meaning wolf), is used to describe any Dogface (or these days, Wulver) involved in Submondo activity. While not all Volks wear tracksuits and speak in mangled clichés, popular Ariadnan fiction suggests otherwise, and more than one Volk has simply steered into the stereotype, rather than constantly explain themselves. While it's hardly upright work, many find it honest in its way. Regardless of their feelings on the matter, there's no denying that they make excellent muscle.

ATTRIBUTES

AGI	AWA	BRW	COO	INT	PER	WIL
+2	+1	+3	+1	–	+1	+1

SKILLS

Mandatory	Athletics	Close Combat	Stealth
Elective	Animal Handling	Close Combat	Thievery

EARNINGS

3 + 1Ⓝ

GEAR: Cod (×2), D.E.P., Nitrocaine (×1), Painkillers (×2), Sports Padding (Chest)

SPECIAL: Criminal career; not available to Antipode characters.

CAREER PROFILE

WULVER SHOCK TROOP

"*Airaghardt!*" (Go Forth!) – the Gaelic motto of the Caledonian 9th Wulver Grenadiers Regiment – sums up the mentality of most Wulver strike teams: they hit hard, they hit fast, and if at all possible, they hit first. While studies have been inconclusive as to whether or not Wulvers are any more or less intelligent than their Dogface cousins, there's no denying they have a much easier time communicating, leading some mixed-troop units to rely on them as commanders and field medics. Ariadnan militaries are still learning how best to use their Dogfaces and so how to effectively utilise Wulvers' unique contributions is very much a work-in-progress. Until then, Wulver soldiers can usually be found in the thick of things, riding the blood fury to victory or death... or far too often, both.

ATTRIBUTES

AGI	AWA	BRW	COO	INT	PER	WIL
+2	+1	+2	+2	+2	+1	–

SKILLS

Mandatory	Athletics	Ballistics	Close Combat
Elective	Acrobatics	Command	Medicine

EARNINGS

1 + 3Ⓝ

GEAR: Grenades (1 Explosive, 1 Shock, 1 Smoke), Light Combat Armour, T2 Boarding Shotgun

SPECIAL: This career is not available to Antipode and Dogface characters..

DOGFACE/WULVER YOUTH EVENT TABLE							
D20	**EVENT TYPE**	**1**	**2**	**3**	**4**	**5**	**6**
1–2	Survived	an Antipode assault	a wild animal attack	getting stranded	a natural disaster	a border skirmish	severe drought/ famine
3–4	Survived	kidnapping	sabotage	violent riots	an accident	a shooting	a Submondo raid
5–6	Witnessed	perjury	a murder	an assassination	political corruption	a violent crime	long-term abuse
7–8	Witnessed	betrayal	bigotry	an Antipode attack	hypocrisy	selfless bravery	heroic sacrifice
9–10	Involved in	a cover-up	smuggling	amateur Dog-Bowl	Dog Nation protests	charity work	gang activity
11–12	Discovered	religion	scientific curiosity	artistic talent	sexual attraction	a dead body	archaeological ruins
13	Family Change	parent (re)marries	parent(s) disappear	parent(s) killed	parent walks out	parent(s) incarcerated	parent(s) sent to front
14	Family Change	Wulver sibling born	Dogface sibling born	adopted sibling	1+8Ⓝ new siblings	Divorce	Moved to new nation
15	Succumbed to	galactic propaganda	toxic nationalism	despair	mental illness	peer pressure	loneliness
16	Social Contacts	made a friend in opposite social class	gained mentor (roll on *Ariadna Homeland Table*)	gained contact (roll on *Ariadna Homeland Table*)	gained galactic contact (roll on *Faction Table*)	gained Submondo contact	gained Mercenary contact
17	Entrusted With	an heirloom	a commendation	a task	a legacy	a secret	a Cube
18	Special	gained a 1 Asset debt	gained 1 Asset	gained a Cube – no strings	gained a Cube – strings	gained a 3Ⓝ Asset debt	gained a 5Ⓝ Asset debt
19	Special	learned a galactic language	learned an Ariadnan language	gained blackmail on another faction	gained blackmail on Ariadnans	debilitating condition	Vigour poison 1+5Ⓝ
20	Reroll Twice and Combine Results						

DECISION SEVEN: ADOLESCENT EVENT

Every Ariadnan undertakes a coming-of-age story, but for Dogfaces and Wulvers, these can become epic tales of survival, heroism, triumph, and despair. In other words, quintessentially Ariadnan. For Antipodes, the transition from youth to adolescence is to truly develop a sense of self, awakening to a deeper realisation of reality. As their trinary begins to coalesce into a fully-formed identity, and where the group begins, and the individual ends becomes the dominant question in this formative period.

Dogface and Wulver characters roll on the *Dog-Blooded Adolescent Event Table*. Antipode characters face unique circumstances than the rest of the Human Sphere so they always roll on the *Antipode Adolescent Event Table*.

ANTIPODE EDUCATION TABLE		
D20	**EDUCATION**	**EXAMPLE**
1–6	Scout Training	Forager, forward scout, hunter, scavenger
7–12	Warrior Training	Big game hunter, raider, warlord underling
13–18	Spiritual Training	Blood Tree Speaker, Gentle Embrace Shaman
19–20	Born Wild	Animalistic upbringing, pack hunter

ANTIPODE EDUCATION BENEFITS—MANDATORY				
EDUCATION	**+2**	**+1**	**–1**	**MANDATORY SKILLS**
Scout	Awareness	Agility	Personality	Analysis, Athletics, Observation, Stealth, Survival
Warrior	Brawn	Agility	Intelligence	Acrobatics, Athletics, Ballistics, Close Combat, Resistance
Spiritual	Willpower	Personality	Coordination	Animal Handling, Close Combat, Command, Psychology, Persuade
Born Wild	Agility	Brawn	Personality	Athletics, Observation, Survival

EDUCATION BENEFITS—SKILLS AND GEAR		
EDUCATION	**ELECTIVE SKILLS (PICK 2)**	**GEAR GAINED**
Scout	Acrobatics, Ballistics, Stealth	Observation: Sharp Senses
Warrior	Close Combat, Observation, Stealth	Resistance: Sturdy
Spiritual	Analysis, Command, Survival	Psychology: Counsellor
Born Wild	Stealth, Survival, Thievery	Special: Gain 1 Life Point

CHAPTER 7

ADVERSARIES

Like Human Edge, *Dawn* is a harsh frontier that is still untamed to a large degree. The various factions that comprise Ariadna have carved out their own domains, but remain ever respectful of the challenging conditions and vibrant life that they share their space with. Though they contend with vicious Antipodes, ferocious bears, gigantic deer, and the unforgiving elements, most Ariadnans would not have it any other way, for these foes and challenges make them who they are and provide a bond of comradery that transcends the fractious divides that so often simmer between their cultures. "You haven't lived until you've stalked a Macrofeidh across the tundra during a blizzard", is a popular retort from Ariadnans to their off-world cousins when discussing pursuits beyond *Dawn's* atmosphere.

Separated into animals, hybrids, and humans, the following adversaries include a number of native beasts and human inhabitants that can be encountered across *Dawn's* frontier.

BEASTS

Many and varied are the types and subtypes of animal that inhabit the wilds of *Dawn*, in proportions both numerical and physical that have not been seen for millennium on Earth. Two of the undisputed giants of the wild, however, cause even the Antipodes to tread carefully.

ELITE

ANTIPODE WARRIOR

The original inhabitants of Dawn, the Antipodes are a fierce race of pack hunting predators who would have come to dominate their planet if not for the unexpected arrival, or invasion as they see it, of mankind. Their warriors are led by war chiefs (see *Infinity Corebook* p. 152) although some are enslaved and controlled by human Assault Pack Leaders (p. 96).

ATTRIBUTES						
AGI	AWA	BRW	COO	INT	PER	WIL
11 (+2)	7	10 (+1)	9	6	5	8

FIELDS OF EXPERTISE								
Combat	+2	1	Movement	+1	1	Social	–	–
Fortitude	+1	1	Senses	+1	1	Technical	–	–

DEFENCES					
Firewall	6	Resolve	8	Vigour	11
Security	–	Morale	–	Armour	–

ATTACKS

- **Antipode War Bow**: Range C/M, 1+5 damage, Burst 1, 2H, Biotech, Subtle 2, Toxic 2, Vicious 3
- **Poison-Coated Knife**: Melee, 1+5 damage, Biotech, 1H, Concealed 1, Non-Hackable, Subtle 2, Thrown, Toxic 2, Unforgiving 1, Vicious 1

SPECIAL ABILITIES

- **Common Special Abilities**: Fear 1, Keen Senses (Smell)
- **Clever Hunters**: When in tall grass or forested terrain the Antipode can spend 1 Heat for +2 difficulty to tests to detect them.
- **Feral Roar (2 Heat)**: As a Minor Action, an Antipode Warrior's Feral Roar is a mental attack that targets all enemies within Close range and inflicts 1+2 (Stun, Unsubtle) mental damage.
- **Super-Jump**: Antipode Warriors treat any distance fallen as one zone shorter when calculating damage. Additionally, they can also vault over obstacles up to their own height without penalty and reduce the difficulty of skill tests to move through difficult terrain by one step.
- **Trinary**: The three Antipodes forming a trinary individual can each roll 2d20 when assisting each other (instead of the normal 1d20). Antipodes who are not members of a trinary, however, suffer a +1 difficulty to all tests. If a member of a trinary is killed or removed from their trinary, the remaining members enter mind-shock, suffering an additional +1 difficulty to all tests until they can succeed on a Discipline (D4) test. The difficuty of this test is reduced by one step per minute to a minimum of D1.

ELITE

ARIADNAN BROWN BEAR

Given some of the strange, alien creatures discovered on the planet Dawn, settlers could be forgiven for seeking some normality. So when *Ursus Ariadna* was first encountered, the Rodinan explorers who found it experienced a complex mix of emotions. The thrill of discovery. Relief at something normal-seeming. And raw terror, because, as it turns out, bears are still terrifying.

Colloquially known as the Ariadnan Brown Bear, despite being more of a dull, grayish green colour, the first settlers viewed the creature as something of a calming, normalising presence in the wilds of Ariadna. Even light years from Earth, a "bear is still just a bear" (as the popular saying goes on Dawn)... even if it really looks more like a bipedal buffalo when you get right down to it.

And when you understand how that could be comforting, you're on your way to understanding Ariadna.

ATTRIBUTES						
AGI	AWA	BRW	COO	INT	PER	WIL
9	11	15	5	5	10	8

FIELDS OF EXPERTISE								
Combat	+1	1	Movement	+1	1	Social	+1	+1
Fortitude	+1	1	Senses	+2	2	Technical	–	–

DEFENCES					
Firewall	N/A	Resolve	8	Vigour	15
Security	N/A	Morale	–	Armour	2

ATTACKS

- **Claws**: Melee, 2+7 damage, Piercing 1, Vicious 1

SPECIAL ABILITIES

- **Common Special Abilities**: Grasping, Keen Senses (Smell)
- **Force of Nature**: Don't poke the bear. Each point of Momentum or Heat spent to gain additional dice for close combat attacks or Resistance tests provides two dice instead of one. (The normal maximum of three bonus d20s still applies.)
- **Natural Armour**: The Bear's thick hide provides an Armour Soak of 2.
- **Sometimes the Bear Eats You**: When the Bear makes a melee attack on a grabbed target, it can reroll up to 7.

TROOPER/ELITE

ARIADNAN RAPTOR

The Ariadnan Raptor combines avian and reptilian traits. It can glide for long distances before swooping down on its prey, the Ariadnan Raptor is an incredibly graceful predator, right up to the moment where it becomes mercilessly savage.

Unlike many predatory venoms which cause paralysis, an Ariadnan Raptor's sting seems primarily designed to cause anaphylactic shock. Lashing with its tail-like stinger when its talons dig into a target, the Raptor proceeds to begin its meal while its victim is still alive, often tearing chunks out of much larger creatures.

ATTRIBUTES						
AGI	AWA	BRW	COO	INT	PER	WIL
12	10	8	11	7	4	8

FIELDS OF EXPERTISE								
Combat	+2	2	Movement	+1	1	Social	+3	–
Fortitude	+1	–	Senses	–	–	Technical	–	–

DEFENCES (TROOPER)					
Firewall	N/A	Resolve	4	Vigour	4
Security	N/A	Morale	–	Armour	–

DEFENCES (ELITE)					
Firewall	N/A	Resolve	8	Vigour	8
Security	N/A	Morale	–	Armour	–

ATTACKS

- **Claws**: Melee, 1+5 N damage, Biotech, Toxic 2, Vicious 2

SPECIAL ABILITIES

- **Common Special Abilities**: Grasping, Keen Senses (Smell)
- **Swoop (Elite – 2 Heat)**: After diving from the air and successfully performing a melee attack, an Elite Ariadnan Raptor can spend 2 Heat to immediately perform a second Minor movement action in the same turn (allowing them to swoop back up into the air).

ELITE

MACROFEIDH

The *Megaloceros Ariadniensis* – affectionately termed Macrofeidh by the Caledonians – is often called the king of the tundra. These gigantic deer stand two-and-a-half metres to the shoulder, with both the adult females and males sporting iron-hard antlers that can savage several foes in one sweep. The deep forests of *Dawn* harbour smaller specimens of deer, but the Macrofeidh choose to wander the tundra with majestic dignity. Other than Antipode hunting packs, they have few natural predators

ATTRIBUTES						
AGI	AWA	BRW	COO	INT	PER	WIL
9 (+1)	10	14 (+1)	9	3	8	19

FIELDS OF EXPERTISE								
Combat	+2	1	Movement	+2	1	Social	+1	–
Fortitude	+1	1	Senses	+2	1	Technical	–	–

DEFENCES					
Firewall	N/A	Resolve	10	Vigour	15
Security	N/A	Morale	2	Armour	2

ATTACKS

- **Antler Rend**: Melee, 2+8 N damage, Extended Reach, Knockdown, Parry 1, Piercing 1, Unforgiving 1
- **Hoof Lash**: Melee, 2+7 N damage, Knockdown, Stun

SPECIAL ABILITIES

- **Common Special Abilities**: Fear 1, Keen Senses (Hearing, Smell), Monstrous, Superhuman Agility 1, Superhuman Brawn 1
- **Passive Aggressive**: For herbivores, the Macrofeidh can be brutally aggressive. Each point of Momentum or Heat spent to gain additional dice for close combat attacks provides two dice, instead of one. (The normal maximum of three bonus d20s still applies.)
- **Tundra King**: Macrofeidh are majestic creatures that aren't easily intimidated. They possess a Morale and Armour Soak of 2. Additionally, when making or being subjected to a Psywar attack, Macrofeidh can reroll one d20, but must accept the new result.
- **Unstoppable Stampede**: A stampeding herd of Macrofeidh can cause terrible damage. If three or more Macrofeidh form a fireteam and take a movement action, their attacks gain the Indiscriminate (Close) quality.

ELITE

TARTARIAN BEAR

Despite its name, this massive bear can also be found in Rodina, the forests of Merovingia, and northern USAriadna, but the biggest and most aggressive by far are the Tartarian steppe-dwellers. Similar in features and colouration to Earth's Kodiak bear, these bears can grow to a height of two metres tall at the shoulder when standing on all fours, or four metres when standing on hind legs. Unfortunately, a short fuse and temper that far outweighs their physical size makes them a threat to any non-bear

ATTRIBUTES						
AGI	AWA	BRW	COO	INT	PER	WIL
8	10	15 (+1)	7	5	8	10

FIELDS OF EXPERTISE								
Combat	+2	1	Movement	+1	1	Social	+1	–
Fortitude	+2	1	Senses	+2	1	Technical	–	–

DEFENCES					
Firewall	N/A	Resolve	10	Vigour	16
Security	N/A	Morale	2	Armour	2

ATTACKS

- **Bite**: Melee, 2+8 N damage, Piercing 1, Vicious 1
- **Claw**: Melee, 2+7 N damage, Knockdown, Vicious 1

SPECIAL ABILITIES

- **Common Special Abilities**: Grasping, Keen Senses (Smell), Monstrous, Superhuman Brawn 1
- **Flight, Not Fight**: Few can stand their ground in the face of an angered Tartarian Bear. When attempting an Intimidate Psywar action, each point of Momentum or Heat spent provides two dice, instead of one (the normal maximum of three bonus d20s still applies).
- **Force of Nature**: Seriously. Don't poke the bear. Each point of Momentum or Heat spent to gain additional d20s when making a close combat attack or Resistance test provides two dice, instead of one (the normal maximum of three bonus d20s still applies). Additionally, when making a melee attack on a grabbed target, a Tartarian Bear can reroll up to 7 N of damage.

HYBIRDS

Humanity has many legends of the ghosts and demons that stalk the wilds and prey upon the unwary. Thanks to the Antipode retrovirus, those tales are very occasionally given form. Some species are immune to the virus' effects, while any foetus infected will almost never reach full-term in those that aren't. Very rarely — perhaps 1 in 100,000 — an abomination will be born amongst the natural beasts of Dawn; a horror that even the Antipodes have learned to fear.

RETROVIRUS HYBRIDS

Most native species of Dawn are immune to the Antipode retrovirus, while the females of the remainder very rarely carry to full-term when infected. There are, however, always exceptions to the rule, though in this case they constitute an extreme rarity. The Bukavac and Drekavac are two examples of Dawn beasts twisted into horrifying monstrosities by the untamed fury of the retrovirus. These are the sorts of creatures that spawn ghostly legends to be swapped around the campfire at night. Everyone knows the folklore, though nobody truly believes the twisted fairy tale; nobody who hasn't seen the terrible beasts' work first-hand that is.

With their overall rarity in mind, GMs are encouraged to create their own rural legends that stalk the wilderness fuelled by the retrovirus. Almost all such creatures are super-sized variants of their base species, that then grow even bigger when enraged. Use the Transform and Retrovirus Hybrid special abilities as a guideline, but also consider the base creature's natural characteristics. For example, if the creature is renowned for its grace, consider including Superhuman Agility as standard or as part of the Transform ability. All manner of creatures can be considered thanks to the tender ministrations triggered in male Antipodes when encountering a pregnant female, which means that the base animal doesn't necessarily need to be the largest and fiercest predator on Dawn. A lightning-fast wolverine-type creature or whipping snake whose venom is caustic thanks to the retrovirus will make an equally terrifying and alien challenge to the group. Dawn is a vast, vicious frontier; the retrovirus can be used as a reminder of how wild and untamed it still is

ELITE

BUKAVAC

The fresh-water rivers and lakes of Dawn harbour and sustain many predators and their prey. The Antipodes prize the flesh of the docile, manatee-like Morj that inhabit the shallow waters of several lakes bordering the mountain ranges. Despite very infrequently leading to the Antipodes finding themselves on the menu when they return to feast later, they still let pregnant females slip away with a bite. An enlarged Morj, the Bukavac sports short hair and a fanged maw, but instantly becomes a hulking, terrifying mass of teeth, claws, elongated limbs, and relentless momentum when enraged...

ATTRIBUTES

AGI	AWA	BRW	COO	INT	PER	WIL
6	9	16 (+1)	9	3	10	10

FIELDS OF EXPERTISE

Combat	+2	1	Movement	+1	–	Social	+1	–
Fortitude	+2	2	Senses	+2	1	Technical	–	–

DEFENCES

Firewall	N/A	Resolve	10	Vigour	17
Security	N/A	Morale	2	Armour	3

ATTACKS

- **Bite**: Melee, 2+9N damage, Piercing 1, Vicious 2
- **Claw**: Melee, 2+8N damage, Knockdown, Vicious 1
- **Constriction**: Melee (only against a grabbed target), 2+9N damage, Piercing 3, Stun, Vicious 2

SPECIAL ABILITIES

- **Common Special Abilities**: Fear 1, Keen Senses (Smell), Inured to Cold, Menacing 2, Night Vision, Superhuman Brawn 1
- **Transform (1 Heat)**: Ill-tempered at the best of times, Bukavac aggression grows proportionally with its bulk when angered. At the cost of 1 Heat, a Bukavac can transform into a fearsome hybrid, which grants them the Retrovirus Hybrid abilities listed below, plus the Grasping and Monstrous qualities. Additionally, its Superhuman Brawn rating increases to 2 (which modifies base damage, amongst other benefits).
- **Armoured Might**: The tough, rubbery hide and terrible temperament of the Bukavac grant it a Morale Soak of 2 and Armour Soak of 3.
- **Born to Water**: Born to water, the Bukavac can travel on or below the water's surface at no penalty to movement actions. Additionally, it gains 1 Armour Soak in all locations when within Close range of the surface and when attacked by a creature on or above the surface. Attacks cannot affect a Bukavac submerged beyond Close range of the surface.
- **Primal Fury (Retrovirus Hybrid)**: A frenzied Bukavac can shatter bones and tear limbs. It can reroll up to 6N when making a close combat attack, but must accept the new results.
- **Primal Power (Retrovirus Hybrid)**: The frenzy drives the Bukavac to perform Herculean feats, granting 2 bonus Momentum on any Athletics test.
- **Primal Terror (Retrovirus Hybrid)**: When attempting an Intimidate Psywar action, each Momentum or Heat spent provides two dice, instead of one (+3d20 maximum still applies).

ELITE

DOG-BOWL PLAYER

The cheering crowds. The thrill of competition. Money, fame, and the adoration of people who wouldn't otherwise look them in the eye; is it any wonder that so many Dogfaces try to make it playing Dog-Bowl? The brutal matches can give even hardened soldiers pause, but to a Dogface it represents an opportunity to lose themselves in aggression, to cut loose unafraid; to hold nothing back.

Take two parts rugby, one part streetball, add violence to taste, and you've got the recipe for an intense and brutal sport. Fans cheer on as players clash in savage conflict, blurring the lines between sport and a full-on melee. One might ask why players embrace a sport where heading to the locker room with "only" a few slashes is considered an easy game, but the answer is simple: many have nowhere else to go. And most would do it for free.

ATTRIBUTES

AGI	AWA	BRW	COO	INT	PER	WIL
10 (+1)	9	14 (+1)	12	6	6	6

FIELDS OF EXPERTISE

Combat	+2	1	Movement	+3	–	Social	+1	–
Fortitude	+2	–	Senses	+2	1	Technical	–	–

DEFENCES

Firewall	6	Resolve	6	Vigour	14
Security	–	Morale	1	Armour	2

ATTACKS

- **Claws**: Melee, 2+6N damage, Subtle 1, Vicious 1

SPECIAL ABILITIES

- **Common Special Abilities**: Keen Senses (smell)
- **Transform**: Lurking inside every Dogface is a monster, waiting to break free. At the cost of 1 Heat, they can transform into their Dog-Warrior form, adding +2 to their Brawn, Agility, and Armour. They also unlock the "Dog-Warrior" abilities listed below. At the end of the scene, they return to normal, suffering the Fatigued condition.
- **Celebrity**: Dog-Bowl Players gain 2 bonus Momentum for social skills tests.
- **Hustle**: Those points aren't going to score themselves. The Dog-Bowl Player generates an additional 1 Momentum on Movement tests.
- **Common Abilities (Dog-Warrior)**: Fear 1, Superhuman Agility 1, Superhuman Brawn 1, Menacing 1, Monstrous
- **Snarling Beast (Dog-Warrior)**: All Personality-based tests not based on intimidation are made at +2 difficulty.
- **Super-Jump (Dog-Warrior)**: The Dog-Warrior can vault over obstacles up to their height without penalty. The difficulty of skill tests to move through difficult terrain are reduced by one.

ELITE

DOG-WARRIOR

An adult Dogface resembles a bulky, hairy human, but the difference is more than skin deep (*Infinity Corebook* see p. 153). Moments of extreme stress can trigger a dramatic and sudden physical transformation, adding considerable height, weight, and strength to the Dogface; as well as a primal, aggressive survival instinct. These Dog-Warriors – strongly resembling the werewolves of legend – were initiallyshunned by society, but the pragmatic Ariadnans quickly learned to appreciate their effectiveness in defending Dawn.

While the term "Dog-Warrior" technically refers to the altered physical state, the term has become a colloquial reference for any Dogface employed in a martial profession. Which, considering the paucity of non-violent career options for Dogfaces, is practically all of them.

ATTRIBUTES

AGI	AWA	BRW	COO	INT	PER	WIL
11 (+1)	9	13 (+1)	8	7	7	8

FIELDS OF EXPERTISE

Combat	+3	1	Movement	+2	–	Social	–	–
Fortitude	+2	–	Senses	+2	2	Technical	–	–

DEFENCES

Firewall	7	Resolve	8	Vigour	13
Security	–	Morale	1	Armour	2

ATTACKS

- **Chain Rifle**: Range C, 2+7 damage, Burst 1, 2H, Spread 1, Torrent, Vicious 1
- **Teseum Chopper**: Melee, 2+7 damage, Unbalanced, Non-Hackable, Piercing 4, Vicious 2
- **Claws**: Melee, 2+5 damage, Subtle 1, Vicious 1

GEAR: Light Combat Armour (Dogface-Compatible)

SPECIAL ABILITIES

- **Common Special Abilities**: Keen Senses (smell)
- **Transform**: Lurking inside every Dogface is a monster, waiting to break free. At the cost of 1 Heat, they can transform into their Dog-Warrior form, adding +2 to their Brawn, Agility, and Armour. They also unlock the "Dog-Warrior" abilities listed below. At the end of the scene, they return to normal, suffering the Fatigued condition.
- **Common Abilities (Dog-Warrior)**: Fear 1, Superhuman Agility 1, Superhuman Brawn 1, Menacing 1, Monstrous
- **Aggression (Dog-Warrior)**: Possessed of unmatched primal fury, the Dog-Warrior's attacks might not always connect, but they hurt like hell when they do. When making a Combat test, they can reroll up to 4 but must accept the new result.
- **Snarling Beast (Dog-Warrior)**: All Personality-based tests not based on intimidation are made at +2 difficulty.
- **Super-Jump (Dog-Warrior)**: The Dog-Warrior can vault over obstacles up to their height without penalty. The difficulty of skill tests to move through difficult terrain are reduced by one.

ELITE

DREKAVAC

As if Tartarian bears and Antipodes weren't enough to contend with, the latter will very infrequently spawn an abomination of the former that can stand toe-to-toe with several trinaries at once. Extremely aggressive, murderously territorial, and ever-hungry, these beasts are given a wide berth by their neighbours. Humans on *Dawn* had never encountered one of these abominations until the harsh winter that spawned the Third Antipode Offensive, which also caused the Drekavac to prowl eastwards in search of their favourite prey: the Antipodes themselves.

ATTRIBUTES

AGI	AWA	BRW	COO	INT	PER	WIL
7	10	16 (+1)	7	4	8	11

FIELDS OF EXPERTISE

Combat	+2	2	Movement	+1	1	Social	–	–
Fortitude	+2	1	Senses	+2	1	Technical	–	–

DEFENCES

Firewall	N/A	Resolve	11	Vigour	17
Security	N/A	Morale	2	Armour	3

ATTACKS

- **Bite**: Melee, 2+9 damage, Piercing 1, Vicious 2
- **Claw**: Melee, 2+8 damage, Knockdown, Spread 1, Vicious 1

SPECIAL ABILITIES

- **Common Special Abilities**: Fear 1, Keen Senses (Smell), Menacing 2, Monstrous, Superhuman Brawn 1
- **Transform (1 Heat)**: Violent and murderous at all times, an angered Drekavac is nigh unstoppable. At the cost of 1 Heat, a Drekavac can transform into their terrifying hybrid form, which grants them the Retrovirus Hybrid abilities listed below. Additionally, its Superhuman Brawn rating increases to 2 (which modifies base damage, amongst other benefits). Finally, the Drekavac now suffers a Wound following eight or more Vigour damage (instead of seven), gains the Knockdown quality on all of its attacks, and can spend 1 Momentum before attacking to add the Stun quality to its melee attacks for the current turn.
- **Armoured Might**: The tough hide and violent temperament of the Drekavac grant it a Morale Soak of 2 and Armour Soak of 3.
- **Primal Fury (Retrovirus Hybrid)**: A frenzied Drekavac can shatter bones and tear limbs. It can reroll up to 6 when making a close combat attack, but must accept the new results.
- **Primal Power (Retrovirus Hybrid)**: The frenzy drives the Drekavac to perform Herculean feats. It generates 2 bonus Momentum on any Athletics test.
- **Primal Terror (Retrovirus Hybrid)**: When attempting an Intimidate Psywar action, each point of Momentum or Heat spent provides two dice, instead of one (the normal maximum of three bonus d20s still applies).

ELITE

WULVER

Wulvers are the children of human and Dogface parents (see *Infinity Corebook*). Sterile and distrusted because of their notorious tempers, Wulvers are few in number and have struggled to find a place in Ariadnan society, with many ending up as muscle for local gangs and other disreputable organisations. Unlike Dogfaces, Wulvers cannot transform. However their natural form is much larger than an average human to begin with and covered with long, thick fur, lending themselves readily to nicknames like "wolf-man" and slurs like "lycan". Although statistically more intelligent than Dogfaces, their reputation is muddied because they cannot avoid being carried away by the blood fever inherited from their Antipodean forebears. The wild look, the furious cries, and the instinctive movement towards danger are the warning signs of a Wulver charge.

ATTRIBUTES

AGI	AWA	BRW	COO	INT	PER	WIL
8	8	14 (+1)	7	7	5	7

FIELDS OF EXPERTISE

Combat	+1	1	Movement	+1	–	Social	–	–
Fortitude	+1	1	Senses	+1	–	Technical	–	–

DEFENCES

Firewall	4	Resolve	4	Vigour	8
Security	–	Morale	–	Armour	2

ATTACKS

- **AP Rifle**: Range M, 1+5 damage, Burst 2, 2H, Piercing 2, Vicious 1
- **Claws**: Melee, 2+6 damage, Subtle 1, Vicious 1

GEAR: Ballistic Vest; no Cube

SPECIAL ABILITIES

- **Common Special Abilities**: Fast Recovery (Vigour 1), Fear 1, Keen Senses (Smell), Menacing 1, Monstrous, Superhuman Brawn 1
- **Blood Fever**: After suffering any Wound in combat, a Wulver must make a successful Discipline test with a difficulty equal to the number of Wounds they have suffered or succumb to the blood fever – an overwhelming bloodlust that urges them to destroy the source of thier pain and frustration even if it's to their own detriment. (This effect can also be triggered as a Metanoia Effect.) In this state they receive +4 Morale and +2 to the damage of melee attacks, but suffer a +2 difficulty to all Discipline tests and other tests requiring mental concentration. Exiting the Berserk mode requires a Standard Action and a successful discipline test with a difficulty equal to the number of Wounds they have suffered (minimum 1).
- **Wulver Charge**: When suffering from the Blood Fever, Wulvers can move up to two combat zones and make a melee attack as a Standard Action.

HUMANS

Despite their varied ancestry and fractious natures, Ariadnans all share some common traits borne from their hardships and sense of planetary patriotism. It takes all manner of people to ensure that communities endure, and special types of character to respond to anything that threatens them.

ELITE

ANTIPODE POACHER

Most people fear, misunderstand, and loathe the Antipodes. The odd few, however, understand them all too well, but only in a cold, calculating way that evaluates each member of the species as a potential source of income. These remorseless hunters make their living through hunting Antipodes illegally, as their furs and organs are highly valuable on the black market—both at home and off-planet. The more unscrupulous poachers join or lead tourist expeditions into the wilderness and entice Antipode attacks so as to gather skins under the guise of defending themselves against the savage beasts.

ATTRIBUTES						
AGI	AWA	BRW	COO	INT	PER	WIL
9	10	10	9	8	7	10

FIELDS OF EXPERTISE								
Combat	+2	2	Movement	+1	–	Social	+1	–
Fortitude	+1	1	Senses	+2	1	Technical	+2	–

DEFENCES					
Firewall	8	Resolve	10	Vigor	17
Security	–	Morale	1	Armour	2

ATTACKS

- **Axe**: Melee, 1+7 N damage, Unbalanced, Non-Hackable, Thrown, Vicious 1
- **Heavy Pistol**: Range R/C, 2+6 N damage, Burst 1, Unbalanced, Unforgiving 1, Vicious 1
- **Light Shotgun**: Range C, 1+6 N damage, Burst 1, Unbalanced, Knockdown

GEAR: Light Combat Armour, Survival Rations

SPECIAL ABILITIES

- **Antipode Anatomist**: Experts in hunting their particular quarry, they gain +2 N to all damage rolls against Antipodes.
- **Performing a Service**: Most poachers believe they're not only supplying demand, but also performing an Antipode eradication service. Their arguments can be enticingly believable. They can reroll one d20 when making a Persuade test, but must accept the new result, and gain 1 bonus Momentum if successful.

ELITE

ASSAULT PACK LEADER

Given the taks of organising and leading an Antipode pack in the field, the Assault Pack Leader has a job few soldiers envy. They must train for months in gruelling environments among captured or captivity-bred Antipodes. Each pack is made up of an Antipodes trinary which has been biochemically altered to be receptive to the Leader's commands and surgically altered to respond to an Antipode Control Device (see *Infinity Corebook* p. 361). Packs can sniff out enemies or traps with uncanny accuracy, and their speed, stealth, and brutality serve as a disruptive spearhead when thrust directly into enemy lines.

ATTRIBUTES						
AGI	AWA	BRW	COO	INT	PER	WIL
10	8	8	10	12	12	10

FIELDS OF EXPERTISE								
Combat	+1	1	Movement	+1	1	Social	+2	2
Fortitude	+1	1	Senses	+1	1	Technical	+1	1

DEFENCES					
Firewall	12	Resolve	10	Vigour	8
Security	–	Morale	1	Armour	2

ATTACKS

- **Light Grenade Launcher**: Range M, 2+4 N damage, Burst 1, Unbalanced, Munition, Speculative Fire + Grenade qualities
- **Marksman's Rifle**: Range L, 1+5 N damage, Burst 2, 2H, Unforgiving 1
- **Pistol**: Range R/C, 1+4 N damage, Vicious 1
- **Knife**: Melee, 1+3 N damage, 1H, Concealed 1, Non-Hackable, Subtle 2, Thrown, Unforgiving 1

GEAR: **Light Combat Armour, Antipode Control Device**

SPECIAL ABILITIES

- **Assault Pack**: With their control device, a Pack Leader can coordinate their pack with a single thought. The fireteam formed by their pack can include Elite Antipodes. Unlike other fireteams, the pack can perform Reactions and pays one Heat less than the normal cost for doing so.
- **Pack Leader**: Leaders and pack members draw strength from their packs. They and their pack members benefit from a +2 Morale Soak when leading a pack (included in their profile above).

NOTES

- Antipode Warriors fighting under the control of an Assault Pack Leader have a locational beacon implant. If the Pack Leader is no longer capable of controlling them, they will usually retreat.

ELITE

LOUP-GAROU

Even the most steadfast Dogface defender of the Dog Nation will agree that a rampaging ball of teeth and claws poses a problem for the average community, though the agreement is always accompanied with a sense of pride and satisfaction. Baton rounds, plastic bullets, and tear gas have proven completely ineffective against Dogfaces and Wulvers in the grip of a frenzy, which resulted in the need for an effective agency that could contend with their unrelenting rampages. Created as a joint task force to specifically contend with Dogfaces and Wulvers, the elite Loup-Garous are trained to prevent, contain, and neutralise any threat posed by their hybrid cousins—or sometimes even the Antipodes themselves. Despite being trained to find non-confrontational solutions before anything else, all-too often the only answer is to neutralise the aggressor with precision targeting.

ATTRIBUTES						
AGI	AWA	BRW	COO	INT	PER	WIL
9	8	9	9	9	9	10

FIELDS OF EXPERTISE								
Combat	+2	1	Movement	+1	1	Social	+2	–
Fortitude	+1	1	Senses	+1	1	Technical	+1	–

DEFENCES					
Firewall	9	Resolve	10	Vigour	9
Security	–	Morale	2	Armour	3

ATTACKS

- **Knife**: Melee, 1+4 N damage, 1H, Concealed 1, Non-Hackable, Subtle 2, Thrown, Unforgiving 1
- **Pistol**: Range R/C, 1+4 N damage, Burst 1, 1H, Vicious 1
- **Sniper Rifle**: Range L, 1+6 N damage, Burst 3, Unwieldy, Unforgiving 2

GEAR: Medium Combat Armour, Tactical Webbing, Adhesive Shell Reloads for Sniper Rifle (×3)

SPECIAL ABILITIES

- **Defuse**: Loup-Garou are trained to talk Dogfaces away from the brink, or take them down if they can't. They can reroll one d20 when making a Coax or Negotiate Psywar action, but must accept the new result. Additionally, when interacting in face-to-face Psywar tests with a Dogface or Wulver, each point of Momentum or Heat spent provides two dice, instead of one (the normal maximum of three bonus d20s still applies).
- **Detain**: A Loup-Garou will usually seek to detain a frenzied Dogface or Wulver before resorting to lethal measures. Nonlethal attacks made against a Dogface or Wulver benefit from 1 bonus Momentum.
- **Drop**: Sometimes, there is no choice other than to permanently put down a Dogface or Wulver. Loup-Garou gain +2 N to all damage rolls against Antipodes, Dogfaces, and Wulvers.

ELITE

IRMANDINHOS PROCURER

The Irmandinhos are known to be rough and ready. They are also the go-to outfit if you need to obtain something quickly, quietly, and – more often than not – illegally. Supply and demand is second nature to the Irmandinhos, which is arguably of higher priority than their military functions. An entire logistical web has been spun across the surface of Dawn and beyond, with most threads pulsing back and forward from Bienvenue Station. The procurers are the face of the network, the people you're likely to be directed to if you go seeking their services. Just check that your comlog and personal possessions are intact once they're finished with you.

ATTRIBUTES

AGI	AWA	BRW	COO	INT	PER	WIL
8	9	10	8	8	10	10

FIELDS OF EXPERTISE

Combat	+1	1	Movement	+1	1	Social	+2	1
Fortitude	+1	1	Senses	+2	–	Technical	+1	–

DEFENCES

Firewall	8	Resolve	10	Vigour	10
Security	–	Morale	1	Armour	2

ATTACKS

- **Knife**: Melee, 1+5Ⓝ damage, 1H, Concealed 1, Non-Hackable, Subtle 2, Thrown, Unforgiving 1
- **Boarding Shotgun**: Range C, 1+6Ⓝ damage, Burst 1, 2H, Knockdown, Medium MULTI (Normal/AP Shells)
  - *AP Shells*: Piercing 2
- **Pistol**: R/C, 1+5Ⓝ, Burst 1, 1H, Vicious 1

GEAR: Analysis Suite, Fake ID 3, Light Combat Armour, Negotiator's Suite

SPECIAL ABILITIES

- **Brotherhood Trained**: All Irmandinhos receive regular training from veterans of the Irmandade. They can reroll up to 2Ⓝ when making a ranged attack, but must accept the new results. Additionally, they reduce the penalty for firing at a range other than the weapon's optimal range by one, to a minimum of 0.
- **Cost of Procurement (1 Heat)**: Irmandinhos are skilled at inflating costs for their services. They can pay 1 Heat when making a face-to-face test as part of haggling for the provision of their goods. If the Irmandinhos succeeds at the test, the final cost of the goods is increased by 1 Asset.
- **Kinesics Expert**: Procurers are excellent at understanding their client's needs and limits through body language. When making an Analysis or Psychology test, they can reroll any dice that did not generate a success on the initial roll, but must accept the new results.

ELITE

USFIRST!

Most USAriadnans make no apologies for their separatist leanings. They believe USAriadna should become an independent nation and they demand explanations from all who do not share their view. To make matters worse, it's all too often their belief that violence is the only means to secure understanding and appreciation for their cause. Concentrated largely in the south of the country – and particularly in the impoverished city of Madison – these American supremacists tattoo their faces with the stars and stripes and advocate for USAriadna separating from Rodina via brutal war.

ATTRIBUTES

AGI	AWA	BRW	COO	INT	PER	WIL
8	7	9	8	8	8	9

FIELDS OF EXPERTISE

Combat	+1	1	Movement	+	–	Social	+1	–
Fortitude	+1	1	Senses	+1	–	Technical	+1	–

DEFENCES (TROOPER)

Firewall	4	Resolve	5	Vigour	5
Security	–	Morale	1	Armour	1

DEFENCES (TROOPER)

Firewall	7	Resolve	9	Vigour	9
Security	–	Morale	2	Armour	1

ATTACKS

- **Plasteel Pipe**: Melee, 1+5Ⓝ damage, Unbalanced, Improvised 1, Non-Hackable, Stun
- **Light Shotgun**: Range C, 1+4Ⓝ damage, Burst 1, Unbalanced, Knockdown
- **Pistol**: Range R/C, 1+5Ⓝ damage, Burst 1, 1H, Vicious 1

GEAR: Armoured Clothing

SPECIAL ABILITIES

- **Browbeater (Elite)**: The USFirst! use heated vitriol to cajole new members into their ranks. They gain 1 bonus Momentum to Intimidate Psywar actions.
- **Might Makes Right (1-3 Heat)**: Members of USFirst! are unyielding in their belief. They benefit from a Morale Soak of 2, but can also spend 1 Heat to improve their Morale Soak by 1, to a maximum of 3 Heat and 3 additional Morale Soak.
- **Perpetual Threat**: USAriadnans live on the front line of Antipode incursions, so most ensure they can defend themselves. Members of USFirst! can reroll 2Ⓝ when making a ranged attack, but must accept the new results.

TROOPER

112 EMERGENCY SERVICES

The 112 Emergency Service was established in Merovingia when it became clear that they needed a coordinated plan for rescue operations after the First Antipode Offensive. Since many Merovingian villages were often isolated and far apart, the government trained their rescue personnel in a wide array of emergency response methods. The average 112 Emergency Service member is able to provide emergency medical care, assist in putting out dangerous fires, and stand shoulder to shoulder with Ariadnan soldiers in defence of the public. The 112 Emergency Service model was so successful that the Ariadnan government decided to implement it across Dawn, and since its implementation there has been a noticeable decrease in loss of human life to accidents.

A member of the 112 Emergency Service will always put their life on the line to attempt to rescue or administer assistance to those in need, and will only withdraw if they feel the cause is completely lost or their actions would lead to more harm.

ATTRIBUTES

AGI	AWA	BRW	COO	INT	PER	WIL
8	9	9	7	8	7	8

FIELDS OF EXPERTISE

Combat	+1	–	Movement	+1	–	Social	–	–
Fortitude	+1	–	Senses	+1	–	Technical	+1	1

DEFENCES

Firewall	4	Resolve	4	Vigor	5
Security	–	Morale	2	Armour	1

ATTACKS

- **Teseum-Edged Breaching Axe**: Melee, 1+7Ⓝ damage, Unbalanced, Anti-Materiel 2, Non-Hackable, Piercing 2, Spread 1, Vicious 2
- **Light Shotgun**: Range C, 1+5Ⓝ damage, Burst 1, Unbalanced, Knockdown
- **Pistol**: Range R/C, 1+5Ⓝ damage, Vicious 1

GEAR: Armoured Clothing (Firefighter's Uniform), Basic Medical Supplies, Portable Rescue Supply Kit

SPECIAL ABILITIES

- **Courage Under Fire**: Members of the 112 Service rapidly learn to tune out the battle around them. They can reroll one d20 when making a Discipline test, but must accept the new result.
- **Emergency Responder**: 112 Service Members can reroll one d20 when making a Medicine test, but must accept the new result. Additionally, they do not suffer the normal penalty for using a MedIKit to perform a Treat action at range.

NOTABLE PERSONALITIES OF DAWN

BRIGADIER BRUANT

Brigadier Jacques Bruant, Sous-Officier des Métros, survivalist extraordinaire, spectre of the Commercial Conflicts, butcher of the Paradiso First Expeditionary Corps. A Merovingian with a penchant for getting things done by any means possible, he has become legendary amongst the Ariadnan military for all the wrong reasons; the very whisper of his presence is used to scare recruits and unsettle superiors alike.

Steeped in blood and gore from the very outset of his military career, Bruant has worked hard at his reputation for brutality and endurance. Towards the start of the Ariadnan Commercial Conflicts and mere days into his very first assignment, Bruant found himself cut off from his unit and chained to a corpse with Yu Jing forces closing in. Forced to dodge enemy patrols and furious Antipodes alike, he dragged himself and the body of Sergeant Lacomte clear of the fighting only to face suspicion and doubt over Lacomte's manner of death, as some were certain Bruant himself was responsible.

Since then, he has built a reputation as a man who bears deep, unrelenting grudges. A man who for whom anything is in the cards in the name of survival, whether it his own skin or those of his fellow countrymen on the line. It is perhaps this last fact that ensures he remains on active duty despite his questionable methods.

NEMESIS

JACQUES BRUANT

ATTRIBUTES

AGI	AWA	BRW	COO	INT	PER	WIL
10	10	12	10	8	9	11

FIELDS OF EXPERTISE

Combat	+3	3	Movement	+2	2	Social	+1	–
Fortitude	+2	2	Senses	+2	1	Technical	+1	1

DEFENCES

Firewall	9	Resolve	14	Vigour	14
Security	1	Morale	3	Armour	2

ATTACKS

- **Knife**: Melee, 1+5 damage, 1H, Concealed 1, Non-Hackable, Subtle 2, Thrown, Unforgiving 1
- **Pistol**: Range R/C, 1+6, damage Burst 1, 1H, Standard, Vicious 1
- **D-Charge**: Explosive Charge, 2+6 damage, 1H, Anti-Materiel 2, Comms, Disposable, Piercing 3, Spread 1, Unsubtle, Vicious 2
- **Molotok**: Range M, 1+7 damage, Burst 3, 2H, Spread 2, Unsubtle

GEAR: Digicloak, Light Combat Armour, Multispectral Visor 1, Survival Kit (Temperate)

SPECIAL ABILITIES

- **Common Special Rules**: Threatening 2
- **Blood and Brutality**: An experienced campaigner, Bruant has honed his military skills across many battlefields. He can reroll up to 3 when making a melee or ranged attack, or one d20 when making a Stealth test, but must accept the new results. Additionally, he reduces the penalty for firing at a range other than the weapon's optimal range by one step (to a minimum of zero). Further, each Momentum or Heat he spends to gain additional dice for a Close Combat test provides two dice, instead of one (+3d20 maximum still applies).
- **Penchant for the Unconscionable (2 Heat)**: Bruant has no qualms with taking extreme measures to complete his mission. He can spend 2 Heat to ignore any Psywar effect that would cause him to retreat. Additionally, he benefits from a Morale Soak of 3.
- **Wilderness Warrior**: From the tree-shattering cold of the Dawn's forest to the steaming jungles of Paradiso, Bruant has survived battles fought across many environments. He can reroll any dice that did not generate a success on the initial roll of a Resistance test, or one d20 when making a Discipline, Observation, or Survival test, but must accept the new results. Additionally, he gains 2 bonus Momentum and regains two additional Vigour when taking the Recover Action.

CANDY DOUBLE

Not considered Ariadnan by many an astronomical unit, Candace is nevertheless one of the Human Sphere's most notable celebrities, and she just so happens to be currently located on Dawn.

The titular star of the number one Mayaseries, "The Incredible Adventures of Candy Double", is a name known and loved by billions. Her smash hit sensaseries offers recordings of her audio, visual, emotional, and physical responses to anyone who can afford to purchase the implants that are able to translate the fees extrapolated from her Cube. And her investigations, triumphs, tragedies, loves, and losses offer more than enough emotional feedback capable of shaking up the dullest of days and hooking the average viewer. Lauded as a rich heiress double-crossed by a malicious stepfather who replaced her with a double. Her trials and travails have kept her one step ahead of Special Agent Terry Rowland, who not only pursues her relentlessly because of her fugitive status, but is also fiercely and tragically in love with her.

Following the recent tragic and sensational loss of her soulmate, Anthony, Candy's production team and inquisitive, perfectly formed nose have brought her to Dawn, where she has trodden a seemingly unrelated path that has bounced her from the Yu Jing-held island of Novîy Cimmeria to deep inside the Ariadnan Exclusion Zone. Living on the edge and preaching the motto "it is better to beg for-giveness than ask permission", both her production team and almost the entire Human Sphere await the findings of her sojourn into the mystery of the strange nanoclouds that drift across Dawn.

ELITE

CANDY DOUBLE

ATTRIBUTES						
AGI	AWA	BRW	COO	INT	PER	WIL
9	10	8	9	9	10	9

FIELDS OF EXPERTISE								
Combat	–	–	Movement	+1	–	Social	+3	2
Fortitude	+1	–	Senses	+2	1	Technical	+1	1

DEFENCES					
Firewall	9	Resolve	9	Vigour	8
Security	2	Morale	2	Armour	1

ATTACKS

- Nil

GEAR: Armoured Clothing, mini hover-remotes, cutting-edge sensarecorder augmentations

SPECIAL ABILITIES

- **Best Protection Ever (2 Heat)**: Candice often and loudly touts the fact that she has the best armour the Human Sphere can buy: fame and uninterrupted recording. Following a successful Persuade test made against someone seeking to cause her harm, she may immediately spend 2 Heat to inflict a Metanoia to reinforce her request to remain unharmed. This Metanoia is in addition to any inflicted as a result of her Persuade test.
- **Investigative Fugitive**: Equal parts detective, fugitive, and socialite, Candy is at home when making connections or avoiding trouble. She may reroll one d20 when making a Discipline or Lifestyle test, but must accept the new result. Additionally, any time she needs assistance from one of her broad range of contacts, she reduces the difficulty to find such a contact by two steps, to a minimum of Simple (D0). Further, she does not suffer an increase in difficulty for social tests made with someone of a social class other than her own. Finally, she benefits from a Morale Soak of 2.
- **Mythical Actor**: A large part of the success behind Candy's sensaseries flows from her ability to focus on minute details, tailor her emotions within milliseconds, and convince others that her response is real. She can reroll one d20 when making an Observation or Persuade test, or may reroll an entire face-to-face Observation test, but must accept the new result. Additionally, when attempting to deceive an opponent, she gains 2 bonus Momentum per Momentum spent, instead of 1 (+3d20 maximum still applies). Finally, she gains 2 bonus Momentum when making Persuade tests.
- **Skin-deep Augmentations**: Candy has been graced with the best sensarecording tech on offer, something which her benefactors wish to keep secure. She is always considered to be recording her surroundings. Additionally, she benefits from a Security Soak of 2.

THE UNKNOWN RANGER

The legend of the Unknown Ranger has been in existence since the dark days of the Separatist Wars. The myth is built around the tale of a Ranger officer who lost his entire command and was himself left for dead. Swearing eternal vengeance on his enemies, he requested release from active service so as to dedicate his existence to vanquishing those who decimated his unit and aiding any USAriadnan soldier in their direst hour of need.

Despite the years that separate that tumultuous time, the legend of the Unknown Ranger continually resurfaces thanks to sporadic sightings. The USAriadnans claim his is an immortal soul that will return to the lands of the living whenever the needs of their country or military are at their most urgent. Outsiders scoff at the myth and state the claim that he is a convenient and deniable asset to be wheeled out when the USAriadnans wish to divert the blame. Still images of the same figure hiding behind a blacked-out face drawn from different decades across several battlefields always silence these critics. With old photos and numerous accounts of his single-handed relief of the siege of Decatur, his slaying of Chief Ice Deadwood during the Second Antipode Offensive, or his solo defence of Deadwood towards the end of the Commercial Conflicts forever in circulation, no one can deny that there at least is some truth to the awe-inspiring legend of the Unknown Ranger.

There are a select few who know the truth of the Unknown Ranger, more information for which can be found on p. 7 of this book.

ELITE

THE UNKNOWN RANGER

ATTRIBUTES

AGI	AWA	BRW	COO	INT	PER	WIL
10	10	11	10	9	9	11

FIELDS OF EXPERTISE

Combat	+4	3	Movement	+2	2	Social	+1	–
Fortitude	+2	2	Senses	+2	1	Technical	+1	–

DEFENCES

Firewall	10	Resolve	13	Vigour	13
Security	–	Morale	3	Armour	5

ATTACKS

- **Knife**: Melee, 1+5 N, 1H, Concealed 1, Non-Hackable, Subtle 2, Thrown, Unforgiving 1
- **Teseum Shield**: Melee, Unbalanced, 2+6 N, Anti-Materiel 2, Full Defence 3, Non-Hackable, Knockdown, Vicious 2
  - *Full Defence*: Using the Close Combat skill, the weapon may be used to make Parry and Guard Response Actions against ranged attacks in addition to melee attacks. Further, it grants Armour Soak X against melee and ranged attacks, where X is the Full Defence rating.
- **Heavy Pistol**: Range R/C, 2+6 N, Burst 1, Unbalanced, Unforgiving 1, Vicious 1
- **Rifle**: Range M, 1+7 N, Burst 2, 2H, MULTI Light Mod, Vicious 1

GEAR: Light Combat Armour, Shield of the Unknown Ranger (Teseum shield), Digicloak, Survival Kit (GMs choice)

SPECIAL ABILITIES

- **Common Special Abilities**: Menacing 2
- **Ageless Doom**: The Unknown Ranger is a deathly spectre of renowned martial capability. He may reroll up to 2 N when making a melee or ranged attack, but must accept the new results. Further, he reduces the penalty for firing at a range other than a weapon's optimal range by one, to a minimum of 0. Finally, he reduces the Heat cost of Defence or Guard Reactions using the Close Combat skill by 1, to a minimum of 0.
- **Ghostly Legend**: The Unknown Ranger is renowned for making spectral appearances in the thick of battle, only to fade away just as quickly. He may reroll one d20 when making a Stealth or Thievery test, but must accept the new result. Additionally, any Momentum spent to add dice to his Stealth test adds two d20s, instead of one (+3d20 maximum still applies). Finally, he may substitute Stealth for Thievery when attempting to bypass physical security measures.
- **Spectre of Death**: The Unknown Ranger's reputation often precedes him. He may spend 1 Heat to gain the Fear 1 special ability for 1 round.
- **Ultimate Survivor**: The Unknown Ranger has survived the ravages of time and Dawn's deadliest environments. He may reroll one d20 when making a Discipline or Survival test, any dice that did not generate a success on the initial roll of a Resistance test, but must accept the new result. Further, when making a Resistance test to avoid a status condition, the difficulty of the Resistance test is reduced by one (which may eliminate the need for a test). Finally, when tracking an opponent, he reduces the difficulty of the test by one step, to a minimum of Simple (D0).

UXIA MCNEILL

A slender red-haired woman with a towering temper and foul mouth to match, Uxia McNeill is a passionate and wild woman who lives life on the edge. She bounced from schools to bortsals from an early age, until finally becoming a prominent figure in the "Scots Razors" street gang. From there came a stint with the Irmandinhoes and various attempts at regular jobs, though the latter were only attempts to throw the authorities from her trail.

She entered the Caledonian Army's recruiting office with her infamous cocksure attitude and fully expected to be laughed right back out. Fortunately for her, the recruiter took note of talents that she took for granted and sent her on to basic training. Bouts of detention for insubordination and general unruliness somehow eventually led to the Highlander SAS Regiment, where she has put her bold thinking, evasion skills, and appetite for destruction to good use. Some say it is only a matter of time before her attitude lands her in trouble that she won't be able to escape, particularly as her behaviour frequently borders conduct that would result in a dishonourable discharge for anyone else. Others know better thanks to the devastation she leaves in her wake with her seemingly endless supply of grenades and her trusty "Ramona".

NEMESIS

UXIA MCNEILL

ATTRIBUTES

AGI	AWA	BRW	COO	INT	PER	WIL
12	12	8	10	10	8	10

FIELDS OF EXPERTISE

Combat	+2	2	Movement	+4	3	Social	+1	–
Fortitude	+1	1	Senses	+2	2	Technical	+1	1

DEFENCES

Firewall	11	Resolve	11	Vigour	9
Security	3	Morale	5	Armour	5

ATTACKS

- **Knife**: Melee, 1+3, 1H, Concealed 1, Non-Hackable, Subtle 2, Thrown, Unforgiving 1
- **Teseum Blade**: Melee, 1+4, 1H, Non-Hackable, Parry 1, Piercing 2, Subtle 1, Vicious 1
- **Boarding Shotgun**: Range C, 1+8, Burst 1, 2H, Knockdown, Medium MULTI
- **D-Charge**: Explosive Charge, 2+6, 1H, Anti-Materiel 2, Comms, Disposable, Piercing 3, Spread 1, Unsubtle, Vicious 2

GEAR: Light Combat Armour, Multispectral Visor 1

SPECIAL ABILITIES

- **Appetite for Destruction**: From a young age, Uxia has enjoyed working to tear down the establishment and swim against the tide, often striking where her foe is weakest or overwhelming them with a blitzkrieg mentality. She can reroll one d20 when making an Analysis or Observation test, or up to 3 when making a ranged attack, but must accept the new results. Additionally, she can draw a weapon or other item as a Free Action, does not need to have a weapon in hand to respond to attacks, and can always make a Defence or Guard Reaction so long as she has a free hand and a weapon within Reach (this can only be done once per turn). Further, she may spend a Minor Action during combat increase the Burst rating of her weapon by 1, and can use a Free Action to swap ammo loads (unless the weapon has the Munition quality). Finally, if she succeeds at a ranged attack and spends Momentum or an Infinity Point to attack the same target with the same weapon, the difficulty of the attack is decreased by one step, to a minimum of zero (this can only be used once per turn).
- **Explosive Temper**: Uxia's explosive temper is reflected in her desire to blow things up. She may reroll one d20 when making a Tech test, but must accept the new result. Additionally, she gains 2 bonus Momentum when setting an explosive charge.
- **Raised on the Streets**: Uxia pretty much raised herself on the streets. She possesses a Thievery Expertise of 3 and Thievery Focus of 2. Additionally, she may reroll one d20 when making a Stealth, Survival, or Thievery test, but must accept the new result. Further, when making an Education or Persuade test to interact or relate with criminal elements, she gains 2 bonus Momentum. Finally, she may substitute her Thievery test for Stealth when attempting to escape from the scene of a crime, con job, heist, or other Thievery task.
- **Foul-tempered Loud Mouth**: Uxia's conversational techniques consist of shouting everyone down and cursing as much as possible. She increases the Complication Range of her social tests by 2.

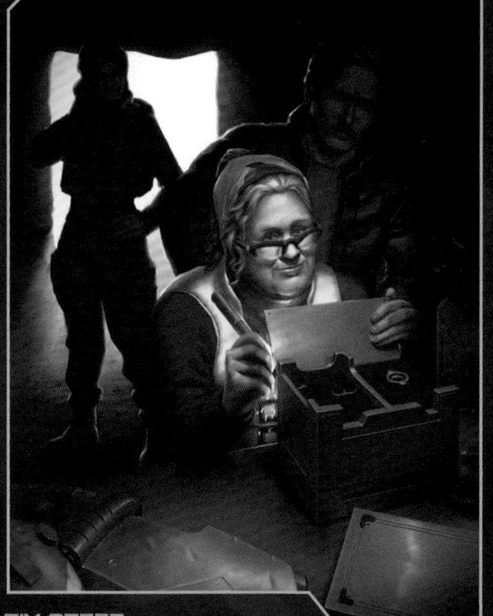

TIM STEED

NEMESIS

DANYKA MILLARD

ATTRIBUTES

AGI	AWA	BRW	COO	INT	PER	WIL
8	9	11	10	11	9	12

FIELDS OF EXPERTISE

Combat	+1	1	Movement	+3	3	Social	+3	1
Fortitude	+2	2	Senses	+3	3	Technical	+4	4

DEFENCES

Firewall	15	Resolve	14	Vigour	13
Security	–	Morale	–	Armour	1

ATTACKS

- **Akrylat-Kanone Adhesive Launcher**: Range M, 1+7 N damage, Burst 1, Unwieldy, Area (Close), Immobilising, Knockdown, Munition, Nonlethal
- **D-Charges**: 2+6 N damage, 1H, Anti-Materiel, Comms, Disposable, Piercing 3, Spread 1, Unsubtle, Vicious 2
- **Pistol**: Range R/C, 1+5 N damage, Burst 1, 1H, Vicious 1

GEAR: Armoured Clothing, Powered Multitool, Survival Kit

SPECIAL ABILITIES

- **Backpack Full of Treasure**: Like most Dozers, Danyka has learned to keep various pieces and parts on-hand, just in case. Each point of Heat paid to gain additional dice on Technical tests provides two dice instead of one. (The normal maximum of three bonus d20s still applies.)
- **Keep it Together**: Danyka's knack for repairing machinery is phenomenally reliable. When making a Technical test to repair an object or construct, (i.e., something with Structure and Faults, as opposed to Vigour and Wounds,) she can reroll any dice that did not generate a success, but must accept the new results.
- **Lightning Edge**: Something about working under pressure brings out the best in Danyka. She adds 1 bonus Momentum to successful Technical tests made during action scenes.

DANYKA MILLARD (DOZER / ENGINEER)

"You the Dozer?"

A greased-covered face peeked under the alien sarcophagus.

"And you are?"

"Colonel Newton. I´m now in command here. What can you tell me?"

Danyka hastily crawled form under the strange capsule, took a deep breath and looked around the cave system (right under Skara Brae!) where she was located: the walls were lined with a glowing moss she had never seen before, probably the bioluminescent product of a chemical exchange with whatever was contained in the sarcophagus and now that it was gone, the moss was slowly withering, plunging the cave into darkness.

The bedrock slowly smoothed around the area where a depression held the small ovoid capsule-like sarcophagus.

Danyka was sweating when she turned to face the impatient colonel, this was definitely not something she was prepared to say out loud when she woke up that morning.

"This is alien tech, Sir... Ma'am!" She hesitated. "Neither human nor Antipode. Someone, somehow stuffed it here a very long time ago and now is missing a piece, or more precisely, its contents!"

Danyka could not believe she actually had said that to a colonel. From the looks of the woman in front of her, neither did the she.

"Would you say the finding of this... thing was an accident?"

Danyka turned to the tunnel that lead to a secret room under the now-ruined research facilities: there were several biohazard crates and a scanning station destroyed by gunfire (no bodies in here, though).

"This is not an actual laboratory... they were looking for something and were prepared for it with all this gear... what did you say they were doing here?"

"I did not, supposedly Phoenix Industries was working in quantronics... clearly they weren't... Sargeant Fraser! Send the Greys to pick up all the galactics involved with Phoenix before they fly away with whatever they found and contact Stavka immediately, tell them we are sending our Dozer to brief them about this situation..."

She then turned to Danyka: "You have two hours to understand what these things are before your flight. Have you ever visited Mat'?"

APPEARANCE

Danyka wears the standard Dozer fatigues, but with an extra helping of machinery grease all over them. She rarely wears her helmet as she is usually fixing the traktors and vehicles of her battalion.

ROLEPLAYING

- Tends to talk to machinery in endearing tones
- When nervous or excited she talks to herself
- She is suspicious (even superstitious!) of ALEPH´s Lhosts and Posthumans

BACKGROUND

Born in Cailleach, Danyka always had a thing with machinery: it made her feel comfortable and secure. Her parents owned one of the few repair shops in the small city and Danyka always knew she was going to work with machines for a living.

She thought all of her life's dreams had come true when she got into the Caledonian Engineering College in Scone, but then she got an invitation to join the Dozer Corps. She joined up just for the opportunity to travel across Ariadna, but after her first deployment in action – against an illegal Teseum mining expedition during which her emergency repairs on the munition-carrying traktor mul saved the day – she realised the thrill of working on the lightning edge of life and death.

Her work that day against the mercenaries hired to protect the mines earned her first commendation and the respect of the soldiers of the 5th Caledonian Rifles she fought with. But most importantly, she knew she had found a new place in life: not in faraway Cailleach, but in the midst of battle, where her machines need her most.

DON JUAN (DOZER (DESPERADO / FORWARD OBSERVER)

DJ LUDOWICI

NEMESIS

DON JUAN

ATTRIBUTES

AGI	AWA	BRW	COO	INT	PER	WIL
9	12	13	11	8	7	10

FIELDS OF EXPERTISE

Combat	+3	3	Movement	+2	2	Social	–	–
Fortitude	+4	1	Senses	+2	2	Technical	+1	–

DEFENCES

Firewall	9	Resolve	14	Vigour	7
Security	–	Morale	–	Armour	1

ATTACKS

- **2 Americolt Eagles**: Range R/C, 2+8 N damage, Burst 1, Unbalanced, Piercing 1, Non-Hackable, Knockdown, Vicious 1
- **Unarmed Strike**: Melee, 1+5 N damage, Stun, Subtle

GEAR: Armoured Clothing (Leather Duster), Motorcycle, Smoke Grenades (×3), Whisky

SPECIAL ABILITIES

- **$&#@?!**: DJ has a way with language, much the same as a demolition crew might have with a wrecking ball or explosives. When attempting to threaten, frighten, or otherwise intimidate others, he can substitute his Fortitude skill for Social tests, provided that he swears up a storm. This is rarely a problem.
- **All-Terrain Vigilante**: From his time in the badlands of the USAriadnan south, DJ is used to riding in tough terrain. When piloting a motorcycle, he decreases the difficulty of Movement tests by two, to a minimum of 1.
- **Lone Wolf**: DJ is used to surviving on his own. If he is the only friendly target in his zone, he gains the benefit of heavy cover.

Don Juan slowly crept towards the cliff's edge, overlooking the barren valley traversed by a dry creek. Sweat covered his forehead and his dry lips were pressed in a grim countenance.

Grunting, he pulled out a pair of binoculars.

"Let's see what we got down there... come on, come on!"

As if on cue, movement became evident in the area surrounding the creek: a lanky figure came out in the open followed by several more of the alien figures. After ensuring there were no intruders, the alien signalled and screeched something in the hissing clicks of their language. They gathered into a circle with the one appearing to be the leader sitting in the centre.

"There you are, you filthy maggot!"

Don Juan flipped onto his back and fetched his radio.

"Central? This is DJ, forward observer... yes! Hostiles!...three clicks north, adjust one hundred yards east... What? You Antipode-loving son of a... What? No, I said east goddammit... You tell that filthy grease-licker, mongrel-loving, cheap-ass rookie that he better pay this time! Just target my position!...Full barrage? Five minutes? Let them skinny monsters have it!"

He synced his watch, spat with grim satisfaction, and settled back to watch the fireworks. Then he heard a scream down below. He closed his eyes, not wanting to take a look, already knowing what was going down there.

He cursed deeply when he focused his binoculars on the source of the screaming: a woman. One of the settlers from out east of the Navajo Outpost.

"You have to be kidding me!"

He checked his timepiece: 4:48 and counting... just enough...

"That nomad-smelling Ontos better have as good aim as he brags..." Cursing himself, he mounted the huge motorcycle hidden among the brush, revved it up, and headed like a bat out of hell right into the Shasvastii outpost, heavy pistol blazing. The Desperado was here, hailing the imminent firestorm.

APPEARANCE

Don Juan rides a huge motorcycle, carrying two heavy pistols under his serape, with enough whisky and food in his saddlebags to reach the next outpost. His hat somehow manages to always cover his eyes. He wears old but comfortable army-issued clothing underneath his outlaw look.

ROLEPLAYING

- DJ is a lone wolf who never asks for help or assistance
- Curses a *lot*
- He doesn't let anyone touch his hat

BACKGROUND

Don Juan's life is the typical (but tragic) Exclusion Zone orphan story. His parents settled beyond the Wall, near Coldspring, only to be attacked by Antipodes that same summer. By the time the militia came to help, DJ was the only survivor. He was left with nothing but his father's hat and was taken to Coldspring where he spent the last few years of his broken childhood.

There, he learned how to survive in the wild and on the frontier, quickly growing accustomed to a life carrying the pelts and wares his foster parents sold from town to town. As soon as he could, though, he built his own custom hog and put Coldspring in the rear-view mirror, leaving its sad memories behind for good.

Living wild he embraced the Scalp Law as a means of satisfying his need for revenge on the Antipodes. Later, he would befriend a retired ranger turned farmer who would teach him the finer skills of scouting and reporting information to the local militias. After having heard rumours of aliens infiltrating *Dawn*, he would volunteer as a forward observer in the first Ariadnan expeditionary force shipping to Paradiso in order to be prepared for the new menace threatening his homeland.

CHRISTOPHER YOUNG

NEMESIS

CHRIS YOUNG

ATTRIBUTES

AGI	AWA	BRW	COO	INT	PER	WIL
11	12	9	12	8	8	10

FIELDS OF EXPERTISE

Combat	+3	3	Movement	+1	1	Social	–	–
Fortitude	+2	2	Senses	+3	3	Technical	+1	1

DEFENCES

Firewall	9	Resolve	12	Vigour	11
Security	–	Morale	4	Armour	1

ATTACKS

- **Assault Pistol**: Range R/C, 1+7 N damage, Burst 3, Unbalanced, Vicious 1
- **Sniper Rifle**: Range L, 1+9 N damage, Burst 3, Unwieldy, Unforgiving 2
- **Teseum Knife**: Melee, 1+5 N damage, Concealed 1, Non-Hackable, Piercing 2, Subtle 2, Thrown, Unforgiving 2

GEAR: Armoured Clothing (Highlander Fatigues)

SPECIAL ABILITIES

- **Enthusiastic Rifleman**: "One shot, one kill" is a nice motto and all, but the important part is taking down your target, right? When spending Heat to gain the benefit of using a Reload, he reduces the Heat cost by 1 (to a minimum of 1).
- **Sharp Senses**: Chris can reroll one d20 when making a Senses test, but he must accept the new result.
- **Who Dares, Wins**: The model Highlander, Chris isn't one to back down from a fight… even if he probably should. This irrepressible courage grants him Morale Soak 4.

CHRIS YOUNG (HIGHLANDER / SAS)

The cold was seeping through his bones. They ached, but he couldn't move yet. It was still one more hour to dawn, and he was sure he had heard something down at the base of the small hill he'd positioned on. The moors north of Cailleach were inhospitable to say the least and at some point the temperature fell well below freezing.

Still, the environment was the lesser of his ailments right now. He was tasked with field-testing a new sniper rifle, supposedly scheduled to substitute the old model he was so accustomed to. Luckily for him, there had been Antipode sightings on the outlying mine fields. Unluckily for him, that meant he got to freeze his tail off in the moors.

Focusing again on his task, Young peered from his hideout and stared at an imposing Macrofeidh, the gigantic Caledonian deer, fifty meters from his station. Relaxing a bit, Young contemplated the huge beast as it munched on the wet grass around him for a few moments when a white-grey blur tackled the half-ton herbivore and started ripping into its entrails.

Young didn't have time to curse in surprise as a hideous beast that seemed to be part Antipode and part Tartarian Bear started feeding on the still-agonising beast. His training kicked in and he already had the bloody killer in his sights.

He slowly squeezed the trigger and nothing happened. Confused, Young looked at the weapon and frowned, apparently the ice had gotten inside the mechanism. He hit the rifle until he was positive it would work, then aimed and fired.

The shot went high impacting the beast but not killing it. A howl of pain and fury echoed in his ears, the abomination growled his way, sniffing, and charged.

"Well… better stick to the tried and true I suppose…" He threw the defective rifle at the monster just in spite and drew his pistol and combat knife hoping all that S.A.S. propaganda during boot camp was true for abomination-fighting.

APPEARANCE

Slightly shorter than the average Caledonian, Young has a powerful physique and an amiable countenance when not in on a mission. He looks young for his age. He always wears clean fatigues and very rarely uses civilian's clothes, but in either case he keeps a very clean and proper appearance.

ROLEPLAYING

- Has a very positive attitude
- He is constantly re-arranging his beret in front of mirrors
- Dislikes Rodinan weapons as he believes them to be low quality

BACKGROUND

Chris is a true Caledonian. Since he was a child, the quick-witted boy dreamt of someday joining the prestigious Highlander regiments.

When he became of age he said goodbye to a tearful mother and enlisted with the Volunteers where he excelled in boot camp. Overconfident and full of hubris, he went with his friends to a local pub on their first leave. There, he started bragging until they annoyed one of the patrons. Full of bravado, the young cadet never thought about the consequences of taunting a stranger in Caledonia until said stranger beat all of his squad put together, trashed the pub in the process, and left the bill hanging around his neck.

It was three days later that he discovered that "stranger" was William Wallace. After that, Chris assumed he would be discharged. Instead, he was approached by a Special Service officer and enlisted in the S.A.S., making him one of the most enthusiastic recruits the Service has ever had.

GEOFFREY STRAIN

MALCOLM "ONTOS" CARRICK (DOZER ENGINEER / TRAKTOR MUL CONTROLLER)

NEMESIS

MALCOLM "ONTOS" CARRICK

ATTRIBUTES

AGI	AWA	BRW	COO	INT	PER	WIL
11	12	9	11	10	9	8

FIELDS OF EXPERTISE

Combat	+2	2	Movement	+3	1	Social	+1	1
Fortitude	+2	–	Senses	+2	2	Technical	+2	2

DEFENCES

Firewall	12	Resolve	10	Vigour	11
Security	–	Morale	4	Armour	1

ATTACKS

- **Pistol**: Range R/C, 1+7 N damage, Burst 1, 1H, Vicious 1
- **Traktor Mul-Mounted Uragan**: Range M, 1+8 N damage, Burst 3, Mounted, Munition, Non-Hackable, Unsubtle 2
  - *Airburst Mode*: Area (Close), Grievous, Piercing 2, Speculative Fire
  - *Direct Fire Mode*: Grievous, Piercing 2, Vicious 2

GEAR: Armoured Clothing, Remote Presence Gear, Repair Kit, Traktor Mul with 2 mounted Uragans

SPECIAL ABILITIES

- **Gambler's Luck**: Ontos has incredibly good fortune in combat zones, though it's yet to rub off on anyone else. He can reroll any failed surprise test, and does not pay Heat to use the Defence Reaction.
- **Tank Killer**: Ontos might be an unusual nickname, but Malcom comes by it honestly. When controlling a remote via remote presence gear, he can reroll up to 5 N when making a ranged attack, but must accept the new result.

"Three clicks to the north? You sure? Not west like last time?"

The radio sputtered a string of profanity that made Malcolm chuckle under his breath.

"All right, all right! Don't choke on that filthy tobacco you like to chew. Emmerson's betting a pitcher of beer that the objective isn't with this squad either –"

Another high-pitched tirade of insults.

Malcolm laughed this time and yelled over the insults, "Confirm, three clicks north, correct one hundred yards east, full barrage, five minutes ETA. Confirm."

This time he received a positive answer and he cut the communications, turning to his aide.

"Emmerson! You got yourself a bet! Load the traktor with full payload, Katies this time, on the double we have to party in five!"

Four minutes, thirty seconds later a solemn and focused Dozer Malcolm "Ontos" Carrick was inputting the coordinates on the traktor loaded with the standard rockets used to rain death on USAriadna's enemies, he checked one last time his watch, the multiple rocket launcher and took a deep breath and looked towards the vast jungle canopy where his payload would hit in a few moments.

The target was located inside a ravine in the valley below them. The treeline made it impossible to watch anything beyond trees and vines, but if the forward observer said the aliens were in the ravine, they were there.

Taking another deep breath, he yelled a warning to his aide and sent a screaming and fiery death to the Shasvastii camp.

"You think we hit them?" asked Emmerson while loading the missile launcher, now with a more relaxed attitude.

"Probably, haven't heard from the observer though."

"He probably lost the radio ag –"

Emmerson fell like a sack of potatoes, blood spurting from a hole in his neck. Malcolm immediately hit the ground as another sniper round hit the tractor, disabling the ranging sensors.

"Emmerson! Damned sniper! Must've tracked the smoke of the missiles..."

Malcolm looked for his weapons, they were out of reach and he was pinned behind the traktor by the sniper. He couldn t reach his fallen friend either and that made him mad, really mad.

"You think you are good? I'll show you skill!" He took the control device and turned the turret in the direction the sniper was hiding...

APPEARANCE

A tall and friendly looking man of originally Canadian stock, Malcolm "Ontos" Carrick is carrying a heavy-looking worn backpack. He looks inquisitively at his surroundings and is very straightforward when meeting new people, smiling constantly.

ROLEPLAYING

- He likes bets, especially if they involve explosions
- He is a good but overprotective friend
- All his gear looks damaged but is actually in working condition

BACKGROUND

Hailing from the small city of Four Tracks, Dozer Engineer Malcolm "Ontos" Carrick worked in the mines for a few months after graduating from the Tech Institute at Fairview but found the repetitive chore of blowing holes in the earth rather boring. So he quit and enrolled into the Engineer Corps where he could start blowing holes in more interesting things.

Malcolm could be your friendly engineering teacher if he wasn't obsessed with military machines and making things explode. Although he is not old, he is so comfortable in his role as a field engineer that he has become some kind of legend in the Navajo Outposts beyond the Wall.

He is one of the most reliable artillery specialists in USAriadna and his presence in any theatre is always welcome, ironically his aides usually don't have that kind of luck which is something that troubles him.

JAMES FRASER (CALEDONIAN GREY)

JACOB EVANSYOUNG

NEMESIS

JAMES FRASER

ATTRIBUTES

AGI	AWA	BRW	COO	INT	PER	WIL
11	12	9	12	8	8	10

FIELDS OF EXPERTISE

Combat	+3	3	Movement	+2	2	Social	+1	1
Fortitude	+3	3	Senses	+1	1	Technical	–	–

DEFENCES

Firewall	8	Resolve	13	Vigour	12
Security	–	Morale	–	Armour	3

ATTACKS

- **T2 Boarding Shotgun**: Range C, 1+8 N damage, Burst 1, 2H, Knockdown, Medium MULTI
  - *Normal Shells Mode (Primary)*: Area (Close), Spread 1
  - *T2 Slugs Mode (Secondary)*: Anti-Materiel 2, Piercing 3, Vicious 2
- **Teseum Knife**: Melee, 1+5 N, Concealed 1, Non-Hackable, Piercing 2, Subtle 2, Thrown, Unforgiving 2

GEAR: Medium Combat Armour, Smoke Grenades (×3)

SPECIAL ABILITIES

- **Got Your Back**: Deeply invested in the well-being of his troops, James leads from the front, and hates leaving people behind. He pays no Heat to use the Guard Reaction.
- **The Highlander Way**: Basically the hard way, but up close and personal. When making an attack at Close or shorter range, James can reroll up to 2 damage dice. As normally, these can only be rerolled once.

The transport stopped in front of the Phoenix Industries Headquarters at Skara Brae and unloaded a full platoon of Highlander Greys, they quickly formed up before their officer, a big man with a reddish beard.

"Listen up lads! We have orders from Colonel Newton to bag all of these foreigners before they skip Dawn – "

His briefing was cut short by shots fired from the rooftop of the building where a landing port had just illuminated, signalling an incoming transport.

"Everyone! Cover!"

He cursed almost immediately as his men charged ferociously towards the compound doors screaming the regiment's warcry: "Death to the enemy!" Sergeant James Fraser of the 3rd Highlander Greys regiment grunted as he followed his men in their charge: you simply did not tell a Grey to stand still and take cover in the face of the enemy.

The interior of the Phoenix compound was a veritable maze and although no significant resistance was met after Fraser's men had neutralised the shooter at the roof, capturing the civilians was proving a dangerous nuisance, particularly on the top floor, where mercenaries hired to protect Phoenix's VIPs where putting up a real fight: they had barricaded themselves and had Fraser's men pinned down.

"Corporal! Report!"

"Sergeant! They are well entrenched they are! And that's not all, Fisher just radioed, the transport landed!"

"Well, shoot it down!"

"Can't do it Sergeant! We weren't kitted with that kind of equipment!"

This much was true, and Fraser knew it, he had prepared for close quarters.

"Well, I guess we do it the Highlander way! Follow me lads!"

Fraser rushed into the enemy's fire lane, he felt his body armour take at least two hits while his soldiers tossed grenades over him, blowing up the mercenaries' barricades. Shrapnel hit his face and unprotected arms but he kept running, he had to reach the enemy before they could regroup.

He discharged his shotgun point-blank at one hostile, and beyond them, he could see the stairwell heading to the rooftop and hurried towards it in hopes of reaching the vehicle before its lift-off.

By then, the Greys were securing the room, so he rushed to the rooftop... just in time to see the aircraft taking off, heading south. Fraser sighed while staring at the aircraft fading into the night sky. Something told him he was going to a long-term mission overseas...

APPEARANCE

Heading in your direction is a huge tartan-wearing warrior, with armour plates covering his torso and when fully armed, he is a serious-looking sergeant, with a short reddish beard who looks disapprovingly at civilians and communicates mostly in monosyllables.

ROLEPLAYING

- Follows orders to a letter
- Likes to reflect on philosophical issues
- Distrusts civilians

BACKGROUND

James Fraser was born in Scone to a poor family with only one asset left: a strong work ethic. As the eldest of the Fraser boys, he developed a more mature character and became the responsible one of his family.

With little studies and resources, James couldn't aspire to enter one of the Caledonian universities and becoming a miner wasn't appealing to him so he took the next best choice and joined the army, this time aiming for the best option available to him and ended up as a recruit of the glorious Highlander Greys.

Rising quickly thanks to his devotion to hard work and responsibility, he acquired the rank of sergeant in no time, becoming a valuable asset to his officers and a caring and brave leader of his men.

SCOTT PEITERSON

NEMESIS

SCOTT PEITERSON

ATTRIBUTES

AGI	AWA	BRW	COO	INT	PER	WIL
11	10	9	11	13	7	9

FIELDS OF EXPERTISE

Combat	+1	1	Movement	+2	2	Social	+1	–
Fortitude	+1	–	Senses	+2	2	Technical	+4	4

DEFENCES

Firewall	12	Resolve	10	Vigour	11
Security	–	Morale	4	Armour	1

ATTACKS

- **Assault Hacking Device**: CLAW-3, SWORD-0, SHIELD-0, GADGET-0, IC-1, +3 bonus damage
- **Pistol**: Range R/C, 1+6 damage, Burst 1, 1H, Vicious 1

GEAR: Chameleonwear, Modcoat, Disguise Kit, Surge (×2)

SPECIAL ABILITIES

- **Adaptive Operative**: Like all Zero hackers, Scott is equally comfortable in both quantronic and real space. When making either a Hacking or Stealth test, he can reroll 1d20, but must keep the new result.
- **Natural Born Gymnast**: Twisting and turning, Scott can be as slippery as a greased eel when it suits him. He does not pay Heat to use the Defence Reaction, and generates 1 Heat if his test is successful.
- **Observant**: A devout follower of the Observance, Scott sincerely believes that Our Lady of Knives has been looking out for him. When pressed, he can fervently pray, gaining 1 Infinity Point for 2 Heat instead of the usual 3.

SCOTT PEITERSON (NOMAD HACKER / ZERO)

The compound was on fire and surrounded by the Ariadnans so that was a big NO. The research facilities may be easier to infiltrate right now, after the specialist the locals had brought in to inspect the dig had left with all the big brass.

Grudgingly, he sent a last message to his contact inside the compound in hopes the signal was still open and quietly headed to the research facilities in downtown Skara Brae. By the time he reached the installations, it was night (and colder than deep space, damn this filthy rock!). Fortunately, security was light in the ruined research station.

Zero Operative Peiterson entered the compound easily enough. The first real challenge was the guard posted in front of the elevator shaft that led to the secret laboratory, luckily the control room of the laboratory was unguarded and so Peiterson managed to quietly hack into the elevator controls and activate it so its doors opened behind an already suspicious guard who, upon entering, found himself trapped in an elevator heading to the upper levels.

Peiterson ran to the elevator shaft and rappelled himself down to the secret laboratory in the basement. There, amongst the debris and destroyed machinery, he found a bullet-riddled computer, deftly dismantled it and grunted in satisfaction: nobody had gone to the trouble to check the quantronic drive which was intact.

"Not so clever now, are we Phoenix?" he whispered to himself while plugging his hacking device into the drive.

Seconds later, Peiterson was reading the drive's information and whistled in astonishment. If this information was real, it was going to blow a lot of minds back on Bakunin!

The elevator started vibrating, signalling its decent to the lower levels. Startled, Peiterson looked around frantically for a place to run, beyond some crates marked biohazard was a tunnel, clearly dug by two discarded remotes near its entrance. Jumping behind one of them, he started dismantling it while two guards exited the elevator. He whispered a prayer to Our Lady of the Knives and activated the repeater secretly located in the remote's hardware, sending the information of Bakunin's greatest enemy involvement with Phoenix Industries...

APPEARANCE

A short, pale, wiry, and athletic man, he looks like an ageless gymnast. He has short-cropped hair and is constantly observing his surroundings, as if looking for a way to escape.

ROLEPLAYING

- Talks very fast
- Slightly paranoid and agoraphobic
- It takes a conscious effort to stay still when not in a mission

BACKGROUND

Zero Operative Scott Peiterson grew in Bakunin's Gymnasium Module (Commune D-36), where he was fascinated by the mystery and myths of the Observance and became a devout follower of Our Mother of Mercy. When first deployed, in an infiltration mission at Human Edge, Scott's team was ambushed due to their contact's treachery. After several weeks surviving undercover, Scott, the only survivor of the Zero squad, was rescued by the Moiras, convincing himself it was Our Lady of Knives herself who had interceded for him.

A little paranoid after his brush with death, Scott has considered joining the Sin Eaters as a way to thank the Observance, but first he is sure he will do everything to get revenge on the traitor that blew his team's cover in Human Edge.

Scott is totally loyal to Bakunin and the Social Energy and is extremely conscious of the war against both ALEPH and the alien menace and will do what his nation expects from him in order to stop these two menaces to freedom and the Nomad ideal.

ARAWN, LORD OF ANNWN (WULVER PIRATE CAPTAIN)

ANDREW BROXHAM

NEMESIS

ARAWN, LORD OF ANNWN

ATTRIBUTES

AGI	AWA	BRW	COO	INT	PER	WIL
11	11	14	7	8	9	10

FIELDS OF EXPERTISE

Combat	+4	1	Movement	+3	1	Social	+2	1
Fortitude	+3	2	Senses	+2	1	Technical	–	–

DEFENCES

Firewall	8	Resolve	13	Vigour	12
Security	–	Morale	–	Armour	2

ATTACKS

- **Claws**: Melee, 1+5 N damage, Subtle 1, Vicious 1
- **Americolt Eagle**: Range R/C, 2+7 N damage, Burst 1, Unbalanced, Piercing 1, Non-Hackable, Knockdown, Vicious 1
- **Teseum Claymore**: Melee, 2+9 N damage, 2H, Grievous, Non-Hackable, Parry 2, Piercing 2, Vicious 2

GEAR: Painkillers (×3), Wulver-Fitted Ballistic Vest

SPECIAL ABILITIES

- **Common Special Abilities**: Fear 2, Menacing 2, Monstrous
- **Predator's Instinct**: Like all Wulvers, Arawn has an extraordinary sense of smell. When making a Senses test in which scent would play a factor, he gains +2d20.
- **The Wild Hunt**: Once Arawn tastes blood, he's even more difficult to dissuade than before. When someone in the scene suffers a Wound – regardless of their allegiance – Arawn can reroll up to 4 N when making a melee attack. His bloodlust has a downside, however: he pays double the Heat cost to use the Defence or Guard Reactions.

"The Hunt is on!" the fearsome warriors howled in a frenzy that foretold of blood-shed and chaos. The spaceship had docked in the orbital base, the airlocks were ready to open. A klaxon fused with the pirate's howling, auguring carnage for the residents of the orbital.

"Today we reap Cubes for the Cauldron! Anything else is yours for the taking!"

With a roar, the pirates charged through the widening doorways into the orbital, though none of them matched the savagery of their leader, Arawn, the Lord of Annwn.

An hour of carnage and brutal skirmishing bought them the orbital. The crew of Yu Jing's "Fujian" had fought well, acknowledged Arawn. He preferred slaughter to surrender and despised cowards, slaying any victims who thought they could submit.

A burly man approached Arawn, stopping just out of reach before speaking. "The orbital is ours, Arawn, and the reaping was plentiful. Care was taken not to damage too many Cubes this time..."

"What about my orders to you, Malik?" growled the Wulver through curled lips.

"I... well... the warehouse was there, just like the informer said, but..."

With a roar, Arawn lashed his sword out at a nearby console.

"But what, man?! Do I have bleed you to get you talking?"

Malik retreated a step, "It was a false tip... the warehouse was empty..."

"Place the detonation charges as ordered and get back to Annwn immediately! We ship towards Human Edge. One way or another, that flesh bag owes me a body!"

The Cauldron, Arawn's moniker for the illegal and heretical contraption, had over a dozen bloody Cubes plugged in. Some still blinked, though most were cold and inert. Arawn took a dark satisfaction from the few flickering devices, his victim's "souls" and memories trapped inside until ransomed by their former owner's families or contractors.

"Lord Arawn, Malik finished rigging the d-charges in the reactor room!"

The Wulver licked his lips and nodded. "Disengage and detonate the charges!"

"But, what about Malik?"

"I told that stinking mechanic to hurry, this'll teach him to run faster!" snarled Arawn with a challenging glare, before easing back into the Annwn's command chair, his gaze tugged again by the winking Cubes.

The Black Labs had delivered true with the Cauldron and insertion of his Cube. Each day, each captured memory, brought Arawn closer to his dream. Soon, he would acquire a Lhost body, then take it and himself to the Black Labs to seize immortality. Then the Wild Hunt would truly begin!

APPEARANCE

Huge and animalistic, Arawn has a cunning and cruel glow in his eyes. He is covered with battle scars that criss-cross the Celtic tattoos and motifs of wolves inked all over his body.

ROLEPLAYING

- Brutal and cruel. Amongst the worst criminals in the Human Sphere
- Obsessed with ancient Celtic mythologies and antiquities
- Fixated on obtaining a Lhost, a functional Cube, and immortality

BACKGROUND

Arawn´s only solace during a loveless and solitary childhood in a Caledonian orphanage was an old book of ancient Earth mythology. Through it, he fled his bleak existence and flew with the immortal and powerful. In his teens, he learned of Cubes and the practice of Resurrection Lotteries amongst the other nations, and so grew his yearning. Shunned by Dog-Bowl teams and Dogfaces alike, he left Dawn for the Human Edge mining colonies, soon earning renown amongst the hovels and fleshpots as hired muscle, thug, and worse.

Eventually joining a smuggling crew, he soon mutinied and convinced them to follow him into piracy. Renaming the small ship Annwn (after the Welsh Otherworld), he incurred the wrath of the Yuan Yuan pirates by looting valuable prizes they had already marked for themselves. Arawn's dreams of immortality have recently taken on greater urgency, as his rivals have a missile with his name on it and only a secure backup can possibly save him.

ALASDAIR "SEISHIN-KA" MACIVER (ARIADNAN HARAMAKI ZENSENBUTAI)

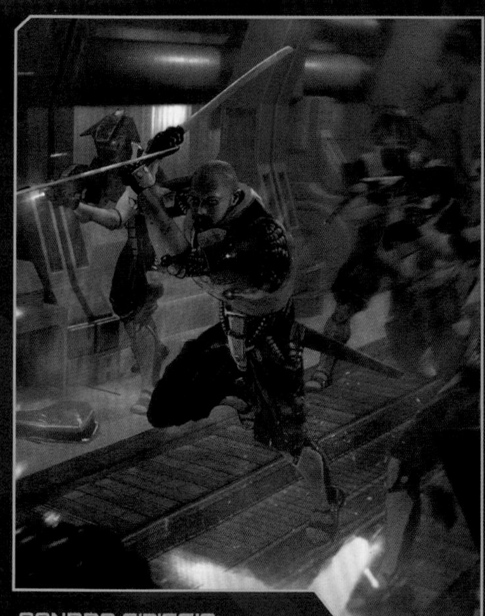

SANDRO CIPICCIA

NEMESIS

ALASDAIR MACIVER

ATTRIBUTES

AGI	AWA	BRW	COO	INT	PER	WIL
14	9	12	8	9	7	11

FIELDS OF EXPERTISE

Combat	+4	4	Movement	+1	–	Social	+1	1
Fortitude	+3	3	Senses	+2	1	Technical	–	–

DEFENCES

Firewall	12	Resolve	10	Vigour	11
Security	–	Morale	4	Armour	1

ATTACKS

- **Ōdachi**: Melee, 2+9N damage, 2H, Anti-Materiel 2, Grievous, Non-Hackable, Parry 2, Piercing 2, Vicious 2
- **Pistol**: Range R/C, 1+5N damage, Burst 1, 1H, Vicious 1

GEAR: Powered Combat Armour

SPECIAL ABILITIES

- **Common Special Abilities**: Threatening 2
- **First Cut**: An intensely disciplined swordsman, Alasdair's strikes are calm, centred, and millimetre-precise. Upon making a successful melee attack, he rolls an additional 4N, provided he has not previously attacked the target in this scene.
- **Zen Warrior**: Harkening back to the words of his sensei, Alasdair clears his mind on the battlefield. He does not pay Heat to use the Defence or Guard reactions, unless the reaction is successful.

"If you think about defeating your enemy, you are not Zen." The proximity horns blared, signalling imminent boarding action to the 14th Haramaki Zensenbutai regiment, or "Unlucky 14th". The heavily armoured samurai looked at their Gunso, Seishin-ka (Steel Spirit), for orders. Lost in meditation, the tall officer remained oblivious.

"If you think about your sword, you are not Zen." The shuttle crashed into the enemy's docking station. The Gunso slowly turned to the six bravest and skilled close-combat warriors in the StateEmpire and nodded. As one, the soldiers donned kabuto and grasped their weapons. Seishin-ka stood, calmly grasped his ōdachi, then strode towards the craft's door and its release switch.

"If you think about death, you are not Zen." Heavy fire erupted from the far end of the loading bay, peppering the shuttle and felling one of the Haramaki mid-charge. Gunso led the way with two-handed sword aloft. He grunted angrily at the soldier's loss, already annoyed by the certainty that high command would chalk the high body count to the regiment's renowned bad luck. Some called it karma for the unit's blackballed status.

"If you think about Zen, you are not Zen. Alasdair, when you understand this, everything you do, will be Zen." After a seemingly endless run, Alasdair "Seishin-ka" MacIver, 3rd Gunso of the "Unlucky" 14th Haramaki Senzenbutai tore into the entrenched enemy that had decimated his squad. Terrified, several of them dropped their weapons and ran, though a few stood their ground. "Domo arigato, Sensei-sama! I will honour your memory once again," whispered Alisdair.

"When you strike at your enemy, do not do it out of hatred, but ensure that your foe falls with your first cut." Sent to recover the Emperor's station, Alisdair struggled to understand why there were still pirates aboard. Two lay dead at his feet, while a third, a woman wielding a short sword, charged towards him. Stepping back and focussing, he struck with a perfect downward cut that ended her rush abruptly. With his squad pursuing the pirates that had fled, he paused in the midst of the carnage to contemplate his work. A groan from one of the bodies on the floor drew his attention. Flicking his wrist to shake the blood from his sword, he stepped towards the badly wounded pirate. "What is your name, dog?" he asked.

"M... Malik..."

"Well Mariku, if you want to live, you will tell me who sent you and why you came here..."

APPEARANCE

A huge, muscled Caledonian with a centred stance and cold features; products of long and intense meditation. Clean shaven, with impeccably spotless armour. Wields an ōdachi (huge two-handed sword).

ROLEPLAYING

- Speaks as little as possible
- He holds his honour and that of his regiment above all
- He is always the first to lead a charge

BACKGROUND

Alasdair's mother hails from Clan MacIver, though she fell in love with a security officer of the YuJing diplomatic envoy in Scone. Despite being deeply in love, Alasdair´s parents suffered insurmountable pressure from their own societies. When his father´s assignment ended, both parents decided young Alasdair would have more opportunities if he also left Ariadna behind. To honour his mother, Alasdair kept his clan´s name. His father soon enlisted him in a little-known Haramaki dojo to learn the Way of the Sword, which eventually led to the honour of participating in the Gekken Kogyo.

He slowly became an outlandish Haramaki. Renowned for extraordinary physical and mental fortitude, swift and powerful blows, prowess with his prized ōdachi, and power armour befitting his size, he soon took to seeking honour and glory on the battlefield in the name of the Army of the Rising Sun.

He has recently been acting as melee support for dangerous Bureau Noir missions. Though he will never pass unnoticed due to his size and features that clash with his cultural attire, his exceptional intuitiveness and well-trained senses are a useful tool in the hands of O-12's Secret Service.

WELCOME TO A CRYSTAL-CLEAR DAWN...

The first great expedition to the stars, Project: DAWN, began with enormous enthusiasm and unprecedented collaboration, but ended in tragedy and isolation. Despite being severed from support, and certain in the knowledge they had been abandoned, the pioneers from the colony ship *Ariadna* refused to waver from their purpose. Alone and forsaken, they bent themselves to the task of surviving on a cold and hostile world.

Since then, the people of Dawn have faced down the bloodthirsty Antipodes and reforged themselves through the Separatist Wars. More recently, following their rediscovery by humanity at large, they fought off the greedy tendrils of the hypercorps during the Ariadnan Commercial Conflicts before accepting a seat amongst the G-5 nations. For Dawn is rich in Teseum, that most precious of metals for which humanity's lust will never be sated, providing Ariadnans with the ultimate bargaining chip.

Renowned for being proud, forthright, and hardy, Ariadnans will happily brawl amongst themselves if given the opportunity. The other nations, however, have learnt the wisdom in not provoking the hornet's nest, as they soon pull together to doggedly defend their homeland and ideals. This sourcebook will allow you to experience Dawn as never before!

- Details on all four Ariadnan cultures — Rodina, Merovingia, Caledonia, and USAriadna, and the state of their union.
- Focused Lifepaths that allow players to become truly Ariadnan, whether Human, Wulver, or Dogface.
- Additional armour, equipment, and adversaries specific to Dawn, including the famed Buffalo armour of the Blackjacks, and stats for the mysterious Unknown Ranger.
- Expanded rules for undertaking trade and seeking profit amongst the Merovingian trade caravans.

www.modiphius.com

ISBN 978-1-912200-34-4
9 781912 200344 >
MUH050223
Printed in the UK